Lady Trader
A Biography of Mrs Sarah Heckford

By the same author
Kruger's Pretoria
Du Val Tonight! The Story of a Showman
Hall Caine: Portrait of a Victorian Romancer
Dear Mr Rossetti: The Letters of Dante Gabriel Rossetti and Hall Caine 1878–1881
The Bulteels: The Story of a Huguenot Family

Lady Trader
A Biography of Mrs Sarah Heckford
Vivien Allen

Protea Book House
Pretoria
2010

Lady Trader – Vivien Allen
First edition, first impression in 1979 by Collins
Second edition, first impression in 2010 by Protea Book House

PO Box 35110, Menlo Park, 0102
1067 Burnett Street, Hatfield, 0083
Protea@intekom.co.za
www.proteaboekhuis.com

Editor: Iolandi Pool
Cover design: Hanli Deysel
Typography: 11 on 13.5 pt Arrus BT by Ada Radford
Printed and bound: Interpak, Pietermaritzburg

© 2010 Vivien Allen
ISBN 978-1-86919-357-7

All rights reserved. No part of this book may be reproduced without the permission of the publisher. No part of this book may be reproduced or transmitted in any form or by any electronic or mechanical means, including photocopying and recording, or by any other information storage or retrieval system, without written permission from the publisher.

Contents

Preliminaries
Chapter 1: Introducing Sarah 15
Chapter 2: The barriers of Young-Lady-dom 23
Chapter 3: Leaping the barriers 31
Chapter 4: Marriage and a hospital 47
Chapter 5: The East London Hospital 65
Chapter 6: Widowhood: Italy and India 85
Chapter 7: South Africa 99
Chapter 8: Christmas in the Free State and a wagon ride to Pretoria 115
Chapter 9: A chapter of accidents 127
Chapter 10: Surprise 139
Chapter 11: Green springs 157
Chapter 12: A lady trader 169
Chapter 13: Return to Pretoria and war 187
Chapter 14: Pretoria besieged 207
Chapter 15: Friends and spirits 219
Chapter 16: Back in business 231
Chapter 17: Ravenshill 243
Chapter 18: The Soutpansberg disturbances 251
Chapter 19: Fresh schemes and a trip to England 265
Chapter 20: War once more 275
Chapter 21: The end of the story 293
Index 303

Note to the First Edition

When quoting Mrs Heckford directly I have retained her use of the word "kaffir" as in her day it was acceptable usage. It is now a term of abuse and whites in South Africa can be, and indeed have been, hauled into court and fined for calling black people "kaffirs". The term "bantu" is equally unacceptable to most black South Africans, who say it is meaningless. I have therefore used the term many of them have told me they prefer: African. Where necessary I have corrected Mrs Heckford's spelling of Afrikaans and African words and names.

The conversations are taken from Mrs Heckford's own writings, published and unpublished, including letters and diaries. Nothing has been invented.

Bristol
1979

Foreword to the Second Edition

Much has changed, both in the East End of London and in South Africa, since this book was written 30 years ago. The London Hospital, now the Royal London Hospital, still exists but has been completely rebuilt. Philpott Street, where Sarah lodged while working at the hospital, has been partly redeveloped but some of the original houses remain.

However, in South Africa, Nooitgedacht ("Surprise" in old Dutch), the Jennings family home, is much altered and the farm is now mainly an estate of holiday bungalows. It is still owned by a member of the Sanders family but the house, slightly altered, has lost its garden and the driveway that used to lead up to it. In the same way the wild country in the northern Transvaal, now Limpopo province, has been developed and the Rain Queen's kingdom has disappeared. Sarah's farm, Ravenshill as she spelt it, was in the hills about 30 kilometres north of Tzaneen. The area is marked as Raven's Hill on modern maps. The primitive timber shack with corrugated iron roof which she built was still there in the mid-1970s, when I was taken to see it by the owner, but was unoccupied and looked to me as if it might soon collapse.

The Pretoria that Sarah knew has become a modern African city. Her account of life there, and in particular of the Siege of Pretoria, makes interesting reading now. Indeed, it has been a pleasure for me to revisit Sarah and all that she achieved. The passage of time seems to make her life even more remarkable.

Ivybridge, Devon
April 2009

Sources and Acknowledgements

For the First Edition

The author's thanks are due to the following for help with research. The staffs of the British Library, the Bristol Central Library, the London Borough of Tower Hamlets Central Library, the Greater London Record Office, the India Office Library, Somerset House, the Central Registry, London, and the Government Archives, Pretoria, South Africa.

Mr John Entract, librarian of the London Hospital Medical School, and Mr Valentine Swain, formerly on the medical staff of the Queen Elizabeth Hospital for Children, gave much help in tracing the hospital's history and information on the cholera epidemic of 1866. Mr Swain kindly provided the picture of the original East London Hospital building. Thanks are due to the Queen Elizabeth Hospital, Banstead, for allowing me to visit the hospital and to the Queen Elizabeth Hospital, Hackney Road, for permission to reproduce the portrait of Dr Heckford.

Mr Brian Fitzelle and the Religious Society of Friends, Dublin, were both most helpful in sorting out the history of the Goff family, and I am particularly grateful to Mr Claude Heckford and Mr Paul Palmer for help with the story of the Heckford family. Coutts & Co, the London bankers, through their archivist Miss M.V. Stokes, provided information on the accounts of the East London Hospital and of Dr and Mrs Heckford which was invaluable. Drs Ann and Angus Luscombe mulled over the descriptions of Sarah Heckford's illnesses and came up with suggestions as to what ailed her.

Mr Menno Klapwijk, author of *The Story of Tzaneen's Origin*, was generous with help from his great knowledge of the history of the northern Transvaal and gave me copies of old maps of the area around Ravenshill. Mr Ted Andrews, of Pretoria, put his unique library and encyclopaedic knowledge of names and places in the old Transvaal at my disposal and also gave me maps and photographs.

There are two people whose help was crucial and without whom this book could not have been written. Mrs Muriel Heckford Sanders, granddaughter of William and Mary Jennings, entertained me on numerous occasions at Nooitgedacht and lent me letters and Mrs Heckford's own photograph and press cuttings albums. She gave me a copy of her history of the Jennings family, *Glimpses of the Past* (printed for private circulation only), and allowed me to copy and reproduce here Lady Nicholson's drawing of Sarah Heckford, together with photographs of her own family. Mrs Dora Graham, daughter of Dora Scrimgeour and Frank Eland and the present owner of Ravenshill, invited me to stay with her and showed me Ravenshill and the Medingen Mission as they are today. She allowed me to copy and reproduce here photographs of her family and Ravenshill, and to read and quote from family letters, including ones written by Sarah Heckford to her mother. She lent me her copies of *Excelsior, True Transvaal Tales* and her mother and Sarah Heckford's diaries for copying.

For historical background I referred to *The Oxford History of India*; *The Oxford History of South Africa*; Eric Walker's *A History of Southern Africa* and the *Dictionary of South African Biography*. For information on the Siege of Pretoria and the First Anglo-Boer War I relied principally on Professor A.M. Davey's thesis "The Siege of Pretoria 1880–1881", published in the *Archives Year Book for South African History, 1956, Part I*; *The News of the Camp*, and *With A Show Through South Africa* by Charles Du Val, apart from Sarah Heckford's own account. At all stages of this work the files of *The Times* and *The Illustrated London News* were indispensable.

Contemporary viewers of the Transvaal scene in the 19th century who provided useful background were Carl

Jeppe, *The Kaleidoscopic Transvaal*; Sir John Kotze, *Memoirs and Reminiscences*; Sir Percy Fitzpatrick, *The Transvaal From Within* and *The Outspan*; Scoble and Abercrombie, *The Rise and Fall of Krugerism*; D.M. Wilson, *Behind the Scenes in the Transvaal*; H.W. Struben, *Recollections of Adventures*; *The Memoirs of Paul Kruger*, dictated to H.C. Bredell; Mrs Lionel Phillips, *Some South African Recollections*; *Brown's Guide to South Africa for Tourists, Sportsmen, Invalids and Settlers, 1893*; H.W. Wilson, *With the Flag to Pretoria* (four volumes).

Present-day writers consulted include Jo Manton, *Elizabeth Garrett Anderson*; Ray Strachey, *The Cause*; C.T. Gordon, *The Growth of Boer Opposition to Kruger*; A.P. Cartwright, *By the Waters of Letaba* and *The Corner House*; T.V. Bulpin, *Storm Over the Transvaal* and *Lowveld Trails*; John Fisher, *That Miss Hobhouse*; John Bond, *They Were South Africans*; Agnes Rissik, *Letters to My Grandchildren* (printed for private circulation only but available in some libraries); Donald Morris, *The Washing of the Spears*; Rayne Kruger, *Good-bye Dolly Gray*. Readers interested in the early days in Pretoria may like to consult the present writer's *Kruger's Pretoria*, which has many pictures of the city as it was when Sarah Heckford knew it, and people connected with it.

Lastly, but very far from least, I owe a great debt to my husband, A.K.W. Atkinson, who copied and printed almost all the photographs that appear in this book, and who put aside his own work to help with hours of research in libraries, to apply his "sub-editor's nose" to sniffing out grammatical lapses, and to type most of the final manuscript. More than that, he put up with Sarah Heckford as an invisible but omnipresent member of our household for a year and with scratch meals and a neglected house while the book was finally being written.

Bristol
1979

For the Second Edition

In preparing this edition, I must again give my thanks to those mentioned above whose generosity of time and effort enabled the original publication. This was the first of my biographies and their contribution to the book remains important to me. However, the passage of time means that a number of them have died, such as my friend Dr Angus Luscombe and my husband, Archie Atkinson.

I am fortunate that friends and family in South Africa have checked some of the changes in the South African settings since 1978. I am grateful to Dr Derrick Hurlin, Professor Bridget Theron and my daughter, Mrs Prue Cowie, all of Pretoria, and stepson Mr Peter Atkinson and his daughter Jacqueline Busa of Johannesburg for help with this edition. Donna Forbes "photoshopped" old pictures to make them usable and prepared the map of Sarah's travels in South Africa.

At Protea Book House of Pretoria Nicol Stassen and his staff have continued to be a great support and my editor Iolandi Pool was helpful in overcoming the distance of 6,000 miles between author and publisher.

With each of my books, my younger son Simon has been involved to some degree and this is no different. I wrote the original manuscript on an electric typewriter and so it was necessary to scan the full text into modern word processing, so that I could edit and update it. He helped with this technical side of modern book preparation and then continued as my informal editor on text and illustrations.

For me personally, the greatest difference is that my dear husband "Archie" Atkinson died in March 2008. He knew that Protea Book House had asked me for this edition and was delighted by that. He was a writer himself, having worked in newspapers throughout his career and having a book published himself just four months before his death at the age of 90. Archie encouraged me from the first time that we met, when he was the editor in charge of the Pretoria Bureau of the Johannesburg *Star* and he engaged me as a reporter. His insistence on a clear and unfussy prose style was invaluable.

Ivybridge, Devon
April 2009

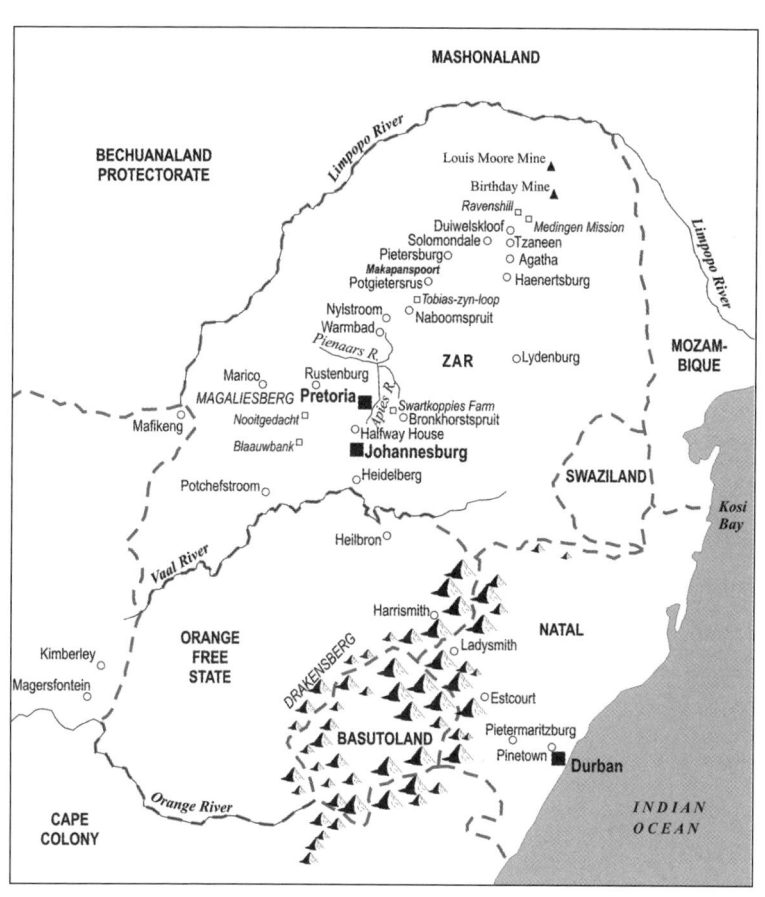

1
Introducing Sarah

"The news of Mrs Heckford's death," read the obituary in *The Times* of 21 April 1903, "comes as a terrible shock to all who knew her; and even those who knew a tenth of her adventures and achievements will feel that her country is much the poorer for her loss. It is not an extravagance, indeed, to describe her as one of the most extraordinary women to whom the British nation has given birth."

Victorian England produced a wealth of extraordinary women, pioneering women, reforming women, champions of Women's Rights, from Elizabeth Garrett Anderson opening up the medical profession to women, to Mary Kingsley exploring West Africa wearing a pair of her brother's trousers – under her dress of course – tied with string at the ankles as protection against insects. From Harriet Martineau to Annie Besant, from Miss Buss and Miss Beale to missionary bishops' wives, they form a fascinating study, and one of them was Mrs Sarah Heckford.

After nearly a column describing her career *The Times* concludes: "Her life will remain an inspiration to noble, disinterested and patriotic endeavour; and her country cannot afford to let it pass into oblivion."

Patriotic endeavour and noble disinterest have gone as far out of fashion as the bustle and corset. However, Sarah

Heckford, who "leaped the barriers of young-lady-dom", as she put it, though they were "armed with painfully sharp spikes", and who got as far from her comfortable upper-class home in London's West End as a leaky shack on a remote South African farm, and who rejected an easy life in favour of working for others and what she called "the real world of the bread-winner", does not deserve oblivion.

In 1905 the Lord Mayor of London rode in semi-state to Heckford Street, in the East End of London, to unveil portraits of Mrs Heckford and her husband that had been presented to the Heckford Street School by her sister. The school has gone but the street remains, a narrow way linking Ratcliff Highway with Cable Street, Stepney. Until then it had been called Collingwood Street. Meanwhile, in South Africa, in the cemetery in Pretoria's Church Street West, a granite headstone had been erected over a simple grave recording that, with her husband, Dr Nathaniel Heckford, she had founded the East London Hospital for Children.

She had been born Sarah Maud Goff in Dublin on 30 June 1839, the child of a wealthy Anglo-Irish family which traced its ancestry back to Goff the Regicide, a major-general in Cromwell's New Model Army. He was one of the jury which condemned Charles I to death. Married to Cromwell's cousin, he reaped quick promotion, a peerage and lands in Ireland. At the Restoration he fled to Massachusetts, where he died in about 1680. His wife and children remained in Ireland and his only son, Richard, was Sarah's great-great-grandfather. The Goffs became Quakers in the 18th century but by the time of Sarah's birth they seem to have left the Society of Friends.

Sarah's father, William, was the fourth son of Joseph Fade Goff, one-time Governor of the Bank of Ireland, who had a town house at 3, Mountjoy Square, Dublin and a country seat at Newtown Park, Blackrock. Mrs Joseph Goff was the daughter of George Clibborn, of Moate Castle, County Westmeath, and Hannah Goff so was her husband's cousin. Her brother, John, who inherited Moate Castle, had a daughter, Mary. When William Goff announced that he wished to marry Mary Clibborn there was general consternation in the family at the idea of such doubly related cousins marrying. William was obstinate, Mary tearful, and finally they were married in Dublin in 1833 by special licence.

Sarah was their third child, the eldest being Jane and the second Annie. The children inherited from the Goffs and the Clibborns a tradition of service on the part of the men – in the Army, the Church and the Law – and of good works on the part of the women, together with a streak of puritanical intolerance, an independent turn of mind and an assured position in society.

By the 1840s most of William's branch of the Goff family had left Ireland. William's eldest brother, after their father's death, moved the family seat to Hale Park in Wiltshire.

William himself left in 1842, when he took his young family to Germany and settled in Dresden. There is no record of the reason for the move but Sarah seemed to have inherited a grudge against the country of her birth. In a will she made in 1880 she directed her trustees to invest the trust funds in securities or real estate in England or Wales "but not in Ireland". She never went back there.

She was six when her mother died. Mary and William had been married for 12 years. In spite of their families' gloomy prophecies they had remained devoted to each other. William was stricken, and before he could recover another blow was dealt him when Jane died within weeks of her mother.

An able and intelligent man, he had always been moody, restless, unpredictable and independent. He never recovered from the shock of the two deaths and for the rest of his life lived almost as a recluse. Mary's youngest sister, Abigail Clibborn, came out to Germany to look after the two little girls, but after a while William could not bear to

17

remain in Dresden. With his sister-in-law and the children he travelled to Switzerland, where they stayed for more than two years, moving from place to place.

Early in 1848 he left Switzerland and took the children, still with Aunt Abigail to care for them, to Paris, where they arrived in February. They were just in time to be caught up in the revolution that ended the 18-year reign of that prudent, laborious and boring king, Louis Philippe.

It was on 24 February 1848, the second day of street fighting, that the barricades went up and with them the cry of "Vive la Republique". Louis Philippe retired prudently across the Channel to the safety of London. Deciding that Paris in the throes of revolution was no place for his daughters, William Goff followed the King, taking rooms near to where his brother Robert lived at 29 Eaton Square.

For the time being it seemed out of the question to take the children abroad again, though London life was not to William Goff's taste. Few visitors came to the house and Annie and Sarah had no other children to play with except when, at rare intervals, cousins who lived abroad or in Ireland came to see them on visits to London. William was generous to the children, spending money freely on them but not spoiling them or indulging in luxuries. Routine was strict, especially lessons; food plain but wholesome; housekeeping frugal.

Though Annie was older, William Goff made a particular companion and confidante of Sarah, never talking down to her but treating her as an adult.

On the surface their life seemed settled and assured. For more than a year they remained in London and Sarah celebrated her ninth birthday in June 1849. Then suddenly, without warning, William left the children with their aunt and went back to Dresden. A few days later he was found dead, sitting on Jane's grave. It seems likely that he committed suicide.

Almost before the news had time to sink in Sarah contracted a severe infection, probably tubercular. In a letter many years later she wrote, "I fell dangerously ill and woke up from delirium to find myself despaired of by the best Physicians at first and then doomed to be lame for life." It also left her with a slight hump on her right shoulder. As an old woman she used to say cheerfully that she always made her own dresses because they had to have a pocket for the hump, but she was self-conscious about it and insisted on being photographed from her left so that it did not show. She recovered only slowly and for a long time could not live a normal life. "I think that this gave a concentration to my thoughts and feelings which they would not otherwise have had," she wrote in 1888, looking back on the invalid years.

But there were other and almost as drastic changes in Annie and Sarah's lives. Their father had left them to the care of his youngest brother, their bachelor Uncle Robert, who agreed to make a home for them and their devoted Aunt Abigail. They were thrust into another world and their whole upbringing changed.

Uncle Robert, in his niece's words, "was a thorough man of the World, in that strangely limited sense which the term is used for, a splendid and delightful type of it – quite unlike my father who was a man of much greater abilities but who had a contempt for the world".

Captain Robert Goff had very definite ideas on what constituted the Whole Duty of Woman: it was to be a success in society. Book learning was all very well if not overdone but "accomplishments" and the "social graces" were what really counted. Women existed to please men and make good marriages. Two lonely, sad and bewildered little girls did their best to conform to what was now expected of them, but their father's training and the influence of their Quaker forebears ultimately triumphed.

Sarah was fascinated by the conversations she heard between Uncle Robert and his many friends, who included the composer of parlour songs and pieces, Alfred Pollock. (Sarah kept all her life a copy of one of his piano compositions which he had signed and dedicated "To my good friend Robert Goff, Esq.") All these friends, according to her, were "strongly tinged with Voltairianism", cynical and sceptical, in direct contrast to the simple, childlike piety of Aunt Abigail, "which I doubt if it would be possible for any woman so well-educated as my Aunt was to possess now [1888] in this present state of social thought".

The emphasis on "accomplishments" introduced Sarah to two arts which gave her joy for the rest of her days: music and painting. She became a competent pianist and her watercolour sketches and portraits, while not outstanding, are something better than the ordinary run of Victorian amateur work. Painting was her great delight and she went regularly to the National Gallery to copy in oils, sometimes as a commission for friends. Her work was well thought of by her family and some of her friends urged her to take it up professionally, but she was under no illusions as to its worth: it was "good, but not good enough". She hated the idea of turning into a hack instead of being able to paint what and how she liked.

Sarah was 20 when Aunt Abigail died on Christmas Day, 1860. The sisters felt their aunt's death perhaps even more than the death of their mother, whom they scarcely remembered.

With their aunt and chaperone gone, Robert decided it would "not be wise" to keep two young women living in the same house with him. A house was taken for them in Warwick Square, Pimlico, then "a very good address". Other residents of the square included two retired admirals, a brace of colonels, an Irish MP and several titled people. Uncle Robert must have thought it eminently suitable and their inheritance was sufficient to support them there with servants, a carriage and riding horses. Sarah had inherited about £15,000 from her father, worth about £14.5 million at 2008 values, so she was a wealthy young woman. She opened an account with Coutts, with whom most of the family banked, on 3 July 1860, when she turned 21.

Now a serious-minded, rather intense young woman, Sarah refused to allow herself to be handicapped by her lameness. "I am not so lame that I cannot walk or ride a horse but too lame to run," she wrote. She had to have saddles specially made for her as she was not able to sit a side saddle (no lady rode astride) which had the horns normally placed. Horses and riding were a lifelong joy to her.

And so she and Annie embarked on an independent life. "I may say that at two and twenty," she wrote, "I found myself possessed of a good fortune and absolutely my own mistress. My Uncle died shortly after and so the last link that bound me to obedience of anyone but myself was broken." Here Sarah, writing more than 20 years later, is not quite accurate. Robert Goff lived on till March 1866.

2

The barriers of Young-Lady-Dom

Her own mistress she may have been, and financially independent, but Sarah still had to reckon with her elder sister, as strong-minded as she was herself, and the influence of her uncles, aunts and cousins who also lived in London.

Sarah longed for real work, for contact with labouring people. Dabbling in painting and the sort of "Lady Bountiful" approach to the poor, which was all that Society approved, was not enough for an intelligent young woman. The barriers of what she called "young-lady-dom" increasingly irked her, but "old ideas and associations and the timidity born of ignorance of all that appertains to practical life" held her back. There is a distinct parallel with the early life of Florence Nightingale, who spent it sitting dutifully at home and was past 30 before she struck out and did the work she felt called to do. "The inert weight of family influence," wrote Sarah, "well nigh choked my life out, for … that which is called life by many is not life at all."

There is no direct record of what she was doing at this time. She did, however, complete a heavily autobiographical novel, *Excelsior*, which seems from internal evidence to have been written about 1884, though there is no date on the title page and the publishers, George Philip, now have no record of it. In a convoluted preface she said she had tried to express:

> The reality of the Ideal, and the unreality of the Material, existence: but I have adhered in all my facts to what is called Truth in the World to which facts belong. I have drawn no single scene in which facts are more prominent than ideas from imagination; they are all studied from material reality, and only slightly moulded to suit the action of the story. It is the same with the Historical allusions made in parts of it; they are all as true as any History can be supposed to be, and, if not true, at least well authenticated. With regard to the characters pourtrayed [sic], which, like all human characters, must partake of the Ideal and of the Material, I can say the same as of the facts mentioned: I have studied them from persons I have known, and I have not absolutely invented any one act or personage.

This we can take as true. Sarah was not gifted with a creative imagination, but she was a shrewd and accurate reporter of what she saw and experienced. Parts of the book are turgid and almost unreadable, the plot at points incredible. Other parts, however, are so vividly written, in such straightforward language, that it is obvious the author is reporting something that actually happened. When we examine these passages, which stick out from the rest of the book, in the light of the known facts of the author's life, it does appear that they are purely autobiographical, and they will be drawn on as such in what follows.

The central character of the book is Illa, clearly a self-portrait, who marries a doctor Sarah calls "Santa-Chiara", but describes in the same terms as elsewhere she describes the man she was to marry, Dr Heckford. Illa's sister, Bella, however, bears little relationship to Annie Goff as we know her and seems to have been modelled on a cousin. At the time the book was published their friends and many relations seem to have accepted that Illa was Sarah and Bella was Annie and that the book was a thinly-veiled autobiography, with the setting of some of the incidents altered and a bit of romancing to colour it as fiction.

The Women's Movement, with its demands for a woman's right to work on equal terms with men and to have the vote, took a big step forward in 1858 with the appearance of the first number of *The Englishwoman's Journal*. An editorial said, "It is work we ask, room to work, encouragement to work, an open field with a fair day's wages for a fair day's work." Victor Hugo had written earlier, "The 18th century proclaimed the rights of man, the 19th shall proclaim the rights of women."

While she was never involved with the political side of the Movement, Sarah certainly knew some of the leaders well and must have been strongly influenced by the new ideas. They concerted ill with "the inert weight of family influence" and her unconventional behaviour scandalised many of her relatives and ultimately led to a complete breach.

Apart from the Goffs, who were a large family, there were her Clibborn relatives, who doubtless added to the "inert weight" Sarah complained of. They also trace their lineage to one of Cromwell's colonels, John Clibborn, born in Westmorland in 1623. He went to Ireland with the Parliamentary army which so cruelly and bloodily subdued the country. Despite this he settled at Moate with his wife, Dinah English. His grandson, James, married a Quakeress with the delightful name of Experience Barclay. There were several marriages between the Goffs, the Clibborns and the Fetherstonehaughs and not surprisingly the family records are tangled. What is clear is that they were for the most part pillars of society, with only the occasional maverick like William. Sarah took after him.

The first time she exerted her independence and shocked her relations was when, soon after she and Annie set up house together, she stopped going to church. Annie reproached her, worried about the reactions of the neighbours. "It may be very wicked of me, but I can't see that it is right for me to go and pretend to be praying, and all that – when I know I am not. It is better for me to stay away," replied Sarah with the honesty that characterised so much of her life. "I only end up criticising the Rubric, and when some infantile curate calls an assembly who are almost all much older than he is 'dear brethren' and proceeds to lecture them on texts from the Old Testament applied to the present day in the most impossible manner I simply want to laugh."

Hankering for a way to be of use, she took to going into the poorer streets and alleys that lay not far from their home, distributing sweets to the children and talking to the women she found there. This shocked and frightened her sister, who called in one of their uncles to remonstrate with her.

"You ought not to be so careless as you are of doing what other girls do. It cuts you off from them little by little and makes you more isolated than you need be," he scolded.

"How do you mean?" asked Sarah, nettled that her efforts to get away from the useless life of girls of her class should earn her a dressing-down.

"For one thing, you have given up going to church, though your sister goes, and you go alone into those back streets near you. Really, you ought not to do it. It will not do at all and is making all your family most unhappy about you."

"I can't see why it should not do," replied Sarah, greatly daring. "Surely there is nothing wrong in my liking to give sweets to the poor little children that live in those horrid places."

"The reason you ought not to do it is that it is too unusual and gets you criticised," came the reply. "In your position, a girl on your own, you ought to be very careful about that. It is not as if you were one of the lady visitors of the parish."

"Oh, I can't go around talking religion to the people and reading the Bible to them, surely you know that," she expostulated.

Afterwards when she came to think about it, though quite sure that she would be wrong to yield to the pressures of convention, she had to admit that her efforts were unlikely to be doing any real good to anyone. With her wonted honesty and self-criticism she admitted to herself that the people she went among frequently took advantage of her and probably laughed at her behind her back. "If only I could work with someone who knew and understood these people," she told her sister.

She continued going to the National Gallery to copy – even making a quite creditable copy of a Titian portrait – and when she could not avoid it she joined in the round of afternoon visits and evening dinner parties with as good a grace as she could muster. Two things she did enjoy: going to the opera and riding in the Park on her pretty bay mare. She rode well and, mounted, her lameness was not apparent. Her habit and veil disguised the slight hump of which she was always so conscious. She was a plain girl, and always ready to point out to anyone how much prettier her sister was, but she knew she appeared at her best riding in the Row.

Through all the criticism and family arguments she increasingly cherished a dream, a dream of becoming unlike other women and leading a life of work, of choosing a path for herself, making a career, self-contained and self-reliant as a man could be. The dream was vague, naïve and insubstantial, but she clung to it. She was without self-pity and was never heard to complain of a fate that had lamed her, but she viewed her chances of marriage realistically. When she fell romantically in love with a much older man, one of her uncle Robert's friends, who did not return her love (possibly did not even know of it), she did her best to smother her feelings and concentrate on finding a career. But what career to choose?

A first visit to the East End of London had made a lasting impression on her and heightened her feeling of the essential wrongness of so much poverty and suffering existing side by side with the life of luxurious leisure lived by her family and friends. She had always liked the City. "There is a feeling of real life about it, which there is not in the West End," she said. "I like to look at all the people coming and going. They all look busy – that is what I like in them, as if they had something they felt they must do, not like most people in the West End, who look as if they were lounging through their lives."

The world east of Aldgate was something else, however, and she never forgot her first view of it. She described "the row of grimy butchers' shops that usher in the East End on leaving the City by Aldgate, the sickly-looking eating shops with a curiously-variegated pudding and big pieces of meat always in the windows; the wonderfully cheap articles of dress, labelled 'The Newest Fashion,' 'Paris,' etc., in little haberdashers shops"; and a placard with a poetical effusion in praise of a particularly cheap and good cake manufactured by an intelligent member of the society of bakers. She felt saddened at the squalid look of almost everyone she saw.

This burgeoning social conscience was not to let her rest. Later when she knew more of the East End she wrote this about it:

> In that part of London which lies East, North-East, and South-east of the Bank, there is to be found a network of streets whose peculiar dingy look it is impossible to describe, and which must be seen in order to be appreciated. It is as though the accumulated dust which maids-of-all-work have for years been sweeping into corners within the houses which form them, had, in despair of ever being put into a dustpan, forced itself through the bricks, hoping to be borne away by some stray breeze, but had instead stuck to the outside, for it is impossible to believe that their dingy griminess can arise from anything as wholesome as open-air dust, or smoke escaped from a chimney. An unenlightened enquirer, as he walks through these streets, must always wonder who lives in them, and, even if he sees their inhabitants, must always wonder how they live.

Just when all this unease, restlessness and unformed ambition crystallised into the idea of becoming a doctor is not clear.

It was certainly a novel thought and one she well knew was unlikely to meet with the approval of her family. How to set about it she had only the vaguest idea. She thought the knowledge of anatomy she had gained from her artistic studies would be a help and that in some way the study of mathematics, which had been a hobby for several years, would also come in useful, but beyond that she felt herself without qualifications, as indeed she was. She had heard that medical studies entailed something called "walking the wards" but that was all. She knew one woman had already qualified in America and had been placed on the British Medical Register – Elizabeth Blackwell – "but I expect her family helped her. My family would only say I was mad".

However, she needed help and advice on how to start and diffidently approached one of the family whose counsel she normally appreciated. His reaction was not helpful.

"You don't mean to say that you are thinking of such a thing?" he asked in tones of astonishment.

"Well, I don't know – at least I have thought of it – but…"

"Then put such thoughts out of your head at once. In the first place, of course you don't know, but women can't be doctors."

"But there is a woman doctor now," Sarah protested.

"Oh, that's nothing," came the airy reply. "She must be some sort of nondescript – half woman and half doctor. No woman could ever be a good doctor because women are physically unfitted for it. Then, besides, you don't know what studying medicine means; it would take all their delicacy out of them. No, no! You must put such fancies out of your mind completely."

At one time she would have argued the point but lengthening experience had taught her that stand-up arguments with her family would get her nowhere. She knew too well that this hostility to the idea of women as doctors was almost universal. But the thought of Elizabeth Blackwell and what she had achieved stuck with her.

Elizabeth Blackwell had been born in Bristol in 1821 but emigrated to America with her parents in 1832. She studied medicine and took her degree there in 1849, afterwards coming to London and obtaining permission to study at St Bartholomew's Hospital. During this time she met Florence Nightingale, then still living at home, and undoubtedly inspired her. When Dr Blackwell returned home to America she left behind her the seed of an important new idea, but the ordinary public still thought that women doctors would be "odious, unsexed creatures".

In 1859 Dr Blackwell returned to England and applied to be placed on the British Medical Register. Her application was accepted, the first from a woman. Alarm bells rang all through the medical world, and the following year the door was slammed hard to make sure that no other woman followed her. This was done by the passing of a decree excluding doctors holding foreign degrees from admission to the register.

Women could take degrees and qualify in medicine in France, Belgium, Switzerland, Italy and Spain at that time, but not in England or Scotland where the universities still refused to allow women to matriculate or to be admitted to degrees. The next 20 years were to prove that the tight, lucrative world of medicine was even harder for women to breach than the hoary academic world of the universities.

In March 1859, when Sarah was 18 and already rebelling against the life she was leading, Dr Blackwell gave a series of lectures at Marylebone Town Hall on the suitability of women for the medical profession. Whether Sarah attended those lectures is not known but she was certainly aware of them. However, all through the 1860s the cause of women in medicine seemed to go backwards rather than forwards and Sarah could see no way to achieve her ambition. No way, that is, until the summer of 1866, when the last great cholera epidemic in England struck London.

3
Leaping the barriers

It is ironic that the scourge of a cholera epidemic should have been the key to free Sarah from having her "life choked out" in respectable Belgravia. The disease came to England in ships from Egypt, where pilgrims returning from Mecca had been responsible for starting an epidemic. The earliest cases occurred in Bristol in April 1866, and in May the disease appeared in Liverpool and Southampton. In the first week of July nine deaths were reported in the East End of London and then the epidemic exploded in the crowded, unsanitary streets of Aldgate, Whitechapel, Bethnal Green, Poplar, Bow, Stepney, Mile End and St George-in-the-East, none of which yet had mains drainage – the low level main drain north of the river was still under construction.

Campaign headquarters in the battle against cholera was the London Hospital in Stepney. "People are falling ill every hour," wrote the Registrar-General in the middle of July. "You see them of all ages, children and adults, lying on their beds like people under the influence of a deadly poison; some acutely suffering, nearly all conscious of their fate and of all that is going on around them... Several wards at the London Hospital are full of patients, many of them children in all stages of the disease. The medical men have no rest and with the Health Officers are nobly doing their duty; brave men ready to lay down their lives for their patients. The people themselves are most patient; most willing to help each other, the women always in front and never shrinking from danger. There is no desertion of children, husbands, wives, fathers or mothers from fear."

Extra nurses were desperately needed. Catherine Gladstone, wife of William Ewart Gladstone, who was at that time Chancellor of the Exchequer, had for several years been visiting the wards of the London Hospital under a scheme started by the Bishop of London, who felt that lady visitors could help the chaplain in his work. Canon Scott, the chaplain at the London, had written to Mrs Gladstone at the start of the epidemic, warning her to keep away, but she was made of sterner stuff than that and was at the hospital as usual the next day. She and her husband were also interested in a new order of nursing sisters at All Saints, Cavendish Square. Canon Scott, when the need for more help became urgent, appealed to Mrs Gladstone and she immediately sent several of the sisters from Cavendish Square to the hospital.

The next crisis was in the laundry, coping with many times the usual quantity of linen while the local women were afraid to work there. Following the arrival of the Cavendish Square sisters, six society ladies volunteered to help in the wards and when this became known paid workers for the laundry became easier to get.

The Rev. C.F. Louder, vicar of St Peter's, London Docks, describes conditions in the district of St George-in-the-East that July, "where there is at all times so much poverty and distress: where the drainage is as yet untouched by the improvements made in other parts: where our poor are so crowded from want of house room; where the alleys are so close; where during the hottest part of the day we have fermenting a large manure manufactory in which are collected, in a very mountain of impurity, hundreds of tons of the refuse of the streets, all to be carted to barges on the River. No wonder that, when the cholera broke out amongst us, it should prove most fatal, and that the death rate in proportion to the population should have been higher here than in any other part of London".

The strain on the London Hospital was enormous and the Union workhouses were pressed into service as emergency fever hospitals. Nursing sisters from St John's Home were brought in to help the pauper nurses and Pickford's vans called at the hospitals each night to collect the bodies from the mortuaries as the undertakers could no longer cope. The hospital carpenter at the London hastily extemporised coffins from any wood to hand and painted them black. Mr Nixon, the former secretary of the London who had just taken over as house governor, left an account of the hospital at this time. "Everywhere we had sawdust steeped in carbolic scattered about, and under every bed there was a large bag of it. The beds themselves were sacks of straw, and such was the nature of the disease that, as soon as a patient died or could be removed, we carried away the bed straw and the sack of sawdust, and took them to an open space at the back of the Hospital where we had a bonfire every night. The sufferings of the people were intense and on every hand one or other would be dying."

By 27 July the situation was so bad that Mr Nixon wrote to *The Times* appealing for money and for more "lady nurses" to come forward. Sarah saw the letter.

There was no doubt in her mind: she must offer to go at once. Through the previous weeks the cholera had been a constant topic of conversation and many society people had left London before the end of the Season for fear of it. Sarah, sure that if she could not be a doctor she could at least be a nurse, wrote at once to Mr Nixon. Before the day was out she had a grateful reply asking her to go to the Wapping Fever Hospital, near the London Docks, east of Tower Bridge. Her sister Annie also volunteered but she went to another hospital.

It is easy now to underestimate the bravery of these two young women and the others who volunteered with them.

Vaccination today gives some protection from cholera and with modern treatment it need not be fatal, but even today it can inspire fear among trained doctors and nurses, and the horror and sheer terror with which it was regarded more than 100 years ago can easily be imagined.

The Wapping District Cholera Hospital was a big, dingy-looking building in a narrow street. A group of children huddled near the doorway stared in astonishment at the sight of a well-dressed lady getting out of a cab. Inside Sarah found it was a dismal place with a curious and most unpleasant smell. The porter told her that the doctor in charge was in the men's ward and led her up a series of drab and dirty staircases. At the top she was ushered into a large, bare room, full of truckle beds covered with coarse brown blankets. Each bed was occupied by a pallid man, many with a curious and terrible likeness to each other – the "cholera face".

Sarah shuddered as she followed her guide the length of the ward. She was 26 but nothing in her previous experience had prepared her for this. So eager had she been to tackle a real job that she had scarcely thought about what she might actually be going to do. She was unpleasantly surprised to find herself afraid. At the end of the ward two sisters were putting screens round a bed over which the doctor was bending. "Some poor fellow is dying, Miss, you'll have to wait," said the porter. One of the patients called out, "nurse – water – nurse", but the nurses did not hear him. "Can I give him some, do you think?" she asked her guide and then, deciding that she must take some action to conquer her increasing fear, she poured water into a glass from a carafe that stood on a deal table in the centre of the ward and went across to the man's bed. Supporting his head with her arm she held the glass to his lips. "Thank you, miss," he said with a weak effort at touching his forelock. "Shall I settle your pillow for you? It doesn't look very comfortable," she said meekly, trying to feel like an efficient nurse.

A moment or two later the doctor came to greet her. He introduced himself as Dr Woodman of the London Hospital. Shaking her hand warmly, he said how much everyone connected with the cholera hospitals appreciated the way ladies like herself had come forward to help. He told her there was one other doctor at Wapping, also from the London Hospital, and that from the following day they would have the help of sisters from a nursing order of nuns.

"I suppose you would like to have the women's wards to superintend?" he asked. Fighting down a moment of panic at the thought of such a responsible position when she felt so totally inadequate to cope, she replied that she would. She was led back down the stairs to an identical ward below, where the women were. The nurse on duty dropped her a small curtsey. It was late in the afternoon and the doctor suggested that she go to the lodgings that had been arranged for her in a house nearby and settle in there, reporting for duty the next morning.

When her landlady had shown her into the tiny but scrupulously clean room that had been allotted to her and left her alone she sat down abruptly on the bed and tried to think about what it was she was really attempting to do. Her head was still full of the vague and romantic notions she had so long cherished of carving out a career for herself and at the same time uplifting and improving the poor by her example and her help. Now against that she had to set the reality of the cholera wards in the bleak hospital she had just seen. She thought about the angry and alarmed reactions of her friends and family when she had said what she was going to do. After years of kicking against her conventional upbringing she had broken out. Without knowing exactly what was before her she was quite sure that she had finally scaled the barriers of young-lady-dom and that there was no going back to Belgravia.

Next morning when she reported at the hospital she met the other doctor, Nathaniel Heckford. More than 20 years later, in a letter recalling this time, she wrote: "When at last

I had got outside the narrow barriers of conventionalism I was met on the threshold of my new life by my Husband." It was the crucial event of her life. The influence he was to have on her dominated her as long as she lived, even though they were to have only a few years together.

Nathaniel Heckford was 23 in the summer of 1866. He had been an exceptional student at the London, winning the gold medals for medicine and surgery in the same year. At 22 he was appointed Resident Accoucheur and lectured to students. His roots were deep in the East End of London, though he had been born in India. His family was older than the Goffs, tracing their descent from Sir William de Hackford, Lord of the Manor of Hackford in Norfolk, who flourished during the time of Henry III (1216–1272). In the 18th century one branch of the family moved to London and the first Nathaniel Heckford, who was a customs official, settled in St George-in-the-East. His descendants were all concerned with shipping and the sea, down to Dr Heckford's father, another Nathaniel, born in 1813. In his early 20s he sailed for India and became a Master Mariner. For more than 20 years he commanded a merchantman, trading out of Calcutta along the Burma coast.

His first wife, whom he married in London, died young and he married again in Calcutta. His second wife, Eliza, was almost certainly Eurasian. Their first child, Sarah's future husband, was born in April 1842 and christened in St James's Church, Calcutta. There were four more children, Sarah, Henry, Mary Ellen and George. They had an elder half-sister, Eliza. In 1858 the Master Mariner took the whole family back to London, where he was engaged in shipping and navigation on the Thames until his retirement to a villa in West Ham. Nathaniel was 16 in 1858. His happy childhood in Calcutta so coloured his life that in London he always referred to himself as "an Indian". Friends commented on his "oriental cast of mind" and his "Eastern looks". In 1860 he entered the London Hospital Medical School. When he qualified as MRCS (Member of the Royal College of Surgeons) he set up his plate on consulting rooms at 5 Broad Street Buildings in the City, near the corner of Liverpool Street.

This then was the background of the young doctor who greeted Sarah Goff on her first morning of duty at the Wapping Cholera Hospital. He was extremely good looking, with a dark, clever face and black eyes fringed with heavy, dark lashes, untidily dressed, charming, easygoing, immensely kind and with a passion for children and animals. This passion even extended to black beetles, which he refused to kill on the grounds that "death would probably be as disagreeable to the beetle as it would be to me". At the London his students had found him an admirable teacher, patient and understanding, knowing when to leave them to cope on their own but always on hand if they needed him. It is difficult to think of anyone better to initiate the lame, strange young woman into her new duties.

Such was the pressure on the hospital and the available staff that there was no time to train Sarah: she was simply given charge of the women's ward, a charge she shared with one of the nuns who arrived on the same day. New cases were admitted at all hours. Some were so desperately ill she had at once to send for the doctors and tension would run high, but sometimes the patients were more frightened than ill. Dr Heckford would shrug his shoulders after a brief examination and walk away, leaving Sarah to deal with the case as she thought best. Dr Woodman would say, "Oh, well, put her to bed and keep her warm," and they would stroll out of the ward for a breath of air and a chat.

Sarah was shocked at first to find that there was what she called "a certain hilarity" when a very bad case came in and a distinct air of disappointment when the patient turned out not to be very ill after all. After a while she reasoned to herself that the doctors and nurses really enjoyed themselves when their work was most needed, and she began to find she shared the same attitudes.

But for all her assurance that at last she was genuinely

being useful, the work was often extremely depressing, and the behaviour of some of the patients shocked her greatly. Some "looked forward with fierce delight to the idea of recovery as to the time when they should be able to revenge themselves by brutal violence on someone who had offended them when they were helpless: others, with the hand of death upon their next neighbour, having to be restrained by threats and almost violence from disturbing their last moments by obscene and blasphemous jokes". She was disgusted by women who flung themselves out of bed, in defiance of the most stringent orders to stay where they were, to grovel on the floor, shrieking to Almighty God to forgive them their many sins before death claimed them, only, she was quite sure, to return immediately to those same sins they so glibly confessed, when they recovered and went home again. Many, of course, did not recover.

She tried hard to be patient and kind with even the worst of the women. She felt that great shame reflected on her own class, "rolling in wealth", that it should let children such as the pathetic creatures who were admitted to her wards, grow up into the women she now saw, and all, she was sure, through lack of education. She did not find all of them bad, not by a long way. There were women who, whatever they were suffering, never complained or demanded attention, and many of the children showed her a spontaneous affection and gratitude for what she did for them that touched her deeply. One attitude was common to all, and this was that they seemed to regard her as something to be wondered at and not touched roughly, a being from a totally different world. It was not unusual for the roughest and coarsest of the women, who would scream abuse at the paid nurses from the Workhouse infirmary, to say, "I can hold it up myself, miss – I'll be dirtying your sleeve," when she raised their heads to help them take their medicine, medicine which they had refused to take from the nurse. Sometimes when this happened they would mutter that they would take it from the nurse next time so as not to tire Sarah out with running after them. She was not sure that she liked this attitude – she so much wanted to be part of the real work of the hospital and not merely regarded as an ornament. She was daily more sure that sterling worth, as she put it, and which she firmly believed to be at the bottom of all human nature, was to be found far more among the poor than among the spoilt rich.

To her surprise she enjoyed night duty. Sitting at the table in the centre of the dreary ward with one gas lamp turned low she often had time to think about the future. Cut off from her usual friends and companions her past life seemed a distant vision. She felt curiously detached. It seemed to her that she was beginning a life in which she would deal with unsophisticated, unconventional people, according to her standards people who were neglected, down-trodden or assisted only as a sort of religious offering. She had seen that many of the outcasts she dealt with disliked that kind of help, and turned only an unwilling ear to the sisters and clergy who visited the wards. She thought she knew better than that. She would go to these people not because it was the right thing to do, but because she genuinely cared for them as human beings, because she felt drawn to them by their very need for help. She would give them the advantage of her education; she would encourage them to strive upwards into her sphere and then beyond it, in other words, to "better themselves".

When she tried to think what her sphere was she began to feel, rather humbly, that she had probably been too spoilt already by luxury and conventionality ever to attain the heights open to an unsophisticated child of the people. Acting on her rather naive and woolly ideas she was frequently disappointed in the reactions of her patients. This did not discourage her. She simply blamed her own lack of knowledge of how to deal with them and tried again.

Her ideas about the future were still vague but she was far too busy to worry about plans. Before long she found that "a brightness" had sprung up around her in the gloomy hospital, that when her landlady called her with a substantial "high tea" before she went on night duty, she was instantly awake, eager to get back to the hospital, and ran up the stairs to the ward when she got there. The sister who had been in charge during the day went over the new cases with her, she did a round of the ward, and then settled down under the half-turned-off gas with her casebook, in which times for giving various medicines were entered, her watch and her textbooks on the table before her. For her hazy notions of studying medicine had become a determination to qualify as a doctor. On one of her free days she had been to a bookseller in the City and had bought copies of *Gray's Anatomy* and the two volumes of *The Science and Practice of Medicine* by Dr William Aitkin.

The under-nurse assigned to help her usually went to sleep and Sarah let her rest as long as things were quiet, interrupting her studies to give medicines or answer querulous calls for water, settling the pillows of restless patients and occasionally going round the beds. Sometimes there were emergencies and the under-nurse would be woken and the doctor summoned but on the whole the nights were surprisingly quiet, considering how seriously ill many of the patients were. Tea was brought to her soon after midnight and gradually everything got stiller, even the drunken cries and shouts in the street outside dying down. The two doctors often came round together about the time her tea arrived, but before long there was a night when Dr Heckford came on his own.

She rose as he entered the ward, ready to make her report and go the rounds with him, but he motioned her to sit down again and drew up the other chair beside her so that they could talk without raising their voices and disturbing the patients. "I've asked them to bring me my tea up here when they bring yours," he said. "You don't mind, do you?" The smile began with his eyes while he watched her carefully and spread to a wide grin as she said, trying not to sound too surprised, that of course she did not mind. "Fancy having a tea party in a cholera ward. A bit different to what you are accustomed to, isn't it?" he asked. There was nothing really she could say to this and they sat in silence for a while, a silence that was getting steadily more awkward when it was mercifully broken by the arrival of the tea.

"You haven't many bad cases tonight," he said, after sipping his tea without saying anything for quite a while. "And one empty bed – that poor girl who died today. You were very sorry for her, weren't you?"

"Yes, I was," said Sarah. "I thought she would have lasted till tonight or I would not have gone away. I wanted her so much to get well."

"Better as she is," said Dr Heckford, and startled her by adding, "I often wish I were dead."

"Dr Heckford," Sarah expostulated. "You oughtn't to say that."

"Perhaps I shouldn't, but I do," he answered.

Sarah knew that Dr Heckford's devotion to his patients was legendary, both inside the hospital and outside. "But think of the use you can be of, that you are of, think how sorry your family would be if you were to die!"

"What do you know of my family?" he asked sharply, a note in his voice she had not heard before.

"Oh – well – er – nothing," she said, trying to cover sudden embarrassment. "I just thought you must have some family."

"Yes, I suppose my family would be sorry," he replied, as if this was an entirely new idea. "But it would be all the same in the end; if one never had to die it would be worth living. As it is, I would rather get it over at once. Well, never mind all that," and he picked up the textbook she had been studying when he arrived.

"Why don't you study medicine regularly? I've often noticed you reading this great book. Why don't you go in for it thoroughly and come out a female MD?"

For a moment she was at a loss, as embarrassed as if she had been caught reading some silly sentimental novel. To have her ambitions brought out and examined so coolly took her breath away. But he was not waiting for an answer.

"You know, of course, of the obstacles that are being put in the way of women qualifying," he went on. "They will be overcome in time, of that there is no doubt. But I don't want you to go on with the idea it will be easy or straightforward. The universities will still not admit women to matriculation and to get admitted as a student at a teaching hospital or to see practice in the wards is well-nigh impossible, but I am not sure it is all a bad thing. All the books in the world won't teach you as much as a few good cases, carefully studied. Nature is only to be understood by learning from herself and if you read books at all it should only be with a view to applying what you read to actual cases, at once. You will need a tutor, however, to prepare you for examinations. If you will accept my help it will be gladly given."

Sarah sat quite still. If she so much as breathed perhaps she would find she had been dreaming. Finally she managed to say, "Thank you," in a voice that did not sound like her own. "Good," he said, finishing his tea. "We'll talk about it and make out a scheme of studies for you next time we meet." He seemed unwilling to leave. He went off to do his rounds of the other wards and then came back to Sarah's.

She must have betrayed her surprise at seeing him back and he was at a loss for an excuse to be there. He looked through the books she had on her table and picked up an edition of Byron's poems. Seeing a bookmark in it he opened it to see what she had been reading.

"Were you reading *Manfred*?" he asked. "That's my favourite work. I read and reread it. It speaks to you of something beyond the grime and toil of this world – of a world ... if one only knew there was such a world..." and he broke off as if unsure how she would take this outburst.

"I'm glad you like *Manfred* too," said Sarah, feeling she

ought to say something but a little startled at his sudden excitement. She thought he looked rather ill.

"Don't it make you thrill and tremble with a strange sort of delight which is half pain, as if you heard the language of your childhood after it had been a dead language to you for years?"

This was a Dr Heckford she had not seen before and she looked at him in wonder. "Yes," she said after a long pause. "Only I could never explain to myself what it was I felt."

"That is because you have been shut up with conventional people who stifled your ideas. What a thing to be a Byron – to be able to hold communion with Spirits, through your own Spirit; but it's all a dream, a sort of magnificent nightmare. We die and are buried and there's an end to us, as far as anyone knows."

She sat up at that. "I don't agree with you at all," she exclaimed. "How can you say there is an end of us – there is an end of our bodies – but that can't be the end of our spirits. It isn't our bodies that make us able to will, to admire, to hope – how can you say such things?"

"But we can't do any of those things if you paralyse our brains, even partially, and that is a purely physical affair. How do you explain that?"

Sarah was somewhat deflated. "Of course you can beat me there. You're a doctor and I'm not. But there is something in me which is better than the best arguments, something which tells me I must aspire – that points upward, upward!"

She stopped in embarrassment at having been so carried away when she was trying to argue reasonably. She felt her cheeks warm.

He shrugged his shoulders. "I believe you may be right, but who can say? You don't talk like most young ladies, but I suppose a young lady who comes down to an East End cholera hospital is not like most young ladies."

There was no answer to that and after a moment's prickly pause Dr Heckford said "Good night." She listened to his footsteps retreating down the stone stairs.

Everything in her ward was quiet; everyone, including her assistant, seemed asleep. Sarah sat and wondered about Dr Heckford. She liked him – but he was so very unlike the sort of man she was accustomed to. He was, she told herself, very handsome, but he did not seem to care about it, even to be aware of it. He never laid himself out to be pleasant but seemed to think that other people ought to humour him. He was at once shy in his manner and yet accustomed to command. He expected to be obeyed – and was. His word was law at the hospital; though Dr Woodman was nominally in command Dr Heckford was at the same time both more liked and more feared. His moods swung from gaiety to depression in a disconcerting way, without apparent cause. His conversation was unlike anything she had ever heard.

He seemed intelligent and well-informed and yet she was puzzled that he seemed to know nothing of the things which she had always thought of as being the interests of a cultivated, well-informed man. The Academy, the opera, balls, Hyde Park, seemed to mean nothing to him. This evening had been the first time she had had a long chat with him alone, but there had often been talks with him and Dr Woodman together. The people Dr Heckford seemed to know well were the poor. His topics of conversation were either his work, the people with whom he was dealing, or an interminable labyrinth of metaphysics, which left her and Dr Woodman at a loss.

There was something about him she could not fathom. He talked to her with a boyish confidence – she knew he must be rather younger than she was herself – but she felt he was not being open with her. There seemed, as she thought over their various meetings, to be some sort of mystery about him. On several occasions he had walked her home to her lodgings when she went off duty, asserting that she would not be safe in the crowded streets, and she had sometimes felt that he took more interest in her than his duties at the hospital necessitated. She tried to examine whether in return she had a more than ordinary interest in him, but dismissed the idea and forced herself back to her duties. Towards dawn was often the dangerous time for serious cases, when they would grow greyer and colder, and she would have to decide whether to call the doctor back. But tonight all was well and soon the day staff came in briskly. She made a last round of her patients, wondering as she did so how many would be there to greet her when she came back on duty, and gathering up her books, walked back to her lodgings alone.

4

Marriage and a hospital

It was now the end of August. New cases continued to come in but it was evident that the end of the epidemic was in sight. Sarah applied herself to the scheme of studies laid down for her by Dr Heckford but she was worried and disconcerted. She had thought that her happiness at the hospital, her eagerness to get back after every break, had been simply the result of useful work at long last and the chance to make a start on a real career. But had it – the "brightness" she had found – just been the result of falling in love? She had loved before, or thought she had, but she had been at all times so aware of her handicap that she had deliberately put love aside, sure that love and marriage could never be for her.

She had yearned to be quite different from other women, self-supporting and self-sufficient. The role of love-sick maiden was one she had no wish to be cast in. It did not fit in with her plans at all. She tried to dismiss the whole idea. Dr Heckford and she had become, as she put it, "great allies", their midnight tea parties a regular thing when she was on night duty. By September, with the cholera waning, there was not such a press of work as a few weeks previously and they had time for long talks that ranged over almost everything under the sun.

She was shocked to learn from Dr Heckford of the conditions under which many of the medical students lived.

He felt strongly about it. "I'm afraid a great many of them go to the bad – drink, and worse." ("Worse?" wondered Sarah to herself, not being able to imagine anything worse than that, but hardly liking to ask for enlightenment. She had heard that medical students were frequently a coarse, rough lot.)

"But they can't all be bad, surely?" she asked aloud. "Of course not," he replied impatiently, but the temptations were often too great for them. "I blame the men at the head of the schools. Why don't they think of the youngsters they meet and teach every day! Why don't they remember that they are not mere learning machines! As it is, one who has gone a little way down himself pulls down the one that is tottering, and they end by all wallowing together!"

He spoke so vehemently that Sarah was shocked, even if she was not sure what he was talking about. "But they are not all like that, are they?" she asked, trying to imagine Dr Heckford as the student he must have been a year or two earlier. "No, not at all, but a great many are and some who might be the best go first," he said, so bitterly that she wondered who he was thinking of and where he had "gone". She was sure from the way he spoke it must be somewhere terrible.

On other nights they had long discussions on religion and morality. Sarah found that his ideas were along similar lines to her own. He seemed to be using their talks to marshal his own ideas, looking to her for help in making his thoughts – "strange and beautiful" they were to her – clear to himself.

In these long, rambling exchanges over their midnight cups of tea Sarah sometimes found herself thinking that he seemed incapable of reasoned, consecutive thought, or less capable than she was herself; at least when it came to philosophical as opposed to scientific topics. She found this odd, when in many ways he was more cultivated than most men she knew. It came out that he was well read in French and German, that Virgil was a favourite of his and that he had read Homer in the original. But on the subject of his family and his origins he never spoke.

This piqued her curiosity. She was not so ill-mannered or insensitive as to probe where he wished to be reticent, so she tried to satisfy her curiosity in another way by casually bringing up the subject of Dr Heckford in conversation with Dr Woodman, who appeared to be a close friend as well as a professional colleague. Dr William Bathurst Woodman, who was 30, had made a hobby of languages. He later translated a German medical work into English and was co-author of *Medical Jurisprudence and Toxology*. He was greatly liked and respected by his colleagues, but his life ended tragically when he committed suicide at the age of 40.

Heckford, he told Sarah, was a clever doctor with a flair for diagnosis and a most able surgeon with a promising career ahead of him. In response to further roundabout questioning he said he thought he had heard somewhere that Dr Heckford had been born and brought up in India. That was all. Dr Woodman no doubt had a quiet chuckle to himself at this approach. Sarah was convinced she was the soul of discretion, preserving a purely professional relationship, but the midnight tea parties and the long whispered tête-à-têtes had not gone unmarked by either the staff or wakeful patients.

"God bless yer, Miss, I 'opes you'll be very 'appy. 'E's a lovely gentleman," Sarah was taken aback to receive from an old woman one night just after Dr Heckford had left. The budding romance undoubtedly cheered the patients, though Sarah was resolutely sure that her demeanour was such that no one could have a glimmer of her feelings for Dr Heckford, or that he had any towards her other than those of instructor to student or doctor to nurse. A delusion such as most women in love have at one time or another.

Once it was decided that she should study for her MD there were many talks and plans for her future. She explained to him that she had to think of her sister as well as they shared a house. "But if my sister marries, as she probably will one day," said Sarah (though Annie was nearing 30), "then I have sometimes thought that I would like to have a small hospital, or a school, or both together, in some poor district, possibly a model farm. If I do become a doctor I will be better able to help neglected people and civilise the people round me. I've often thought over just where I should apply my diminutive efforts."

"But that is my dream, exactly!" said Dr Heckford. "How have you got hold of it?"

"Then why don't you try to make your dream a reality?" she asked. "You are in a much better position than I to do such things and if you really want to you should try."

"Looking at me lounging on this empty bed and pulling my moustache I suppose you think me a lazy indolent fellow, but it is not as easy as all that," he replied, and that was the last said on the subject at that time.

By late September most of the cases were convalescent, Dr Woodman had begun dismissing the temporary staff and the excitement was over. He told Sarah they would probably be closing in another two weeks.

The cholera had taken a terrible toll. According to the returns of the Registrar-General nearly 8,000 people had died, more than half of them in the East End of London.

Finally, the day came that Sarah had been trying not to think about: the London was ready to cope on its own again and the emergency cholera hospitals were to be closed. It had been borne in on Sarah that she had come to depend on Dr Heckford's daily companionship and the thought of having to forgo it was painful.

The London Hospital Management Committee passed a resolution: "Resolved that the most grateful thanks of the Committee are due to those ladies who, throughout the period of the formidable outbreak of cholera, so nobly and efficiently gave their valuable and untiring services to alleviate the sufferings of the patients in the cholera wards." A copy of this resolution was published in *The*

Times and *The Daily Telegraph*, and each "lady volunteer" was presented with a Bible suitably inscribed by the Duke of Cambridge. The regular staff – doctors, nurses, servants, porters and "others who had rendered special services to the patients during the recent visitation" (the carpenter with his black-painted coffins?) – were given more tangible rewards in the shape of gratuities.

And so, presentation Bible and all, Sarah found herself abruptly at home with Annie in Warwick Square, the cholera hospital to be remembered for ever "with a weird brightness round it". She felt completely out of place. Though she could not help – against her better feelings – enjoying the awe with which her cousins who had spent the summer in the safety of Eastbourne regarded her and her sister, she felt desolate at the parting with Dr Heckford. Nothing had been said to encourage her to hope their relationship would continue. He had her address and had promised to call to see if she wished to continue her studies. She had the address of his lodgings in Stepney, at 65 Philpott Street, conveniently close to the London. The house, one of an 18th century terrace, is still there. She longed to invite him to dinner, but the last strands of conventionality held her back.

In those first days back in Warwick Square Sarah lived in a perpetual state of astonishment. She had been scolded and as good as told she was a disgrace when she had announced she was going to nurse in the now-defunct cholera hospital. She returned to find herself a heroine, petted and fêted, admiringly talked about by the very same people who had been swiftest to condemn her before the event. She found herself asked out here, there and everywhere as someone that everybody wanted to meet. She wondered whether she or all the others were mad.

In a quiet moment at a party given for a young cousin who was about to go overseas with his regiment, her host told her, "You are much changed, you know, altogether changed. You are an independent young woman now, with an air of quiet decision about you that you did not have before."

"Yes, I feel changed," she admitted. "I think you come to look at life in a very different way after you have been in a hospital like that cholera hospital for a while, not just as a lady visitor to the wards but working there and getting to know the patients."

There seemed to be no time of the day when she did not think about the hospital – and Dr Heckford. She had a perpetual reminder of him in the form of a young girl named Margarite (she spelt it that way) who had been a servant at the hospital. She was a pretty, dark-haired, frail girl of 17. One evening when Dr Heckford had been walking Sarah back to her lodgings he had told her that Margarite, whom he thought "a very superior kind of girl", was doomed by tuberculosis unless she could be got away from her grim surroundings in a slum home. He asked Sarah if she could help. He told her frankly that he had no money himself and did not know of anyone else but herself who might be able to help the girl. It was decided that Margarite should be sent to her and Annie's house to be trained for "good service" under their lady's maid. This might seem a strange suggestion to us but at that time the true nature of tuberculosis and how it was transmitted was not understood. Because several cases frequently occurred within one family it was thought to be inherited, not passed on by infection. Hence Dr Heckford's willingness to have a girl with "consumption" living with Sarah and her sister.

When Sarah had stood on the hospital steps saying good-bye to the two doctors on the day she left, Dr Woodman had said, "You will think about us when you've gone, won't you? You won't forget us?" Sarah had replied that of course she would not and had pressed them both to call on her and her sister. Dr Woodman turned back into the hospital; holding her hand, Dr Heckford had said, "I may come and see you sometimes, mayn't I? You must let me be your guest in that little room at the top of the house you told me about, that you had made into your studio. That would not be proper, though, would it? You are going back to the world of proprieties now."

Dr Woodman had called at Warwick Square about a week after her return, taken tea with them, chatted affably and departed, but Dr Heckford had not come. Each day that he neither called nor wrote was like a week. It was impossible to settle to the scheme of studies he had given her. She was distant to her friends, her thoughts constantly elsewhere.

And then he did call. He chose to arrive just as lunch was about to be served and the house was full of people. Sarah and Annie's solicitor had called to talk business with them, the subaltern cousin who was off to India had brought his fiancée to see them and an old family friend from Ireland had dropped in.

Dr Heckford was disconcerted. It did not seem to have occurred to him that Sarah could have any other life than her studies, that she might not be sitting alone at home waiting for him as she had waited for their midnight tea and talk sessions at the hospital. He apologised for interrupting a family meeting and arriving unannounced at an inconvenient time. He would call again another day. The military cousin, however, would have nothing of it. Everyone must celebrate his engagement and his coming departure overseas, Sarah must order another place to be laid and Dr Heckford must stay. "We all want to know what she's been up to. Dashed fine job you people did," he bellowed. So Dr Heckford stayed, hoping he did not look as awkward as he felt.

Sarah sat at the head of the table hardly daring to look at him. She was torn between joy that he had come and annoyance that he had picked the one time when it was not possible for them to be alone. For his part Dr Heckford talked studiously to the subaltern cousin and ignored his hostess. She became more and more exasperated as the meal progressed and she had to lend an ear to her cousin's fiancée's prattle about their forthcoming wedding and preparations for the voyage to India.

Soon after lunch the young couple departed in a cab, seen off at the door by Annie and Sarah. As they turned to go back upstairs to the drawing room Annie said, "You go on up to the studio and I'll send Dr Heckford up to you. I can quite well deal with our legal friend on my own; when he has gone I'll call you both down for tea."

"Annie, I can't, I'll come back to the drawing-room with you," Sarah pleaded, afraid of what she really wanted.

"Nonsense," said Annie briskly, having weighed up the situation over lunch to a nicety. "Up you go and do as you are told for a change."

Exactly what was said in the studio that afternoon, or when Dr Heckford proposed – if it was indeed he who made the proposal – is not known, but there was not a long interval between his visit to Warwick Square and their marriage. The wedding took place according to the rites of the English Presbyterians at the Little Portland Street Unitarian Chapel, near Oxford Circus. The date was 26 January 1867. The register was signed by Annie and Dr Woodman, presumably bridesmaid and best man, the minister, the Rev. James Martineau, and the Registrar, Thomas Tindall.

At the time of their marriage Sarah was 26, Nathaniel 23. When the engagement had been announced, everyone had assumed that, with Sarah's money and the house in Warwick Square, Dr Heckford would set up as a consulting surgeon in the West End. With his brilliance, charm of manner and good looks he would undoubtedly have had a most lucrative practice in a short time. Annie would live with them and a bright future would be ahead for all. That, however, was not how either Sarah, Annie or Nathaniel saw things. Dr Heckford had always dismissed the idea of a comfortable West End practice – the idea bored him and he made no bones about it, though the prospect would have been alluring to many of his contemporaries at the London. Evidently, however, Sarah had proposed this course, as she reported him as saying, "What is the greatest result you look forward to in that sort of life? Why do you want me to go in for it? The most it would lead to would be our wasting our time trying to please people instead of trying to help them; in our frittering away in ostentatious living almost as much money as we should make, and in giving parties to people we should not care for and who would not care for us; and at the end perhaps I should become Sir Nathaniel Heckford. What a glorious ambition! Let us stop and work in the East End – it will be much better."

Likewise he refused to rush into print, though urged to publish by colleagues who knew the contribution it could make to professional success if he were to make himself known in this way. "When I have a really instructive case I will bring that forward," he said. "What good will it do to bring my name forward? That is what fills up more than half the medical papers – men puffing themselves." Nathaniel could hardly have afforded to take such a high tone on his own. He opened an account with Coutts on 6 April 1867, with a cheque from Sarah for £41/12/3. A few small dividends were received but the account never held more than £40 or so at a time and it was closed on 19 May 1869.

Annie did not approve of unmarried sisters living with married ones and moved out into lodgings. She lived in lodgings for the rest of her life, ending up in Cintra Park, Upper Norwood. She kept her interest in matters medical, as is attested by her letters to the papers over many years concerning vaccination, compulsory hospitalisation of plague and fever cases (she did not approve), anti-vivisection, the need for health education and the Notification of Diseases Act.

As for Sarah, she was so deeply and overwhelmingly in love that had Nathaniel announced they were going to live in an igloo in the Arctic she would willingly have packed up and followed him there. Quite likely they stayed on in

Warwick Square for a while, Nathaniel commuting to his consulting rooms in the City, but the house was given up before the end of 1867. They may for a time have moved into the ground floor sitting room and one bedroom that comprised his lodgings at 65 Philpott Street. Certainly before they had been married for very long they were living in the East End, having taken the consumptive Margarite with them as their servant.

By this stage we have a better account, though by no means a full one, of Sarah's life: *The Story of the East London Hospital*, which was published to raise money for the hospital building fund in 1887.

There were long, earnest discussions as to what they should do. "We determined to work out our theories of life as it ought to be, on thoroughly new principles," Sarah wrote. "We were sometimes undetermined as to what to do, but we agreed that we must do something to show how much happiness might ensue if persons of means and culture would devote themselves to elevating those less fortunate than they."

This was neither as smug nor as patronising as it might sound to us today. It was perfectly honest and typical of the troubled social conscience of a section of the upper classes in mid-Victorian England. What was less typical was that Sarah and Nathaniel had the courage of their convictions. They gave up a comfortable life in a luxurious home in Belgravia to live and work in one of the poorest areas of the East End. They were also atypical in that they did not act out of conventional Christian beliefs. They acted according to moral and ethical principles which were part a British sense of justice and fair play, part a rather ill-digested Oriental mysticism. If that sounds muddled, it was, as anyone who reads the chapters of her novel *Excelsior* in which Sarah records their philosophical discussions and speculations will soon find.

One evening Nathaniel arrived home from a visit to friends on the staff of the London and scarcely greeting his wife burst out with, "I tell you what we must do: we must start a children's hospital. It is the thing most needed, and will do the most good. It is THE great need of the East End and we must do that and nothing else!"

He was right about the need for children's hospitals. They had for long been opposed, though there were dispensaries for children, the idea being that children should be cared for by their mothers at home. In theory this was all right, but Dr Heckford, with his knowledge of the East End and his experience of visiting patients in their homes – something he had always been willing to do at all hours of the day and night – knew too well that the only hope most sick children in the East End slums had of recovery was a stay in hospital, away from the insanitary, overcrowded conditions and poor diet in their homes. The Manchester Children's Hospital had opened as early as 1829 and the Kensington Children's Hospital in 1840; Great Ormond Street had been opened in 1852 but in 1867 no hospital admitted babies under two years old.

The inspiration was Nathaniel's but to Sarah this was also her great moment. Her vague yearnings were now channelled into a definite course and she threw herself into it headlong. All her life, whenever she undertook a project – and there were many of them, some of them distinctly odd – she would drive herself until she collapsed from exhaustion. When her legs would no longer hold her up she would go to bed, to rise in a remarkably short time and fling herself back into her work with a passionate determination, quite often charging ahead in a fury of impatient enthusiasm that meant unnecessary labour.

Now that she once more knew what she had to do, as she had known in the cholera epidemic, there was no holding her. With Margarite she tramped the streets of the East End at all hours in the hunt for premises. In his spare time Nathaniel joined in the search. They quartered the parishes of Shadwell, Ratcliff and Stepney and were almost in despair when a Dissenting minister named Benn told them about two old warehouses, one with a sail loft, at Ratcliff Cross, close to the river in Butcher Row, which were empty. "The price asked was £2,000, an exorbitant sum, but we were so hopeless of finding anything else, and so impatient to begin, we agreed to it," Sarah wrote. They were certainly held to ransom as the usual price for such a property was around £600.

Nathaniel's may have been the inspiration but the money to finance it was Sarah's. She sold £4,000 worth of Midland Debentures to see the hospital started – a substantial slice of her capital. She was quite sure they could live frugally, but there had to be funds for the hospital. She was never at any time in her life "good with money" and simply hoped they would get by somehow.

On 7 November 1867, a meeting was held in Nathaniel's consulting rooms at Broad Street Buildings at which an Interim Committee of Management was appointed, one of whose members was Nathaniel's father, Captain Nathaniel Heckford. Then an active man of 54, he worked hard as a committee member all through the early years of the hospital. When it became rather grand, with royal patronage, the Bishop of London as chaplain and titled ladies on the committee, he retired.

The formal minutes begin with a "preliminary meeting" held on 1 January 1868, at Nathaniel's consulting rooms. Apart from Nathaniel and his father those present were the Rev. E.R. Jones, Dr Barnes, Mr A.A. Caesar (whose appointment as dispenser was later to cause a monumental row), Mr Edward Whiston, Mr George Reid and the Rev. J.B. Burnaby.

Nathaniel told the committee that his aim was to establish a Children's Hospital in freehold premises which he had already purchased. He offered to guarantee all expenses up to £500 a year, "or more, if necessary", for two years. He also said that "whether seconded by the public or not" he intended to start at once with ten beds, to live on the premises "and to undertake the medical supervision".

The minutes record that "those present were unanimous in their opinion with respect to Dr Heckford's munificent offer, and they were all determined to second his good intentions to the best of their ability". Sarah basked happily in the glow of praise for her adored Nathaniel's "munificence". She never let it be known that the money was actually hers. Dr Barnes told the committee he had seen the premises at Ratcliff Cross and considered them suitable, especially as they were near the river "which secured a constant atmospheric change".

Another meeting was held a fortnight later. A prospectus had been printed and sent out and more subscriptions and offers of help had come in. At this point Dr Elizabeth Garrett's name first appears in the records. She had promised a subscription of a guinea a year. The first Englishwoman to be placed on the Medical Register, she had been one of Nathaniel's students at the London Hospital, though two years older than him.

Everything was now ready for work to begin. Sarah's own account of the opening of the hospital cannot be bettered.

> It was delightful work now. We moved the furniture and electrified Ratcliff Cross by the sight of the van and its contents. Some of the articles were too large to pass up the narrow stairs, and had to be hoisted through the windows, whilst a crowd of excited youngsters in the streets acted chorus as each article was removed from the van, crying "Here comes the sofa! Here come the fenders! Oh! Look at the gold, oh!" – their minds not having yet grasped the idea "all is not gold that glitters", which delusion caused our little drawing-room to be described by one privileged to see it as being "all furnished in gold", owing to a buhl cabinet and some ormolu ornaments. When our rooms were settled they looked very pretty; in the ward above them ten little iron bedsteads awaited their inmates; I painted "East London Hospital for Children and Dispensary for Women" on a board; we fixed it above the warehouse door, and on the 28 January 1868, the first anniversary of our wedding day, the hospital was opened.

That the hospital was needed was soon attested by the patients who crowded it. During the first year there were 312 inpatients and 4,624 outpatients, many of them women. Dr Heckford gave up his private practice, partly because he wanted to devote his whole time to the hospital, but also because he was anxious that it should not be thought that in founding it and appealing for funds he was trying a covert form of professional advertising. From that time (May 1869) on, Sarah's account at Coutts shows numerous payments to Nathaniel of sums from £5 to £20, indicating that she was making up to him the income he was losing.

Sarah was the hospital's matron and she soon gathered a staff of young nurses, including Margarite, all between 19 and 24 years old, Arthur Caesar – known to everyone as "Julius" – who acted as dispenser, a cook and servants. Someone had presented them with an old perambulator which was the hospital's "ambulance".

"We hardly knew where time went," wrote Sarah, "and took but little account of it; indeed, we worked so late, and were called up from our sleep so often, that day and night got somewhat mixed up; added to which I often went out to attend women in their confinements, and my husband constantly attended patients at their own homes, besides doing amateur work as a nightly visitor in haunts where the police were afraid to go alone. It was dangerous, no doubt, and I always felt thankful when he came home safe; but he had a great influence over the people, and it was part of our scheme for reforming the neighbourhood. No one who did not live near the Ratcliff Highway then can have an idea of what it was. I have seen men and women fighting and rolling together in the gutter before the hospital doors; have heard the shrieks of a woman in the opposite house until they were stopped by her being felled to the ground, and left weltering in her blood by her drunken husband, whilst her children stood aside in terror; and although we could see all from the windows of the wards, have been powerless to interfere because the poor creature had not called 'Murder!'

"I have seen my husband stand unarmed in the midst of a yelling mob, which the police were afraid to approach, and have heard his voice rise above the din and quell it, whilst he appealed to the better nature of those wild men and women, until at last they would disperse, the very combatants bidding him 'Good-night and God bless you, sir!' But as time went on the civilizing effect of the hospital began to be felt. I do not wish to paint these poor people as better than they are, but I think it speaks volumes in favour of the wretched population seething around 'The Highway', that not only my husband, but that I also, alone have traversed their streets and alleys at all hours of the night and early morning, with a watch and gold chain round my neck, a diamond ring on my finger, and a valuable brooch fastening my dress, yet have not been molested."

The East London was the first hospital to admit babies. Their ward, on the top floor of the second warehouse, was a complete innovation in the hospital care of children. An early visitor was Dr Murray, editor of *The British Medical Journal*. In the edition of 8 February 1868 he wrote a description of the hospital, pointing out that while there were thirty to forty hospitals in the wealthy West End, only the London and one or two others served the million inhabitants of the East End. Until now, he added, there had been no children's hospital there at all, and he pleaded for generous support.

Dr Murray was to prove a good friend to the hospital, not least because he introduced his cousin, Skelton Anderson, who became vice-chairman of the management committee. This was a particularly happy appointment and made none too soon. Both the Heckfords were hopelessly unpractical and Mr Anderson, an executive in his uncle's shipping firm, brought management experience to bear on the hospital's affairs.

Nathaniel had recently made the acquaintance of Dr Murray and had asked him to lunch to see "our bantling". He was to go over the hospital after the meal.

"We seldom indulged in luxuries," wrote Sarah, "and our

cooking was of the simplest; but this being a special occasion we determined to rise to it, and, in solemn conclave with the cook, I determined to attempt strawberry tartlets. The excitement produced in the kitchen by this announcement was great: it was generally felt that a superior effort was about to be made for the good of the hospital.

"Dr Murray came and partook, all unconsciously, of the tartlets. Whilst he was in the wards, after lunch, Mr Heckford descended to the subterranean kitchen to see that all was in order there. It was an unevenly paved, murky apartment at best – a cellar in disguise – but at that particular moment an accidental slip of the foot had upset a pailful of water which made small pools in the inequalities of the floor. 'Wipe it up, quick,' said my husband. 'Dr Murray is just coming down. You'll get us a bad report.' 'What!' exclaimed the girl addressed. 'After all them tarts?'"

One aspect of the management of the hospital which drew favourable comment was the excellent training that was given to the nurses. They also gave their nurses what no other hospital did at that time, a pleasant sitting room of their own where they could have their meals and relax when off duty. As numbers grew another house was bought opposite the warehouse to provide residential quarters for the staff. Sarah and her husband did not choose their student nurses for their educational qualifications but more often because, like Margarite, they were girls in need of help, and they responded with a devotion to the hospital which contributed largely to its success. Margarite, in particular, proved an able student. She studied anatomy, learned to use a stethoscope and watched post-mortems. She became an invaluable nurse despite her own precarious health. The Heckfords watched her carefully and made her take extra rest when they thought it necessary. One day during a post-mortem she startled them both while they were examining the lungs of a patient who had died of a peculiar form of tuberculosis. "That is the same sort of case as mine, sir, I think, only worse?" she said in tones of disinterested scientific enquiry.

The loyalty that their staff displayed glowed in Sarah's memory till the end of her life. When funds were low and they had to give some of the nurses notice because they could no longer pay them, they came in a body to Sarah and Nathaniel to say that if things were bad they would work without pay, just so long as the hospital could stay open. One of the nurses was a good dressmaker and Sarah urged her to get work elsewhere as they could not pay her what she could earn with her needle. But she pleaded that she could never be so useful or so happy anywhere else and she wanted to stay. Which she did – on a salary of less than £12 a year.

In her history of the hospital Sarah discoursed at some length on "distinctions of rank". She said that one thing she had learnt was "that there is as much refinement and elevation of thought to be found in the homes of the poor as of the rich".

"It is a difficult idea to grasp, unless in the midst of such work as ours was... A woman who has to lock up her baby's corpse into the only cupboard she has, along with the bread and sugar, in order to prevent her remaining little ones from wasting her scanty stores, or being frightened at the dead body while she is away at the hospital waiting for the certificate of death; a man who cannot but allow his wife's corpse to be opened in his own room, perhaps lying on his one table, in order that the professional scruples of her medical attendant may be satisfied before giving the same necessary document; or a child who hears the most private concerns of its parents' life ruthlessly discussed by a parish officer, is liable to harden on the outside; but within there may be, and often is, as refined a nature as can be found amongst the most delicately nurtured ladies or gentlemen."

In this school Sarah herself certainly toughened up – she had to if she was to go on with the work she had set herself – but she never lost her fierce sympathy with the victims of deprivation or injustice wherever in the world she found them, nor ceased while she was living to try to do what she could to better their lot. In their partnership she was the driving spirit, Nathaniel a softer and less abrasive character. "You were meant for the man and I the woman," he often said to her.

But for all their dedication and hard work, the happy comradeship of the two of them with their staff, the help of Dr Murray, their management committee and the visiting consultants, funds were not coming in. It was at this point that they had another visitor: Charles Dickens. He became a close friend and his death in June 1870 greatly distressed Sarah.

5

The East London Hospital

It was Dickens's visit which really set the seal of success on Sarah and Nathaniel's project, success which meant that what *Macmillan's Magazine* (February 1870) described as "an Ark by the Riverside in the midst of a dreary sea of suffering and hunger and cold" kept afloat. It led indirectly to a fine, purpose-built hospital in Shadwell and to royal patronage. The country branch at Banstead, named the Queen Elizabeth Hospital for Children, was opened in June 1948 by the then Princess Elizabeth. Sarah and Nathaniel's foundation is now amalgamated with the Queen's Hospital, Hackney, and known as the Queen Elizabeth Hospital for Children, in Hackney Road. The Shadwell hospital was closed in 1963 and the building has been pulled down. The Heckford ward at Banstead, which is now used as a mental hospital, commemorates the founders.

A legend at Banstead, when the children were still there, was that Sarah haunted it. The story went that when a child was desperately ill, if Sarah's shade was seen in the ward, it recovered, if not, it died. How anyone knew the ghost *was* Sarah's, or how, if it were, her shade was supposed to have found its way to the Banstead branch, opened many years after her death, no one has explained.

To return to the great day of Dickens's visit, the excitement among the staff when it was known he was coming was enormous. The cook, a stout party, hid herself and peered at the great man from her concealment. She explained afterwards that she had a dread of being "took off" by the famous novelist. One has to sympathise with her, thinking of some of his female creations. After showing him round the hospital, Nathaniel took Dickens to see some of the poor people living in the neighbourhood.

In the article Dickens subsequently wrote, which was published on 19 December 1868 in his magazine *All the Year Round*, he gives the impression that he stumbled on the hospital during a walk through the East End. However, from Sarah's account it is obvious that someone told him about the hospital and he invited himself, or else he was asked to go and see it by someone connected with it.

The article, with the title "A Small Star in the East", was afterwards reprinted in pamphlet form to raise funds for the hospital, but its appearance in the magazine brought an instant response. A letter arrived addressed to Nathaniel in childish handwriting, saying "my Mamma has read the story of your hospital to me. I am six, and would like to give the money in my money-box for the little children". It was, as Sarah put it, "the poetical beginning of an influx of money and help". Letters arrived in such numbers that they sat up half the night replying to them and acknowledging donations.

It is worth quoting Dickens's article extensively as it is the fullest account of the hospital in its earliest days that we have, rounding out Sarah's own story and the brevity of the minutes of the management committee.

> I found the Children's Hospital, [he wrote] established in an old sail-loft or storehouse, of the roughest nature, and on the simplest means. There were trap doors in the floors where goods had been hoisted up and down: heavy feet and heavy weights had started every knot in the well-trodden planking; inconvenient baulks and beams and awkward staircases perplexed my passage through the wards. But I found it airy, sweet and clean. In its seven-and-thirty beds I saw but little

beauty, for starvation in the second and third generation takes a pinched look; but I saw the sufferings both of infancy and childhood tenderly assuaged, I heard the little patients answering to pet playful names, the light touch of a delicate lady laid bare the wasted sticks of arms for me to pity; and the claw-like little hands, as she did so, twined themselves lovingly around her wedding ring...

A young husband and wife have bought and fitted up this building for its present noble use, and have quietly settled themselves in it as its medical officers and directors. Both have considerable practical experience of medicine and surgery; he, as house-surgeon of a great London Hospital; she, as a very earnest student, tested by severe examination, and also as a nurse of the sick poor, during the prevalence of the cholera. With every qualification to lure them away, with youth and accomplishments and tastes and habits that can have no response in any breast near them, close begirt by every repulsive circumstance inseparable from such a neighbourhood, there they dwell. They live in the Hospital itself, and their rooms are on its first floor. Sitting at their dinner table they could hear the cry of one of the children in pain. The lady's piano, drawing materials, books and other such evidences of refinement, are as much a part of the rough place as the iron bedsteads of the little patients. They are put to shifts for room, like passengers on board ship. The dispenser of medicines (attracted to them, not by self-interest, but by their own magnetism and that of their cause) sleeps in a recess in the dining room, and has his washing apparatus in the side board.

Dickens described Sarah and Nathaniel's pride in the alterations they had been able to make, moving or putting up partitions, installing a stove that had been given to them for the waiting room and the conversion each night of the tiny consulting room into a smoking room! Colourful prints and Sarah's paintings decorated the wards and:

A charming wooden phenomenon of a bird, with an impossible top-knot, who ducked his head when you set a counterweight going, had been inaugurated as a public statue that very morning; and trotting about among the beds, on familiar terms with all the patients, was a comical mongrel dog, called Poodles. This dog (quite a tonic in himself) was found characteristically starving at the door of the Institution, was taken in and fed, and has lived there ever since. An admirer of his mental endowments has presented him with a collar bearing the legend, "Judge not Poodles by external appearance." He was merrily wagging his tail on a boy's pillow when he made this modest appeal to me.

Sarah could never resist a doggy appeal. She owned a succession of dogs throughout her life and almost all the photographs of her that have survived include at least one of them. The children throve in this most uninstitutional atmosphere. The dispenser, "Julius" Caesar, was "really the life of the hospital" and the children adored him. He was general factotum and if a child wanted anything it was as likely to ask him as to call the nurse. "His advent in the ward, whither he always betook himself after dinner," said Sarah, "was heralded by a shriek of delight and a universal romp; and many a time he would catch up a baby and run downstairs with it sitting on his shoulder, to show it the glories of our private apartments, whilst on the occasion of impromptu festivities in honour of the birthdays of our nurses and servants, his genius for making people enjoy themselves was invaluable."

Dickens remarked as something worthy of mention that the children's mothers made good use of visiting hours and that even the fathers came on Sundays.

There is an unreasonable (but still, I think, touching and intelligible), tendency in the parents to take a child away to its wretched home, if on the point of death. One boy who had thus been carried off on a rainy night, when in a violent state of inflammation, and who had been afterwards brought back, had been recovered with exceeding difficulty; but he was a jolly boy, with a specially strong interest in his dinner, when I saw him.

As well he might have. The prime causes of the diseases which brought the children to the hospital were starvation and the insanitary, crowded conditions of their homes. Good food and hygiene were the best medicine. Dr Heckford instituted a system of aftercare for discharged patients, who were invited to dinner every now and then, as were some hungry children in the neighbourhood who never had been patients. Dickens ended thus:

> An affecting play was acted in Paris years ago, called *The Children's Doctor*. As I parted from my Children's Doctor now in question, I saw in his easy black necktie, in his loose buttoned black frock coat, in his pensive face, in the flow of his dark hair, and his eyelashes, in the very turn of his moustache, the exact realisation of the Paris artist's ideal as it was presented on the stage. But no romancer that I know of, has had the boldness to prefigure the life and home of this young husband and young wife, in the Children's Hospital in the East of London.

The help that followed the publication of "A Small Star in the East" arrived not a moment too soon. The sudden relief from the crushing anxiety of the previous months was a shock in itself. It was decided to celebrate with a grand Christmas party, which was fixed for Christmas Eve. Two hundred children from the streets around the hospital were invited. One committee member lent a magic lantern and Sarah invited friends from the West End, asking them to dress as they would for a party in Belgravia so that the children could have the thrill of seeing ladies in beautiful dresses and jewellery – who might have been creatures from another planet.

The nurses were each presented with a dress of white book muslin with a red sash, to their great delight. The Christmas tree was put up in the operating theatre and a "grand tea" served in the outpatient department, where as soon as tea had been cleared away the magic lantern show was given. In addition there was Punch and Judy with Dog Toby in attendance and a barrel-organ for music. The hospital, decorated with flags and evergreens, "offered a quaint appearance filled with motley guests".

But in spite of the fun, the toll of long hours, hard work and anxiety over money began to take effect, not only on Sarah and Nathaniel but on the consumptive Margarite, whose declining health began to worry them seriously. Just at that time an American woman asked Charles Dickens if he knew of a pleasant, trustworthy girl to be maid and companion to her little daughter on a tour through France, Italy and Switzerland. He introduced Mrs Johnson to the Heckfords and they begged her to take Margarite. They asked that she should not be treated as a servant but as one of the family, paid no wages but given the extra comforts needed by an invalid. The Heckfords said they would provide her with a dress allowance and pocket money. Mrs Johnson agreed, and treated the girl with great kindness. The letters that came back to the hospital from Margarite in the following months surprised Sarah, they were so well written and showed how much the girl had developed since the days of the cholera hospital.

Despite Dickens's help, as 1869 wore on money was again short; not enough was coming in to meet increasing expenses. Sarah does not specifically mention it at this time but they adopted a little girl of about ten years old, Marian Matthews. Who Marian's parents were, or how she came to be adopted, is not known but there is a strong supposition that she was a patient at the hospital. A picture of her in Sarah's photograph album shows a plump, rather smug-faced child with dark, wavy hair.

They skimped and saved and tried to "make every shilling do duty for one-and-sixpence" but when, just before Christmas, they had paid the monthly accounts all they had in hand was two-and-elevenpence of the hospital funds and a balance of three pounds at Coutts. It was evident they could not go on and reluctantly they decided to close two of the wards. This was the occasion on which the staff came in a deputation and refused to be discharged, offering to work without pay till times were better. Many faces were streaked with tears. In vain did Nathaniel explain it was not just their poor wages that were proving the breaking point but the patients' keep.

In a defiant gesture they decided to give another party,

this time on New Year's Eve. That same December, soon after the lachrymose staff meeting, there was a fund-raising evening of amateur entertainment given at the London. Sarah and Nathaniel were invited and although they had little inclination for merrymaking they decided they had better accept. The fiat had already gone out for reducing the scale of the Children's Hospital's work but no actual changes had been made. Walking home gloomily from what she described as "the brilliant little affair at the London", Sarah thought bitterly how hard it seemed that the relatively rich London should continue to be fed while their struggling little hospital, for all the genuine need that it was meeting, was dying of starvation.

"We had not heart left even for lament," wrote Sarah, "and we walked in silence. I was taking off my bonnet in my room when my husband came in quickly, waving a letter in his hand. 'What do you think this is?' he asked, 'Look, a thousand pounds!' 'Nonsense, how can you talk so?' I exclaimed; but he held it before my eyes: it was – it really was – a note for one thousand pounds, sent anonymously!" They were stunned with relief and it was the next day before they could really grasp what had happened.

New Year's Eve came and with it the committee and friends of Sarah and Nathaniel, 200 former patients and an artist from *The Illustrated London News*. His drawing was published in the edition of 8 January 1870. It shows an odd-looking gentleman with long hair, drooping moustaches, and a holly-wreathed hat standing in front of a toy-laden Christmas tree in the girls' ward. Poodles sits on a bed in the foreground, elegantly dressed ladies and gentlemen sit and stand around and Sarah and Nathaniel are on the left of the picture.

The party was a great success. The report that accompanied the *I.L.N.* picture described the events of the evening, including the Punch and Judy in the boys' ward, "which, from the roars of laughter, seemed to be thoroughly appreciated". It added that the pressing need for expansion of the work meant they must appeal for funds and that during the two years of the hospital's existence 7,155 outpatients had been treated and 597 inpatients. It was a staggering number for a makeshift hospital in a sail loft.

The party became legendary in Ratcliff and, as far as "the poor" were concerned, was a wonderful success to be recalled long after. Sarah was amused many years later to hear an old woman recount how that night she had seen for the first time an incredible sight – ladies and gentlemen in evening dress – and that they had been regaled with turkey and champagne in a room lit by Chinese lanterns. "I did not destroy the harmless illusion," said Sarah, "but my memory must be strangely at fault if there were either turkey or champagne provided, although I know there was some very weak mulled wine."

The euphoria created by the party soon faded, however, as the new year brought the certainty that Nathaniel had contracted tuberculosis, or, in the terminology of the day, "was in a consumption". The source of infection could well have been Margarite, though they must both have been constantly in contact with the disease in the course of their work. "We shall neither of us live long," he told her. "You have the sickness too."

As he felt his health failing Nathaniel became feverishly impatient to see the hospital soundly established but subscriptions were once again falling off and the committee, on whom so much depended, seemed to him to be lacking in initiative and not working as hard for the hospital as he thought they should. One evening when he was feeling particularly dispirited he said to Sarah, "There is only one thing. The Committee won't pull together until they know that the place absolutely belongs to them. They have some idea that we want to put ourselves forward. Let us give them the freehold. They must work then."

Sarah suggested that the committee be offered a nominal leasehold on a long term, but Nathaniel thought that would make no difference. She reminded him that if he gave away the freehold he gave away the right to dispose of the premises as he saw fit. They had long decided that the sail loft could only be a temporary home for the hospital and that somehow money must be raised for a proper building. They had intended that as soon as the hospital was properly housed the warehouse would be used for a Lock Hospital, that is, a closed hospital for the treatment of venereal disease in women, "in the hope of thereby being able to combat disease morally as well as physically".

Admission to a Lock Hospital carried a terrible stigma, as bad as prison or the workhouse. Under the Infectious Diseases Act of 1863 any woman suspected of being a prostitute could be arrested and forced to submit to a medical examination. If found to be infected she was consigned to a Lock Hospital under a court order for treatment and detained there until cured. The Act was bitterly opposed by the Women's Movement, and also the whole concept of the Lock Hospitals. The idea of using the Butcher Row building for such a purpose was originally Nathaniel's, and Sarah's support of it is one of the instances that show she was not a wholehearted supporter of "The Cause" in every particular.

When Sarah reminded her husband of his plan he said sadly that he had given up the idea as hopeless. "We shall never live to do it. Let us make sure of the future of our one scheme. We shall never do more, if even we can manage that. If we die before it is fairly started it will be ruined. The committee must work, and they won't until they feel the place is theirs."

Sarah admitted there was some truth in what he said, but it was only the conviction that his life was being endangered by constant anxiety about the hospital that at last brought her to give her consent. Not that it was needed. The Married Women's Property Bill was before Parliament but was not actually passed until August 1870. Before the Act became law the whole of a woman's property became her husband's as soon as they were married. He may have been obliged to say in church "with all my worldly goods I thee endow", but in fact the boot was on the other foot: she endowed him. Nathaniel, however, was too honourable to take his wife's money and do what he pleased with it without her agreement. He had also come to rely on her judgement. Had he not said that she should have been the man and he the woman? So the deed was drawn up and signed – to the astonishment of the committee.

For a while it seems to have galvanised them into action, but the effect did not last long. It was at this moment that Ashton Warner was appointed secretary of the hospital, and Sarah soon realised that at long last its affairs were in capable hands.

Meeting the new secretary in his office every day and seeing how calmly, firmly and conscientiously he set about disentangling the hospital's affairs, Sarah felt that there was a hope that the work they had begun would continue. But she was not entirely happy at the changing atmosphere at the hospital. "The life of fun and frolic was gradually fading away like the dew of early morning before the noon-day glare. We could not understand why this should be, and we rebelled fiercely against it."

We may find it difficult to understand how they could ever have found the hard and frequently distressing work of the hospital "a life of fun and frolic", but it is a revealing remark. So also is her comment that to them the hospital did not mean "a mere hospital", however well appointed and well managed. To them it meant "a system by which widely different classes of society might come to appreciate their unity, and learn to develop the good which is in all alike, disguised under various aspects". No committee, she conceded, could be blamed for finding it impossible to realise this idea but she began to hope that Mr Warner might take it up and help them to work it out.

It was in the early part of 1870 that another important appointment was made at the hospital. At a meeting of the Board of Management in February, Nathaniel "spoke in favour of inviting Miss Garrett to join the Hospital, which he knew she was willing to do". The proposal was not well received. The minutes record a discussion among the members as to whether or not it would be advisable "to make any innovation by introduction of female physicians, which would be a grave step for a hospital in its infancy". The general public, on whom the hospital depended for the voluntary subscriptions that kept it going, still abhorred the idea of women as doctors, and it was to be some time before opinion came round. In June 1872, Queen Victoria wrote to her eldest daughter, the Crown Princess of Prussia, "The case of the women is one which I have a very strong feeling upon. I think they should be sensibly educated – and employed whenever they can be usefully, but on no account unsexed and made doctors (except in one branch), lawyers, voters, etc. Do that, and you take away at once all their claim to protection on the part of the male sex." Sarah would never have agreed with that, but the Queen was far from being alone in her opinions.

On 16 March Nathaniel returned to the subject of Dr Garrett at a meeting held in Granville Wright's office. He urged the committee to appoint Dr Garrett because it would strengthen the body of supporters of the hospital, rather than the other way about. He pointed out that she had recently founded her own hospital, which was to be associated with a medical school for women. He urged them to "strike out a new path in expectation of gaining the suffrages of the public". Some of the committee feared her appointment would alienate the greater part of the medical profession and thus greatly damage the hospital, but others, including some of the doctors, were in favour. Skelton Anderson, as the hospital's financial adviser, was wary of anything that might upset the subscribers. He knew the area well and did not think a woman would be suitable for such a tough job, despite all that Sarah had done. He changed his mind, however, after meeting Elizabeth Garrett and the proposal to appoint her was carried unanimously.

This first appointment of a woman honorary at any British hospital was announced in *The Times* on 22 March and Dr Garrett took up her duties on 23 March 1870.

She had qualified by taking the examinations of the Society of Apothecaries, having been unable to gain admission to a university in the face of the immense opposition in the 1860s. She had been placed on the register, the first Englishwoman to be so recognised. The Society of Apothecaries took fright and closed their examinations to women. Dr Garrett had hoped to receive her MD from a British university but it was impossible, so she went to Paris in June 1870 to take their final examinations and returned triumphant to London a fully fledged MD. She was convinced that only by her becoming not just a good but a great physician could the prejudice against women doctors be overcome.

Conditions at the East London Hospital appalled her. The medical work was brilliant and the children did well but the haphazard administration angered her. She found the work gruelling, and heart-breaking when a child saved by devoted nursing had to be returned to the squalor which had caused its illness. The death rate among children in the district distressed her. She had always liked and admired Dr Heckford, but Sarah was another matter. She could not do with what she called "Mrs Heckford's airy-fairy ideas". The two women were strongly contrasted and Dr Garrett told Skelton Anderson that she and Sarah were "not so made as to be capable of much active friendship". As Sarah nowhere makes any mention of Elizabeth Garrett we cannot be sure what she felt about her in return.

Dr Garrett embarked on a course of trying to get practical reforms introduced. This was not likely to have endeared her to Sarah. Her first move was to tackle the chaos in the outpatients department, and she drew up a new system to bring order to the noisy crowds who attended. The committee thought a man should be put in charge but she rejected with scorn the idea that a woman could not control the department. Skelton Anderson backed her up in the committee. During this time she wrote frequent letters to him about hospital affairs which are preserved in the Fawcett Library and her comments make a telling contrast to Sarah's own story of the hospital.

Real trouble, however, arose when Dr Garrett's investigations reached the dispensary. When she looked into the books and records she was dissatisfied with the way that drugs were bought and kept. She became sure that a great deal of money was being wasted. She was both surprised and angry to find that "Julius" Caesar had no qualifications for the job. "I shall move to have this department set in order," she wrote to the vice-chairman on 20 August. "The dispenser does not know his business and there is no supervision, no check either upon him or the wholesale druggist." This really stung Sarah and she flew to Mr Caesar's defence with a round declaration that she and Dr Heckford had every faith in him. The committee tried to subdue Dr Garrett but she stuck to her point and used every opportunity she could to bring up the dispenser's lack of qualifications. However, 18 years later, Arthur Caesar was still a member of the Board of Management.

By autumn it was plain that Nathaniel's health was failing fast. He was ordered to spend the winter in Italy or Egypt. As Sarah naturally was to go with him a matron had to be found to take over at least some of her duties. One candidate for the post, which carried the then generous salary of £70 a year, told the committee "the inconvenience and bad arrangements were so overwhelming that she could not undertake the office". However, after a Mrs Fisher had been engaged as housekeeper, Miss Pollock took the post of matron "on a monthly engagement".

In October Sarah and Nathaniel set out, intending to go to Egypt, but by the time they reached Italy Nathaniel was too weak to travel further. They settled down at the quaint and comfortable hotel of the Cappuccini at Amalfi. The balcony of their room had a view of bays and headlands along that beautiful coast. The peace and balmy weather restored Nathaniel and he began to recover but the storms at the hospital pursued them to their haven. Nathaniel watched every post for letters and there were even telegrams between Amalfi and London. None of this was conducive to an improvement in his health. But worse was to follow.

During the previous summer Nathaniel, who was the most friendly and trusting of men, had met a Dr Baron von Seidewitz. They had become friends and Nathaniel had invited him to see outpatients at the hospital for a while. He had not checked the Baron's qualifications or references and had gone off to Italy leaving the Baron in charge of outpatients, though Dr Leonard, the house surgeon, had a poor opinion of him. When battle was joined in December 1870, Dr Garrett warned the committee that if Dr Baron von Seidewitz proved incompetent his acting as consultant in Dr Heckford's absence could seriously damage the hospital. She said that, whatever the committee might think of Dr and Mrs Heckford's right to put a personal friend in as a consulting physician, such a person should not have actual charge of patients. Finally she moved on 13 December that the Baron's appointment had been made irregularly and should lapse. No one on the committee would second this but they did agree to tell Von Seidewitz that it was "absolutely necessary for him to be registered as a qualified medical practitioner in the United Kingdom". Dr Garrett also got through a motion "that a competent person be appointed to enquire into the quality of the drugs supplied to the hospital".

Like a dog worrying a rat she would not let the matter of the Baron's qualifications rest. At Amalfi Nathaniel fretted over the insult to his friend and the damage the fracas might do to the hospital, where Dr Leonard, the house surgeon, was now also under threat of suspension.

At the end of February news reached Nathaniel from his father that the Baron was about to be told he must produce acceptable medical qualifications or resign forthwith, and that there were problems in Dr Leonard's position. The committee had told the house surgeon that he should resign as he was not experienced enough to carry on without Dr Heckford's supervision. The committee had been bitterly divided and debate acrimonious. Nathaniel read the letter carefully several times and then decided he must return to London. It was evening. Sarah had been sitting on the balcony watching the sun go down, enchanted at the scene before her. Nathaniel came out and leaned on the rail, looking at the light dying over the sea. "Well," he said, "When shall we start?"

Sarah was snatched out of her reverie and felt a cold grip on her heart. For him to go back into the teeth of the March winds and to the hard work of the hospital meant, she was sure, certain death within a year. She told him the decision must be his, she could not even advise, but it was useless his going back unless it was to work and to do that would be to write his own death warrant. If he made a supreme effort he might put things right at the hospital, but it would kill him. Would it not be better to leave the hospital to its fate for now, rest a while longer and get his health back so that he could work perhaps for years longer? "But the hospital would be ruined," he answered stubbornly. Sarah did not reply. Sitting there miserably in the dusk she knew that if he felt it right to go back that was what he was going to do. Later, when it was all over, she had no doubt that they had made too much of the difficulties at the hospital and the threat these formed to its continuance and success, but it was hard to see it at the time.

Recounting that evening at Amalfi she added, "My faith in a Providence of which we are at best but instruments, and often mere tools, was very faint and vague. I believed in him, and in myself, practically more than I believed in anything else."

Nathaniel gazed out over the darkening sea as if taking a final farewell of Amalfi. Then he turned to her at last and said, "We'll go home. It's true, I shan't see next year, but the hospital will be saved. What is my life against the good of numbers? The hospital must go first."

By the time they reached England Nathaniel was ill again. They stayed with friends a little way out of London, Sarah managing to persuade Nathaniel that the murky air of the East End in March would be immediately fatal. They were delighted by a visit from Margarite, who was passing through London with Mrs Johnson. Sarah went to the station to meet her and gasped at the young lady who came down the platform to greet her. "It was our Margarite, and yet not our Margarite. Even before she spoke there was an indescribable something about her which is so seldom met with but in one who, if not born, has, at least, from childhood been bred a 'lady'. But Margarite was one; by every turn of her face and figure, by every action, every word, even by the intonation of her voice." The transformation from slum child to young lady was a triumph and they "rejoiced accordingly". It seemed the vindication of their whole philosophy and they were as delighted as Professor Higgins. It is an intriguing possibility that Shaw may have read *The Story of the East London Hospital* – it was reissued in 1904 – and found in Margarite the seed of the idea that flowered as Eliza Doolittle.

But rejoicing did not last long with some of the committee still demanding Baron von Seidewitz's removal. On 10 April Sarah and Nathaniel attended a committee meeting at which Nathaniel managed to smooth things over a little. It was Nathaniel himself seconded by Sarah, who put forward the motion that the Baron be told that as he, Dr Heckford, had now resumed his duties, the committee would recommend the Baron's appointment by the next Annual Court in May, provided he obtained a United Kingdom qualification within six months of that date. Skelton Anderson moved that the Baron not be appointed until he had qualified but that was defeated. Nathaniel's motion was carried by five votes to three.

The Baron claimed to have a Paris MD, but when the

committee tried to trace it they failed. Sarah, and more especially Nathaniel, were hurt and embarrassed but there was nothing more they could do at the time. Shortly afterwards Skelton Anderson and Elizabeth Garrett were married. She continued to practise as Dr Garrett Anderson.

During the summer a site in Glamis Road, Shadwell, was found and bought for the new hospital building. Work began on drawing up a new set of regulations suitable for such an institution as the East London Hospital would now be.

By October Nathaniel was worse. At the last committee meeting of the month Sarah – unable, she felt, to leave him even for a few hours – asked leave of absence from her post as Visiting Governor. Hoping that sea air, even if not Italian, would help, Sarah went with Nathaniel to Ramsgate, where they took rooms in The Paragon. "Julius" Caesar and Ashton Warner both came down to visit them. Finally Nathaniel was confined to bed, but despite his weakness continued to work on the proofs of the new hospital rules which had been sent to him for checking.

On 12 December an important committee meeting was due. The Baron's six months' grace was up and his resignation was to be demanded. Sarah and Nathaniel had prepared a last-ditch defence of their friend but Nathaniel was very ill and seemed to Sarah to be sinking fast. She did not want to leave him but he insisted she must go. Reluctantly she consented. Ten of the committee were already assembled at the London Tavern when Sarah arrived. She was grateful for her father-in-law's presence and support. Three more members hurried in just after the proceedings had begun. Sarah felt the tense atmosphere and knew she had a battle on her hands.

A letter from the Baron, tendering his resignation, was read. The chairman, Mr Scrutton, told the meeting he had written to his agents in Paris. They had searched the Medical Register as far back as 1836 but there was no record of the Baron's name.

At this point Sarah rose to explain that she had herself seen the Baron's name recorded as an MD of Paris, "but that probably during the excitement of the Emperor's leaving France the records might have been destroyed". She was of course referring to the Franco-Prussian War which had culminated in the fall of Paris and the surrender of Napoleon III at Sedan at the beginning of January that year. It was a last desperate plea which she must have known would be impossible to substantiate, even though she and Nathaniel had probably passed through Paris on their way to Amalfi before the Siege, when they could conceivably have checked the records themselves. The committee, however, remained sceptical. The Rev. J. Kennedy moved that the Baron's resignation be accepted and a letter expressing appreciation of his services to the hospital be sent to him. Sarah seconded it. Skelton Anderson then moved an amendment that the resignation merely be accepted, with no letter of appreciation. "Debate continued," say the minutes, and Anderson's amendment was carried. It must have been a bitter pill for Sarah.

It was night when she got back to Ramsgate. Nathaniel's first words were to ask the result of the meeting. He had been lying all day with his watch beside him, impatient for the time when he knew Sarah would be speaking in the Baron's defence.

"He was dying," Sarah wrote in her history of the hospital, "and was at times delirious. Indeed he had known for some time that there was no more hope. 'I have done so little,' he said once, 'and I hoped to do so much, but I suppose it was worth living for to do that little?' Shortly before he died he told me that I must try to feel that it was better for him to die than to live, for that, broken as his health was, he should only cause me to waste money and thought in carrying a worn-out creature from place to place, instead of devoting both to helping those who might yet be useful. 'You will be able to do much more good without me than with me,' he ended. 'You will not be long in following me, but you must see the hospital settled.'"

Nathaniel Heckford died early on the morning of 14 December 1871. He was 29 years old. His body was taken to the hospital, where it lay for a day in his old consulting room. Crowds of women and children filed through, weeping. Next day he was buried in the Goff family plot in the cemetery at Woking.

6
Widowhood – Italy and India

Sarah was 32. "What should I do without you?" Nathaniel had said to her once when they were at Amalfi. "You calm me, you arrange my ideas, you help me understand my own thoughts. I should go mad without you."

Sarah knew what she had to do now she was without Nathaniel. She had to go back to work at the hospital. His words to her at the end, "You will not be long in following me," were constantly on the edge of her consciousness. She was driven on by the thought that she had not much time and that the work must be completed.

She and Nathaniel shared a belief in a spirit world. She had taken from him the idea that every man and woman on earth was there because a spirit was trying to work towards perfection, and that some were more "experienced" than others, having worked their way through many previous lives. She believed in an all-pervading Supreme Spirit, a "self-existent creative Being". Though Nathaniel was not an avowed, practising Buddhist, many of his beliefs were in accord with the Buddhist religion, imbibed during his early years in India. This accounts for his refusal to kill as much as a cockroach: to the Buddhist all life is sacred and to kill even an insect is murder. Sarah came to hold this, too. Friends remembered it of her after her death. She would carefully capture any insect found indoors and carry it outside unhurt, saying firmly, "I live here and you live there," as she released whatever it was in the open air.

Buddhism teaches the way of liberation through ethics and discipline, which had a great appeal to Sarah. It is also a creed of detachment, which accounts for Nathaniel's fatalism towards his illness and the "death wish" that he expressed on at least one occasion, the longing for Nirvana. Sarah was, at least nominally, a Unitarian but many of her ideas do not fit that pigeonhole.

"You are my master, my guide. I cannot touch you," she once said to Nathaniel. He told her that if he died before her he would linger at the edge of the spirit world waiting for her.

This thought sustained her. She loved him with an all-absorbing devotion but she was not one to waste time in mourning or parading her grief. She had a gold locket with Nathaniel's picture – a gaunt young man with a lock of hair falling over his eyes – and with a snippet of his dark, wavy hair in it. She wore it until she died.

She returned to her post as Visiting Governor and immersed herself in the details of the planning and building of the new hospital, sometimes drearily, often wearily, with the constant aching thought that Nathaniel was not there to share the work and the joy of seeing their plans fulfilled. She was convinced she also was consumptive and had not long to live and she drove herself unsparingly.

In the year following Nathaniel's death, 1872, in spite of her involvement with the hospital, she found time to put down on paper the ideas and beliefs which had been maturing over the previous ten years or more. The result was published in London by Field and Tuer under the title *The Life of Christ, and its bearing on the Doctrines of Communism*. This short book – it can be read in an evening – is the key to Sarah's whole life. It opened with a letter of dedication to Marian Matthews Heckford. Dated 4 March 1873, it read: "My dearest Child. I dedicate this little book to you, not only as my adopted child, and as one I love as my own, but as the representative of the many children and young girls with whom my husband and myself came into affectionate contact during our connection with the East London Hospital for Children, and from whom we learnt more than from any books we ever read. To you then as their representative, and as one from whom I have learnt many invaluable lessons, I dedicate this book, in token of gratitude. Whether you may now, or in after life, agree with the opinions expressed in it or not, I know that you will always believe that they are the result of honest thought."

The book begins with a brief discussion of the divinity of Christ. Sarah said that she herself did not believe in it and had not done so for a long time. She objected, however, to "scepticism which attempts to discover flaws in His conduct and strives to lower a noble character". Even though the idea of the divinity of Christ "is unfounded, it is at least a grand idea, a superb magnification of the old Grecian idea of the demigods". She then left the subject, saying that it had been discussed by numbers of people who were more competent to debate it than she was.

She went on to say she was writing the book to show how Christ's teaching could be applied "in dealing with the social problems of the present age".

The next few chapters are devoted to a sketch of Christ's life on earth which is in effect a commentary, rather than a history. While not showing any great profundity it does indicate a thorough knowledge of the gospels, and indeed of the whole Bible, which could only have been gained by long and thoughtful study. The Quaker background of her family made its contribution, and so did the works of Priestley, Darwin, Huxley and Marx, with which she seemed to be familiar, though the only person she actually quoted was Octavia Hill. She laid emphasis on the Eastern nature of Christ's teaching as she saw it, and the light it threw on the existence of a universal Supreme Being.

The last section of this surprising little book begins, "In

the present day, when social reformation is more or less the theme of discussion in all ranks, but when it is principally discussed by those who will not only gain most by it, but who are daily acquiring more power to enforce their views, I think it is of great importance that those who have a great deal to lose by the undeniable growth of communistic doctrines should study them honestly, and whilst rejecting the dross, refine the pure gold which is in them. By doing so they, the most educated portion of the community, will lead, instead of being forced to submit to, the dictates of the revolution which is coming, and may materially help to make it a purely moral one." She was well aware of how what she was saying would be received. "Immorality of all sorts, and that greatest immorality of all, cruelty, has generally been the result of communism as put into practice by the poor. Hence it is hardly to be wondered at that the rich have come to regard communism as but a synonym for rapine and bloodshed. Yet its enlightened advocates tell one that it is a code of morality which might have been approved of by Christ himself."

Society is divided into the working class and the idle class. "The wealthy banker, the prime minister, the elegant and fascinating wife, who whilst apparently amusing herself really keeps his party together, are all of the working class: so is the dock labourer, and so also is every good mother in the midst of her children, provided she cares for and educates them herself instead of handing them over to others." The idle class consists of those who cannot work, either from infirmity or because they cannot find work, including "the daughters of the rich, to whom good useful work would be a luxury, but to whom prejudice denies it", and "the thoughtless and frivolous", who can be found in the public house, the workhouse and the prison as well as "in the haunts of those with money to command". She appealed to the rich and idle, "the inheritors of capital, small or great", because "it is not selfishness but simply want of thought which prevents its members from endeavouring to carry out, to some extent at least, the teaching of Christ as regards social reform". The commandment which bears most on this question is "Go and sell all thou hast and give unto the poor and come and follow me", to which "Love thy neighbour" comes second. She interpreted it as, "Give all you have to those in want and come and earn your living ... by curing the sick and teaching the ignorant... It is a duty to earn your own living, honestly and conscientiously and it is a duty to give to others the means of living, if such means are in your possession." This might be by giving employment to others who had no work. Those who had an independent income could use it to keep themselves while they did unpaid social or charitable work, but rather on the lines of St Paul's "it is better to marry than burn", asserting that it was better to work for your keep if you could. The "nobility of work" is a constantly recurring theme.

She was particularly insistent on the need for the proper education of girls so that there shall be "no more half-taught girls going out as second-rate governesses".

There would be, she knew, "a phalanx of objections" to her ideas. Many of the "rich and idle" were convinced that "to work for one's livelihood means to be a drudge ... with no enjoyment or amusement", an idea "peculiar to ladies". She demolished this concept, and also the one that if you took up charitable work you must give up parties, theatres and dressing well, "and that you must be grave and benevolent, not frisky or laughter-loving". There were a number of earnest, serious-minded women constantly bent on "good works" and Sarah thought their attitude misguided.

There follows an exposition of the uses of capital both to create wealth, to diffuse it more widely and to promote employment ... but without education nothing could be achieved. "The labour market is at present glutted with men who are too ignorant to do anything but the commonest work, too ignorant to understand even the simplest abstract idea of justice, or any other principle of action, but whose very ignorance, whetted by their want, makes them excellent tools to the hands of an ambitious demagogue or enthusiastic communist. To talk to these men of a just distribution of wealth means to incite them to plunder the rich. This is the dross of communism: the refined gold lies in the principle that it is the duty of every human being to work for his livelihood."

Finally she turned to the bearing of Christ's life, death and teaching on the laws against suicide. The subject might appear foreign to communism, she said, but it was not. "The enlightened communist" based his theories on the idea that each human being should regard himself not as an individual but as a member of a community and should be ready to sacrifice himself for the good of that community. That sacrifice could conceivably be life itself. She made an impassioned plea for the right to take one's life if it had become unendurable and said there was nothing in the Bible against it (which must have raised a few eyebrows). She went on to say that it might not be necessary actively to take one's own life to commit suicide. To act in a way you know was likely to lead to your death without trying to avoid it could be called suicide and on these lines she argued that the Crucifixion was suicide. Jesus had warning of His arrest and knew what would happen, but made no attempt to escape, going quietly with the soldiers who arrested Him. This, she argued, pointed to suicide being in some circumstances justifiable and that there should be no law against it.

How widely this book was read is impossible to tell, but it revealed a great deal about Sarah herself and explained much of what she did and believed. She was a quiet revolutionary, an idealist who abhorred violence, cruelty and injustice, and who had the courage of her convictions.

A few months after her return to the hospital Margarite came to see her. Mrs Johnson had gone back to America and she wanted to come back to nurse at Ratcliff again. "You'll be dead in three months if you do," said Sarah bluntly. She was used to facing facts squarely, however unpleasant, and expected others to do the same. "But I can't be idle," the girl pleaded. "It is against everything Dr Heckford taught me." Sarah relented and Margarite returned to her old work. The doctors were delighted to have her back and she worked until she collapsed while going to attend a patient. She died exactly a year after Nathaniel and was buried at Woking beside him.

By the summer of 1874 Sarah, practising what she preached, had given away most of her capital. What remained she put into a trust, for which an account was opened at Coutts on 31 July 1874. The trustees were her friends Ashton Warner and Dr Frances Morgan – now Mrs Hoggan. Occasional sums of £100 to £150 were paid to Sarah and her current account gradually dwindled until it was closed in 1882.

In the summer of 1875 the foundation stone of the new hospital building, in Glamis Road, Shadwell, was laid by the Duke of Westminster. By the autumn of 1876 it was complete. With the land it had cost £15,000 and a further wing was planned as soon as more money was available. There would be a total of 180 beds.

At last Sarah felt she could let go. Her work for the hospital was done and she could leave it in good hands. Ashton Warner, who was still the secretary and was to hold the post for quite a while yet, had become a close and trusted friend. She felt that she could hand the hospital over to him "as a mother parts with her daughter in marriage, with something of pain but more of thankfulness".

One crisp day with the first sharp edge of winter in it she went over the still-empty building with Mr Warner. They went through the echoing wards and corridors, slowly, savouring the details of planning and decoration, down to the beautiful graining on the massive polished wooden doors. In the hall she stood before a mosaic plaque on which red and black lettering on a gold ground recorded that Nathaniel Heckford, MD, MRCS, "Founded this institution at his own cost in a warehouse at Ratcliff Cross, January 28, 1868. He Lived For It and died a few days after the site of this building was purchased by the Committee of Management of the hospital." A border of green leaves and red flowers enclosed the inscription and a space at the bottom that was left clear. Nearly 30 years later her name was added with the words, "widow of the above, who shared with her husband all the trials and anxieties associated with the early history of this Hospital and died 18th April 1903". Also hanging there was a portrait of Nathaniel with an inscription saying it was presented by his widow. It is now at the Hackney Road hospital.

As she walked out of the main entrance it was with a pang that the work would now go on without her, that she would have no part in the life of the hospital in its new home. She had made up her mind to leave England. When the hospital was officially opened on 5 May 1877, by the Duchess of Teck, Sarah was in India.

She had not gone there direct. A few days after her tour of the hospital she had left with Marian, then just turning 17, for Italy. Nowhere does she say why she left England but the most likely reason was her health. Another was finance. She had done as she promised Nathaniel and seen the hospital started in its fine new home. Now it was time to give more attention to both Marian and her own health. Amalfi had so benefited Nathaniel, until the storms at the hospital caught up with him, that Italy was an obvious choice. It was also, for English people, cheap. To return to Amalfi without Nathaniel would have been too painful so she chose Naples instead. They arrived there at the end of January 1876.

For all its beauty Sarah found Naples "commonplace", at least on the surface, though seen at first from the sea it looked "a veritable City of Romance". She described the fishermen "and their quaint dwellings cut in the sandstone rock, their half-naked ... babies, playing on the shore and tumbling about in the clear water; their nets, and their boats, and their wives with bright handkerchiefs tied round their heads, all making a pretty picture of Southern life". She contrasted this with the fashionable public gardens, which she found dull, though "if you arrive at the hour of the promenade you are deafened by the cracking of whips; but after all there are not many private carriages, and few of those are well appointed". Of the smarter equipages most were likely to belong to members of the Camorra, "that famous society of thieves and murderers". It still ruled Naples in 1876, she said, and murders were common occurrences, taken "as things of no account".

To Sarah the most interesting part of Naples was the Old Port. "If you walk through the maze of narrow streets you will see Old Naples much as it was when Masaniello raised his cry of Liberty."

She passed scathing comments on the "mummeries" that took place on saint's days – so completely foreign to her Protestant upbringing. The warren of subterranean passages which ran beneath the streets and communicated with the wells in the houses intrigued her. Thieves used them to get into the houses at night to rob and sometimes to murder, coming and going through the well shaft. "Hence in Naples, when locking up the house, the most necessary thing to observe is that the little door communicating with the shaft be well closed and barred, and it is always a good precaution to sleep with a loaded pistol in the room."

She found lodging for herself and Marian with a widow and her old mother, who came from an aristocratic family but had fallen on hard times. Not surprisingly, Sarah was not able to sit back and enjoy being idle. She was shocked by the cruel treatment of animals that she saw around her and before long was involved in a one-woman campaign on behalf of the ill-treated and overworked cab horses of Naples, which brought her a certain measure of notoriety. Word also spread around, probably through her landlady, that she had some knowledge of medicine and soon patients too poor to afford a doctor were arriving at her door.

At this time malaria was rife in the plains of central and southern Italy and she saw many bad cases of fever.

When she and Marian had been in Naples a month or two a relative of their landlady introduced them to a young lawyer, who rejoiced in the rolling patronymic of Enrico Guiseppe Cipriano Longobardi. He swept Marian off her feet. Within a short time they were engaged and were married at the end of the year.

For the first time since the days of the cholera hospital, ten years before, Sarah was on her own with no one to consider but herself. So she went to India, taking a look at Egypt on the way, an eccentric and rather daring enterprise in those days for a woman on her own.

She went first to Calcutta, to work for a charity called the Zenana Mission. Three Zenana Missions and a school are mentioned in the Bengal Directory for 1878 but there is no mention of Sarah Heckford or which one she went to. It is not difficult to imagine her feelings when she reached the city of Nathaniel's birth, where he spent the first 18 years of his life, but nowhere does she tell us about them.

The aim of the Zenana Mission was, as its name implies, to bring medical help to women in purdah. No man could enter the zenana, or women's quarters, so that doctors, who were all men, could not reach them. Sarah had only recently qualified as a doctor but she was greeted kindly everywhere she went and her advice was sought. She is thought to have been the first woman doctor to practise in India.

After a short time in Calcutta she travelled through central India. Perhaps, like others before and after, she looked for a Teacher, perhaps she sought the mainsprings of the beliefs that Nathaniel had instilled in her. Whatever the purpose of her journey, it is evident that she was warmly welcomed in Bhopal, the capital city of the princely state of the same name, where she became for a year or so the resident medical adviser of the ruler, Shah Jahan Begam. This wise and benevolent ruler had succeeded her mother in 1868 and was later succeeded by her own daughter. Her mother was one of the princely rulers who had remained loyal during the Mutiny of 1858 and Shah Jahan Begam's own loyalty and good government were rewarded with the Imperial Order of the Crown of India.

While she was at Bhopal Sarah visited Agra, where she made a watercolour sketch of the Taj Mahal. Other sketches made at this time include views of "the ruined city of Futteepore" and "the ruined city of Mandoo, territory of Dhar, Central India". She kept them to the end of her life.

Whether she was happy in India or not is hard to tell, though it would seem unlikely she would have treasured the sketches she did there if she had not been. It is possible that the climate of central India was too much for her. She certainly had malaria badly while she was there and that might have been the reason why she returned to England about the middle of 1878.

The problem was, with her health precarious, where should she go and what should she do? She remained a member of the committee of the East London Hospital but there was no question of her returning to active work there. In 1878 much attention was being focused on the Empire's newest colony: the Transvaal. The Boer Republic had been annexed to the British Crown in April 1877 by Sir Theophilus Shepstone, who came up from Natal with a small group of policemen and a young lieutenant called Rider Haggard.

The Boers, who had trekked to the Transvaal in the late 1830s, had remained a pastoral people, occupying large tracts of land which they did not greatly improve, living instead off their flocks and herds. They squabbled among themselves, setting up several small separate republics. The Transvaal had become a single state only in 1860. The Boers manufactured little and concentrated on their flocks. As a result traders, almost all of them English or Jewish – which was ironic when the Boers had trekked to get away from the English – had moved in from the

Cape and Natal to supply the goods, from spades to guns, from teacups to pins and needles, which the Boers needed. Simple frontiersmen, they were not particularly good at administering their large and sparsely populated territories. In 1870, while the British colonies of the Cape and Natal had around 200,000 white inhabitants, there were only 45,000 in the Orange Free State and the Transvaal. Land was cheap, opportunities for trading were expanding and when gold was discovered – or rather, rediscovered, for there are ancient gold workings long predating the arrival of the Boers – in the eastern Transvaal in 1867, and diamonds were found in Griqualand West, the British began to turn their eyes towards the Highveld.

After the annexation trade boomed and land speculators moved in. Many, various and frequently strange were the plans for developing the new colony and the promoters published glowing accounts of its prospects, potential wealth and glorious climate. Such indigenous inhabitants as the anopheles mosquito and the tsetse fly were not mentioned, the primitive state of transport and much of the housing were glossed over. Sarah bought a hundred shares in the Transvaal Farming, Mining and Trading Association and prepared to sail for South Africa.

Her friends and family thought she was mad. She joined a group – the only woman among them – who were going out to learn the language and study farming methods with a view to improving agricultural production and to speculate in land. Sarah was 39 years old, lame, and a widow of unsound health, although the climate of South Africa was at this time already being recommended by doctors in England, who knew nothing of the country and its rigours, as being good for invalids.

Sarah's cousin, Gerald Goff, then 23 and an officer in the Argyll and Sutherland Highlanders, was going out to the Zulu wars in Natal and she arranged a passage in the same Union Steamship Company's vessel he was in. Also travelling with Sarah was George Warner – aged 15.

Whether he was related to her old friend Ashton Warner is not clear, nor why he was being shipped off to South Africa before his sixteenth birthday, but Sarah had known him since he was a baby and took him under her wing. She was the more glad to do this as he was the only member of the Transvaal-bound party that she had met before.

They arrived off the port of Durban, or Port Natal as it was then called, early in December 1878. It is at this point that Sarah commences the narrative in her best-known book, *A Lady Trader in the Transvaal*, which was published in 1882. ("Best-known" is a relative term as this book is moderately rare "Africana" in South Africa and almost unknown in Britain.) For the next few years we have a fairly detailed account of Sarah's life and adventures which can be corroborated from other sources. Because of the political situation in the Transvaal at the time the book was published, Sarah changed the names of the people she wrote about to protect her friends still in the country. George Warner, for instance, she calls "Jimmy". As she does not disguise the names of places, such as the farm Nooitgedacht – though she does translate its name into English, "Surprise" – it has been possible to identify many of the people and trace their descendants. The period covered by the book – December 1878 to the middle of 1881 – was an important and eventful one in the history of the Transvaal and of South Africa as a whole.

7
South Africa

The narrative of *A Lady Trader* begins with the Union Steamship Company's vessel lying off Durban waiting for the tug that would take the passengers ashore across the bar. In the 1870s the passage to the fine natural harbour was not dredged out to take sea-going ships. Getting ashore meant braving the basket. A strongly made basket that could hold four people was swung over the deck of the steamer. The passengers got in and clung on while it was swung over the side and lowered onto the deck of the tug, which was bobbing up and down on the tide.

"They were immediately and very unceremoniously tipped out, if they were men. Women and children were somewhat more gently treated," said Sarah, adding that it looked quite easy to break a leg in the operation. Once safely in the tug they were all cautioned to sit fast and wedge themselves in well or they might be swept off while the tug was crossing the "terrible bar". "I expected a frightful drenching at least, but nothing at all happened," said Sarah. She added, caustically, "It was the old story of the mountain and the mouse, and as such, it formed a fitting prelude to life in South Africa, where, as far as my experience goes, everything is exaggerated – dangers, difficulties, beauties and advantages." Many people find South Africa unchanged in this respect today.

She was travelling with a party going to the Transvaal, thinking it might be unwise for a woman with no knowledge of the languages and customs of the country to travel alone. But having been used to managing everything for herself she found it difficult to submit to other people's arrangements, especially when they did not go well. It rained heavily as soon as they got ashore and when they learned that the Zulu porters were on strike she found "it decidedly tried" her. Her companions piled the party's luggage on a railway line, apparently oblivious to the fact that it might be in danger. "I felt very uncharitable towards them," was Sarah's restrained comment. "After a while a number of Kaffirs, with that beautiful disregard of consequences which is one of the pleasing characteristics of the race, sent a line of empty trucks right into it." The ensuing scramble to rescue their bags she found amusing "but it would have been a great relief to one's feelings to have been able to vent one's wrath, if only in words, on those unpleasant Kaffirs, who looked on grinning, but it was no use abusing them, for they didn't understand English, and none of us spoke Zulu".

By the time Sarah and George Warner had managed to board the omnibus which ran between the port and the village of Durban, Sarah was fairly seething. Durban in those days consisted of a straggling line of cottages and small houses, some used as shops, with goods for sale in the windows. There was a railway station and "a nice-looking building where the Post Office was". The bus took them to the best hotel in town – a cottage in a garden. There was a sitting room with a piano in it and a dining room, but none of the appurtenances of a hotel as one understood the term in Europe. Sarah thought it looked like a farmhouse where the owner had suddenly been called upon to put up unexpected guests and was doing the best he could in awkward circumstances.

They were not long in Durban before catching a train to Pinetown, "a pretty place in the middle of scenery that reminded me of an Indian jungle". At Pinetown they transferred to another bus, all of them squeezed tightly together with parcels of all shapes and sizes packed in around them in every available space. The horses set off at a spanking pace over a rough road. Many of the party complained miserably but Sarah enjoyed the run as it took them through beautiful scenery. They stopped at a farmhouse for lunch and got to Pietermaritzburg by sunset. "It is not really a pretty place, although I believe its inhabitants think it is so," said Sarah acidly.

Sarah viewed South Africa with an artist's eye and found it disappointing. There were woods and rocks and ravines, she told her readers, but they must not think it was anything like Switzerland or Italy because it was not: it was "commonplace", the same word she applied to Naples. She evidently thought herself that such an odd choice of adjective needed explaining because she continued that it was necessary to go to South Africa to see what a "commonplace" wooded ravine is, but that once there one would understand it perfectly. She struggled to reason out why scenery which should be extremely beautiful was not in fact so, in her eyes. The answer, she thought, was in the quality of the light.

Notwithstanding this rather crabby reaction to the South African countryside, Sarah sketched and painted on all her travels through the coming years and has left some watercolours which convey an affectionate view of the landscape she came to know so well.

From the scenery she turned to the life of South Africa, or that part of it which she had seen by the time she completed her book, that is, Natal and the Transvaal. She found that it lacked "moral atmosphere", though just what she meant by that is hard to tell. "Life here is a jumble, to use an inelegant but expressive word." There was much in the life there that she and a great many others found attractive. She commented that many who spent all their time in South Africa longing to return to Europe, when they did so found they could not settle there and came back to finish their days in Africa, "though I doubt whether more than two or three of those persons even could have told the characteristic charm which thus recalled them from their old homes".

A week or so was spent in Pietermaritzburg while the party came to an arrangement with a carrier – or transport-rider, to give him his South African designation – a small man with red hair and whiskers whom Sarah described as "an Africander", by which she meant English-speaking South African. He was to take them and their goods to Pretoria, although Rustenburg was their ultimate destination. Just as new arrivals in South Africa today have to do, Sarah had to get to terms with South African English. Having found that the carrier was called a transport-rider, she learnt that one of his vehicles which looked just like a hay wain was a wagon and that the tarpaulin thrown over it to protect the goods from the weather was called a bucksail. The second wagon in the convoy had a tent covering the back half, formed of canvas stretched over bent laths with curtains that could be closed at the back and front. This was where she slept for most of the journey, which took about three weeks. It would have been fine if she had had it to herself, but she had to share it with everything that twelve men, all of them unused to travelling, thought it essential to have handy during the trip – including their rifles, though they only shot one or two birds for the pot the whole way and not a single buck.

Sarah also found that she was expected to ride in the wagon, as South African women did, but this she flatly refused to do and went in search of horses to buy, undeterred by the fact that the journey before her was about 450 miles. It proved difficult to find horses as every suitable mount had been bought up by the volunteers for the Zulu wars. In fact, two of their party gave up the idea of going to the Transvaal at all and enrolled as officers in the Volunteers. As the men they were to command were sullen, ill-trained African levies who spoke no English, while they spoke no African language, Sarah was at a loss to see how they would make out.

Eventually she found a Basotho pony, thin and ugly but willing and surprisingly strong, on which she mounted her young friend, George, and a fat and handsome pony for herself which would have been very good if it had not been the "laziest little horse I had ever seen".

Finally the party was ready to set off. With some idea that they might be going to a wild country and that George would not be much protection, Sarah had one revolver strapped round her waist and another in a holster on her saddle. The situation was certainly tense. In the 1870s the Zulu kingdom was the greatest African domain south of the Limpopo. Its ruler, Cetshwayo, who succeeded his father Mpande in 1872, was the nephew of Shaka, the great leader who had built up the Zulu nation to the pinnacle of its power, and of Dingane. In February 1838 Dingane had slaughtered the Voortrekker leader Piet Retief and his party, after inviting them to a beer-drink to celebrate the treaty to which he had put his mark, giving Durban and its hinterland to the Trekkers. In December of the same year Andries Pretorius led a commando of 500 men against the Zulus and defeated them in a battle in which no whites were killed but 3,000 out of the 10,000 strong Zulu army died. This was the Battle of Blood River, fought on 16 December 1838, which is still celebrated in South Africa as public holiday though not under that name. The commando had vowed before the battle to build a church if God sent them victory, a vow they kept.

Cetshwayo set about rebuilding the Zulu army, and by the end of 1878 the *impis* were spoiling for war, wanting to wash their spears in blood to celebrate his accession. He had reintroduced Shaka's system of conscription and enforced it on all the young men. They lived in barracks in regiments under strict discipline. They were forbidden to marry until Cetshwayo released them, one regiment at a time, from service to him, by which time they were about 40 years old. They were superb warriors, confident and aggressive.

In the 1870s the colony of Natal was a wedge of white occupation separating the Xhosa kingdom of the Transkei from the Zulus. Under the benevolent dictatorship and sound administration of Sir Theophilus Shepstone, whom the Africans liked and respected, there had been a period of stability and peace in the colony. The Africans called Shepstone "Somtseu" and Cetshwayo had invited him to crown him in 1873.

There were few white residents in the Zulu kingdom. Apart from the renegade Scotsman and gunrunner John Dunn, who had been made a chief and provided with a good supply of wives, followers and cattle by Cetshwayo, they were mostly missionaries and traders. Converts were few, however, and trade poor, so that they urged on the British authorities the cause of annexing Zululand as a colony.

In the north, pressure by the Transvaal Afrikaners, who claimed Zulu territory east of Blood River, was increasing, despite their weakness in the face of Sekhukhune's Pedi tribe in the Transvaal, whom they had failed to subdue in a ludicrous campaign when the commandos packed up and went home rather than fight it out. When Shepstone, who had entered the Transvaal in January 1877, declared its annexation to the British Crown on 12 April 1877, Cetshwayo's warriors clamoured to help by washing their spears in Afrikaner blood.

However, when the Boer Republic suddenly became a British colony, Shepstone, who up till then had supported the Zulus in their boundary dispute with the Afrikaners, turned round and endorsed the Transvaal claim. Cetshwayo felt betrayed. By December 1878, tensions in Zululand were reaching breaking point. Sir Bartle Frere had arrived from England to carry out the British Foreign Secretary's policy of federation between the British colonies and the

Boer republics, a policy which was anathema to the Afrikaners. Frere was persuaded by people with an axe to grind that the Zulus stood in the way of this policy, and that there could be no stability in South Africa while there was an independent Zulu kingdom ruled by a man they saw as a tyrant.

This was the situation that Sarah rode into on her fat and lazy little horse. She rode unscathed through Natal and on up into the Highveld while the British faced Cetshwayo with the demand that his army be disbanded. No independent ruler could accede to such a demand and had Cetshwayo tried there were plenty of jealous relatives ready to depose him, take his place and defy the British. As Sarah passed into the Transvaal the *impis*, about 30,000 strong, gathered at Ulundi, the Zulu capital, to be doctored for war and on 11 January 1879 Viscount Chelmsford launched his planned invasion of Zululand. He had about 7,000 British regular troops, the same number of Natal African levies – officered among others by Sarah's shipboard companions, one of whom was to die in the fighting at the hospital at Rorke's Drift – and around a thousand colonial volunteers. They cheerfully expected to sweep on unopposed to Ulundi, but on 22 January the main column was taken unawares at Isandhlwana. The British army lost 600 men in the biggest disaster it had suffered since the Crimean War. The Zulus today remember with pride this defeat of the English.

Sarah's party made an inauspicious start from Pietermaritzburg as there was a misunderstanding between some of the men and the transport-rider as to when they should have their things loaded up. He started off unexpectedly, leaving them and some of their goods behind. For most of the journey Sarah thought him most unreasonable in the way he insisted on the times and places for outspanning and inspanning. However, when she came to ride transport herself she soon found that even the most inhumane driver had to consider the needs of his oxen or he would be stuck on the road.

With the remainder of their belongings tied to their saddles in a variety of parcels Sarah and George set off after the wagons. They were clear of the town when there was a despairing cry from George, who had discovered that most of his parcels had come undone and his property was strewn over the road behind him. Sarah sat and laughed while he got off and collected everything, though she had to admit the way the parcels had been done up was her idea so she should not have laughed. They caught up with the wagons at the first outspan and stowed their parcels in what were to be their homes for the journey to Pretoria. When they started off again Sarah felt her South African venture had truly begun.

As she rode on ahead of the wagons she was exhilarated by the clear air and wide views and the thought of the new project that lay ahead of her in the Transvaal. She had always longed to try farming and now, she thought, she would have the chance to do so. She was nearly 40 and ready for anything. Which was just as well as she was about to have to cope with their first night on the road.

The outspan was on a chilly hilltop swathed in thick, damp mist. As soon as the wagons had been drawn up and plans were being discussed for the evening meal they realised they had made their first mistake. Being all of them new to the country they had not made a firm arrangement with the transport-rider as to what help the natives he had with him would give the party. So the Africans gave almost no help at all, and they had to find water and fuel for the fire themselves. More than that, they had to light the fire. The natives, who looked as if they could have done the same in pouring rain, soon had a fire of their own going a little way off, but the Englishmen struggled a long time to get a smoky fire going in the mist. One of them cooked the supper while the others put up the tent the men were to sleep in. Sarah had a small tent of her own but no one seemed willing to help her put it up so she settled for clearing a space under the wagon tent and sleeping with the luggage. Supper eventually was ready but the cook refused to touch it himself, saying it was "rancid tallow candle, with lots of salt in it". Sarah was ravenously hungry and ate it, but had to agree with the description. The coffee was hot, but there was no milk for it. She disliked it black but found she had to get used to it. It struck her as odd that in a country so full of cattle, milk should be so often unobtainable.

They travelled over miles of dull, undulating country, starting very early each morning, outspanning during the midday heat and travelling again in the evening. It was midsummer and the weather extremely hot. Sarah found it unpleasant not being able to wash or change her clothes, but as the men would not help her pitch her tent and she could not manage it herself there was no help for it. She looked in vain at each outspan for trees so that she could rig up an impromptu dressing room, and was astonished at the treelessness of the country. The noon outspans were particularly trying when there was no shade but under the wagons. She employed the time grooming her horse, finding that it had been one thing to rub down for fun a well-groomed horse looked after by someone else but quite another to clean a hot and dirty one under a broiling sun. Occasionally they came to a tiny "hotel", where Sarah snatched the chance to wash.

When they reached the Drakensberg she looked up at the mountains with respect, having heard many tales of the perils of crossing the range in an ox wagon. They had expected to go straight on into the Transvaal by way of Newcastle and were startled to be told that they were to go by the other road that led into the Free State and reach Pretoria by way of Heilbron and Heidelberg.

Sarah's knowledge of the geography of the country was still hazy but she protested to the transport-rider that this would take them at least 70 miles out of their way, which at the pace of the ox wagon meant a considerable delay. However, the transport-rider said he had to go to Heilbron and there was nothing they could do but grumble and follow. He said he had lost many oxen on the road and had to go to his home at Heilbron to fetch more, but it turned out in the end that it was not oxen he had to fetch but his wife, who wanted to go to Heidelberg to visit relatives.

When it was time to leave the comfortable and hospitable inn at the foot of the Drakensberg, Sarah discovered that her pony had saddle galls, or, as she put it, "its withers were touched by the saddle". She decided it would be best not to ride it for a day or two and told the transport-rider she would go in the wagon. He replied that the wagon would very likely be upset and she had better walk. At this stage the innkeeper intervened to provide for Sarah's use a light carriage, called a spider, drawn by four oxen, which saved the day.

The wagons went on ahead as Sarah's equipage would travel faster. She had been looking forward to the ascent as the country was now more picturesque, but a thick mist came down and she could see little. They found the wagons stuck fast in deep mud. The driver of the spider dumped her in the mud and turned back to the inn.

It was a miserable night. There was no chance of moving any further and it was a struggle to get the men's tent up. Sarah crawled into the wagon, which was on a steep incline, and spent the night with no mattress and trying to prevent herself and everything piled in around her from slipping out.

A sullen dawn found everyone cold and damp. The ponies were warm under their blankets but slipping in the mud, which looked like keeping the wagons fixed for a good while yet. The saddle galls were better so Sarah rode on with George Warner to the next inn on the road, about twelve miles away. They passed a wagon smashed to pieces below the road, where it had fallen the previous day. It was two days before their own wagons caught them up at Willow River.

They were now in the Free State and Sarah was intrigued

to hear a great deal of political talk, much of it anti-British. She was also amused by "a conversation with a gentleman of an inventive turn of mind, who told me some wonderful stories, to which I listened gravely. Whenever something suggested to him that my wonderment was getting too strong he would appeal in a most artless manner to the memory of a friend of his who was there, and the friend always remembered. These two were dwellers in the Transvaal but both, with delightful naïveté, cautioned me not to trust any Transvaalers, as they were all fearfully acute and untrustworthy."

When the wagons arrived Sarah and George set off on their ponies for Harrismith. It boasted two inns and the one they put up at was comfortable, though she disapproved of the dirtiness of the large stable.

For the next stage, to Heilbron, it was proposed that Sarah should travel in the post cart. She did not much like the idea but her pony's withers were galled again and, besides, the men of the party seemed eager to get rid of her for a day or two and she did not like to disappoint them. She bade an anxious farewell to her pony, which went off tied behind the wagon, and settled down on the sofa in the inn's little sitting room with a copy of *Great Expectations* she had found there.

The next morning she was surprised when George arrived, his pony "quite knocked up", saying he had lost the party and had been chased by Africans who threw assegais at him. Sarah found this a tall story, as did everyone at the inn, but turned her attention to what was to be done with George, as the pony could go no further and she only had enough money with her for one fare in the post cart. There was nothing for it but to sell the pony. She was cross with George but felt herself responsible to his parents for his safety and well-being. In the event she was glad to have him with her.

The African driver in charge when they boarded the post cart was quite drunk. A bystander "persuaded" him to leave it (with a whip!) and commandeered a diminutive Khoikhoi, telling him to drive. The Khoikhoi protested he could not drive, but the bystander, who evidently knew him well, insisted he could and ordered him to jump up.

"The vehicle into which he jumped," ran Sarah's account, "and into which I proceeded to scramble, had once been a dog-cart but was now a ruin. The system of pieces of leather and cord, ingeniously twisted together, which attached it to the horses, had, I suppose, once been a set of harness. The horses had certainly once been good, but now they were a pair of vicious, jibbing rips." The Khoikhoi soon proved his mettle as a driver when the horses finally went flying off down the road. Every stop, including one at the Khoikhoi's house to collect his blanket and say goodbye to his wife, meant a battle of wills between horses and driver before they plunged off again.

Each stream, or spruit as Sarah was learning to call them, meant fresh trouble. There were no bridges in those days and the horses were frequently unwilling to go into the water or, having done so, to climb out again. Then the harness started breaking. The driver mended it with strips of leather and pieces of twine from his capacious pockets. When his supply ran out they resorted to the thong of Sarah's hunting crop.

As dusk fell and it turned chilly the driver announced he could not reach the proper outspan and they would have to stop at the next house they came to. They were lucky: the next dwelling was a pleasant cottage where a hospitable young couple welcomed them with a good supper and – at least for Sarah – a clean and comfortable bed. Next morning they would accept no payment but thanks and gave Sarah a cup of strong black coffee without sugar before she and George climbed back into the post cart and set off once more.

Each change of horses seemed to have brought them a worse pair and driving was still a trial. At the next change they were given a bottle of milk and some bread by the farmer's wife. The new horses also refused to start and Sarah was handed the reins so that the driver could help George to push. She couldn't help laughing at their frantic rush after the cart to catch up when it started. The driver had assured her earlier he had broken two ribs only recently but he seemed pretty active when it came to jumping into the moving cart.

He pleaded his broken ribs as an excuse for breaking the regulation which laid down that the driver of the post cart must blow a horn on the approach to any dwelling, which was a disappointment to Sarah, who had looked forward to rattling up with the mails to the sound of a fanfare. She and George both had a try at deputising for the driver, but puff their cheeks as they might all they could produce was a sort of snorting noise.

That night – it was a Saturday – they arrived at a house which seemed to her the most squalid she had seen, not excepting the combination of poverty and dirt she had encountered around the East London Hospital. The "road" approaching it was quite invisible to her. In fact, she had seen nothing she could recognise as a road since they set out. The driver seemed to find his way by dead reckoning over a featureless sea of grass.

The house was a "long, low-roofed cabin stuck down in the middle of the veld, with three stunted trees near it, looking cheerless in the extreme. Our advent was heralded by a barking chorus of gaunt dogs. This brought out seven men and boys. The little Hottentot whispered, 'You must shake hands with every one,' and I descended and immediately commenced operations. The oldest of the men led us into the house, where we shook hands with a woman and a number of girls, big and little, terminating with a baby. All the hands were very dirty".

No member of the family spoke a word of English and Sarah felt desperate at not being able to speak to them. They settled down on benches round the walls of the living room and regarded her seriously. She smiled at the baby, which was well received, and was struggling to form a mixture of English and German that might sound like Dutch when the driver came back from stabling the horses and acted as interpreter. She was astonished to hear that the household consisted only of a man and wife and their children as there appeared to be no more than ten years' difference between the eldest of the men and several others. Eventually more gawky boys came in and shook hands and it turned out there were fourteen children all told.

"They were rich in flocks and herds and yet all but the father, mother and two eldest sons were barefooted; none had stockings, none appeared to be possessed of a brush and comb, or of soap!" said Sarah in amazement. The contrast between the size of the man's landholding and the way his family lived was extraordinary to her English eyes.

They were evidently a devout people for the father said a long grace in Dutch before and after the evening meal. The table had been laid with a cloth and plates with bowls placed on them. There was a big basin of milk and "a dish full of a sort of hard, crisp bread, peculiar to this country and very nice". She was surprised that only the father, George and herself were given knives and forks. The rest of the family had spoons only. One tallow candle illuminated the scene. After grace the mother helped everyone to milk and *boerbeskuit* – as she learnt the "hard bread" was called. The eldest daughter brought in a small piece of mutton which the father cut into three, giving one bit each to her and George and taking the other himself. Sarah felt most uncomfortable that none of the rest of the family had meat and thought it mean, considering the hundreds of fat cattle milling around outside.

Almost as soon as supper was finished a collection of sheep and goat skins was brought in and spread on the benches. The mother beckoned to Sarah and led her into a small room "in which was a big, very dirty-looking bed, a number of little Delft bowls on a shelf, and absolutely nothing else". She was left without a candle, the only light being over the top of the door from the tallow in the living room. There was a window, or rather a hole in the wall with a rough wooden shutter, which she decided to leave open for light and air, but a moment later it was slammed shut and there were sounds of it being securely barred on the outside.

She lay down on the bed – which turned out to have a great number of other inhabitants – fully clothed, and gazed up at the rafters while a barrage of snoring arose from the other room. She had sworn to escape "young-lady-dom", she had turned her back on Belgravia and sought work in the slums of the London docks. She had been into the poorest parts of Naples, seen Egypt and the teeming villages and towns of India, but never before had she felt so far from home, so translated to another world, as she did lying wakeful in that primitive farmhouse in the middle of the Free State grasslands.

Next morning George told her the whole family had slept in the living room. He had shared a bench with one of the sons. None of them had undressed. "Boers never do when they go to bed," Sarah reported, "not even in case of illness. Indeed they think it the height of impropriety to do so – so much so that a Boer who travelled in the wagon of an English Africander, an acquaintance of mine, afterwards said to the wife of the latter, 'I shall never travel in William's wagon again with him. It is so dreadful of him to take his trousers off when he goes to bed.'" One wonders how families of fourteen children were achieved.

After a mug of coffee, they set out early, delivering letters on the way. The letters were in the box on which Sarah and the driver sat. He handed the bunch to her at each stop to decipher the names and addresses. As the names were all Dutch and the addresses quite unknown to her and often illegible she was sure some of them went to the wrong places, but consoled herself that letters must often go astray in the Free State, given this method of distributing them, and that there were probably no more mistakes on this trip than was usual.

8
Christmas in the Free State and a wagon ride to Pretoria

It was 23 December 1878 when they reached Heilbron, which consisted then of about 15 small houses and a few larger ones, stuck down together on a gentle slope in the middle of bare country. From the top of the incline all that could be seen, whichever way you turned, was a grassy plain stretching to the horizon. There was no sign of the wagons or news of them coming in and it seemed clear that Sarah and George would have to spend their first South African Christmas in Heilbron.

The only hotel was on the usual simple plan: a cottage whose front door led directly into the sitting room, which connected with a small dining room at the back. There was one bedroom on each side of these central rooms, occupied by the proprietor and his wife and their large family of children. The guest rooms were out at the back; for access to them you went through the dining room and into the yard. Two of these rooms were allotted to Sarah and George. The others were inhabited by two bachelors who worked in the village. A few other people were table boarders, coming in for meals, which were odd gatherings with conversation that greatly intrigued Sarah. She was amused to hear the shopkeepers of the place regarded as local magnates. Everybody knew everybody else and, like small places everywhere, Heilbron delighted in gossip.

On Christmas Eve the proprietor and his wife gave a dance in the sitting room, their one public room. The guests included the local judge and the magistrate, or landdrost as he was called, most of the shopkeepers of the village and some of their assistants, and a dressmaker – all, of course, with their wives or husbands. Music for dancing was provided by a fiddler and there were some songs, all of them strange to Sarah. Between dances a music box played.

For all her spirit and gameness dancing was one thing Sarah was too lame for. A comfortable chair was placed for her just inside the dining room door where she could watch the jollifications. The scene impressed itself clearly enough on her memory for her to be able three years later to describe it in detail.

"They all danced with great gravity and ponderosity, if I may use such a word, but some clung to each other as they hopped heavily round and round to a waltz tune. Others charged round savagely with outstretched arms, to the imminent danger of their neighbours. Others held their arms stretched down so tightly that they looked as if they were mutually desirous of dislocating each other's shoulders, whilst one couple, a chubby little man and woman, regardless of the time of either the music or the dancing of the others, with a stolid smile on each fat little face, turned slowly round and round as on a pivot. I cannot say how they managed it. Their progression was very slow and they seemed quite regardless of the collisions they came in for. I saw them get a thump from one of the chargers which would have knocked a less steady couple down, but only caused them to totter. But the comicality of their appearance at last tickled me so much that I felt I must laugh if I stayed, so I took myself off to bed."

A communal picnic had been arranged for Christmas Day but there was much lamenting and great woe when the morning dawned grey with drizzling rain. There had been tremendous preparations and a great baking all the week and until ten o'clock there was much running into and out of the hotel and debating whether to go or not. At ten the drizzle let up a little and it was opined that the weather was clearing and that the picnic should go ahead. Rather to Sarah's relief she and George were not included. She was entertained by the arguments and consultations as to who should go in whose wagon, arrangements being complicated when two young men drove up in a vehicle that was intended for a generous load of picnickers and somehow managed to upset it and break it beyond repair, a mishap which was ascribed to the previous night's festivities having been too much for them.

At last all was arranged and every white inhabitant of Heilbron prepared to desert it for the rest of the day. The landlady told Sarah she had killed a chicken, picked a dish of peas and made a plum pudding and that the African servant-girl would prepare these for her and George to dine off. With strict injunctions that they should make themselves comfortable and regard the hotel as their home she drove off with her family.

Soon after the picnic party had left the rain came down again, making Sarah more glad than ever they had not been asked to join the villagers. George, taking the landlady at her word, played the music box interminably, driving Sarah to the borders of insanity. She looked for something to read but in the whole house could find only juvenile stories about good and bad children and a mutilated copy of Scott's *Ivanhoe*.

Dinner was served, minus the peas, which Sarah concluded the "girl" had kept for herself. Towards the end of the afternoon the weather cleared and she and George went for a walk outside the village. She gave him his first lesson in pistol shooting. It would be interesting to know where she had learnt to shoot but she does not tell us.

As they were about to return to the hotel a young man came up and asked them if they were the people who were travelling with a certain transport-rider. When they said they were he told them he owned one of the spans of oxen the driver was using and that he had been distressed to hear that many of them were dead of redwater fever and the teams were flogged unmercifully. Sarah said she was sorry to say it was true. He had news that the wagons were still a day or two away, and invited them to his house for tea.

He was English-born and a small farmer on the outskirts of Heilbron. His wife, who welcomed them hospitably and provided an ample tea, was a local girl, attractive and slender, with a delightful baby. It began to feel more like Christmas – even if it was the middle of summer.

When they got back to the hotel the picnic party had returned and were in a bad temper. Not surprisingly, thought Sarah. Picnicking under a dripping tarpaulin stretched between wagons in a drizzle in the middle of a bare plain was not likely to be conducive to good temper. Mr So-and-so had said this, Mrs So-and-so had done that and the picnic, Sarah concluded, had set the little town by the ears!

Two days later the rest of the company arrived with the wagons and Sarah's pony, which seemed fit and well. However, she had by now heard that horse sickness was likely to be bad beyond the Vaal. She had no idea if the pony was "salted", that is, if it had had the disease and recovered, thus being immune from further attack. It seemed best for her to sell it and when the Englishman offered a fair price she accepted and resigned herself to travelling the rest of the way in the wagon.

The transport-rider unloaded a large pile of goods from the tented wagon at his home, which made things easier. With some rearrangement Sarah managed to make herself tolerably comfortable. At least until they started off. "To jolt hour after hour in an ox-wagon along a dead flat under a broiling sun is objectionable," she wrote. In addition, now being in the wagon all the time she could not escape witnessing the brutality with which the transport-rider treated his animals. His dreadful language, equally to the teams and the Africans with him, she also found hard to bear.

They crossed the Vaal on New Year's Eve. They were in the Transvaal at last and late the following night reached Heidelberg. The trek from there to Pretoria was uneventful but when they were still a day from the Transvaal capital a passing traveller told them it was expected hourly that the Boers would "break out" and enter the town armed. Far from being disconcerted the party was pleasantly excited at the prospect and urged the transport-rider to make speed so that they could witness this interesting happening. There was, however, no uprising at this time and they were disappointed.

They entered the long valley in which Pretoria lies, by way of Baviaanspoort – or Bobian Poort, as Sarah spelled it, translating it, "baboon's entrance". They saw no baboons, though Sarah imagined there must have been troops of them there not long before. As they approached in the late afternoon sun, Pretoria, with its blue gums and willow trees and its enclosing hills, looked more attractive than any place she had seen since they had landed at Durban.

It was almost dark by the time they had outspanned at the top end of the town. She asked the transport-rider which would be the best hotel for a lady to put up at. "The European, on the Market Square, without a doubt," he said. She set off with George to find it. It was not in those days a long walk from the edge of the town to the centre – at what was then the marketplace and is now Church Square. Pretoria was little more than a village and barely 24 years old, having been founded in 1855.

The first recorded white visitors to the area were two Scots traders, Robert Schoon and William McLuckie. They visited Mzilikazi, the break-away Zulu chief who founded the Matabele nation, in his stronghold in the Magaliesberg, just north of where Pretoria now stands, in July 1829. During the next few years missionaries, including Robert Moffat, passed that way. The first Voortrekkers, led by Louis Trichardt, crossed the Vaal in 1836 but kept well clear of Mzilikazi. It was another two years before the first white man struck root permanently in the district.

By the warm January night in 1879 when Sarah and George went looking for the European Hotel, Pretoria was a bustling and rowdy little town – predominantly English-speaking owing to the influx of traders and professional men to meet the needs of the growing republic, a flow which had been encouraged by the annexation nearly two years before. Sixty per cent of the names on a voter's roll of 1880 are of United Kingdom origin.

As they set out Sarah asked the way of an elderly gentleman seated on the stoep of a house near the outspan. She was agreeably surprised he spoke English. He directed them down a road lined with rose hedges. She could hear the water in the furrows on either side of the way – they carried the town's water supply and were a feature of the place – but could not see the ditches in the dark so kept well in the middle. The cottages down the road stood well back in large gardens. With their lighted windows they looked pleasant and homelike after nights in the veld.

The road led to the Market Square, hub and heart of the town, with a squat, white, thatched-roof church in the middle of it. One corner of the square was formed by two low buildings at right angles to one another which appeared to be hotels. As neither had a sign Sarah asked a passer-by which was the European. Neither seemed to her suitable lodgings for a lady but as she had been directed there she felt she should at least enquire. The bar was the most obvious feature of both hotels, each of them crowded with loud-talking men in broad hats, short coats and riding boots. The European had a verandah running the full width of its frontage where more men of the same kind were lounging. It appeared to be the more popular hotel of the two. Looking in from the marketplace Sarah could see it had a public dining room, crammed with men and not one woman. The only way into it was through the bar so, "taking heart of grace, into the bar I walked. It was as full as it could be of the kind of men who frequent bars". A moment's astounded silence greeted her entry.

It is doubtful whether a woman had ever been in there before. Mr Colquhoun, the proprietor, was behind the bar looking as surprised at this apparition as anyone else. Sarah marched up to the counter, introduced herself and said she had been told this was the best hotel for a lady to put up at. When Mr Colquhoun regained his breath he said politely, "I'm afraid you've been misinformed. This is completely a man's hotel, in fact it is not an hotel but simply a restaurant…"

Sarah bowed and apologised and asked if he could tell her where she might go as she could not return to the wagons. "If you will step into my private room I'll send you in some supper," said Mr Colquhoun. "And while you're eating I'll send round to the Edinburgh and the Royal to see if they have a room to spare." George was sent back to the wagons while Sarah enjoyed "a nice little supper" (which seems hard on the lad). By the time she had finished word had come back that both hotels were full. These were still busy days in Pretoria, though the first post-annexation boom was evaporating fast with the growth of more determined Boer opposition to British rule. The town was crowded out. Mr Colquhoun, clearly worried at what was to become of her, said that all he could propose was that she should use a small room near the hotel. The regular tenant was away and had left the key with him. He was sure it would be in order for her to have the use of it for a day or two. An African servant took her to the room in a yard behind a public house. There was a stable next to it and the noise from the bar was tremendous but it was clean and comfortable. A woman's dress hung from a peg and there was a candle on the table.

When the servant had left Sarah investigated the door and window. The door had a lock but there was no way of securing the window. "It was not very pleasant," she said, "for the little I had seen of Pretoria that night made me acquainted with the fact, which further acquaintance only confirmed, that it was a very rowdy little village, and that a woman might better walk about late in London or Paris than in this place. I began to wish I had brought my pistol with me."

She placed a chair on top of the table under the window, hoping that if anyone tried to climb in they would knock it over and wake her up. Then, thoroughly tired out, she fell into the narrow bed, and slept her usual sound sleep. This ability to go right off to sleep wherever she happened to be must have been an enormous asset during her travels. She wrote, about 15 years later, of spending an excellent night and sleeping well wrapped in a blanket on the hard ground, with her saddle for a pillow, under a wagon on a frosty night.

The next morning she woke up hungry. There was nothing for it but to return to the European if she wanted breakfast. The "eating-room" – she does not dignify it with the name of dining room – was filled with men who stared at her with forks halfway to their mouths. The South African habit of staring she found disconcerting, even when she had been in the country a good few years. Mr Colquhoun, however, escorted her to a small table in a quiet corner and waited on her himself, something he did whenever she ate there and for which she was grateful. If women today sometimes find it embarrassing to enter a bar or restaurant on their own, how much more difficult it must have been for Sarah 100 years ago when such a thing was quite unknown.

After breakfast she stood on the verandah to take her first look at Pretoria by daylight. The grassy marketplace was rutted by wagon wheels and hoofs. It appeared that the church would be an island in a sea of mud when it rained. Though this was the main square the buildings enclosing it were single-storeyed, with roofs of thatch or corrugated iron.

"You new in town?" asked a man who was lounging against the railing with his hat firmly on his head.

Sarah gave a stiff little bow in acknowledgement. She

was not yet used to being addressed so casually by complete strangers.

"Then you'll want to know what everything is," he went on, not in the least put out. "This on our right, the next building, that's the Raadsaal, the Boer Houses of Parliament, and beyond, across Market Street, is Robert Lys's house. There's some stores and a bar over that side," he said with a wave of the hand. "Then you see this big oak tree in the corner next to us – that's The Oaks. Everyone meets there. Every Friday there's an auction. If you want a horse or a wagon or a farm, or an erf in town, anything, just you be under The Oaks at eleven sharp on Friday. That's the South African Hotel, next to The Oaks. Opposite us – there with the two gables – that's the parsonage. If you want the Post Office, it's round the back here, behind the Raadsaal."

"Thank you. I'm sure I'll soon find my way around," said Sarah politely.

"Not at all, ma'am. Good-day," and he strolled off down the verandah steps with the barest sketch of raising his hat as he went.

Sarah spent the first day in Pretoria searching for lodgings without any luck and spent a second night in the room behind the pub. The next morning she was on the stoep of the European wondering where to try next when a man raised his hat to her and said, "I believe you are looking for lodgings." She was no longer surprised at being accosted by a stranger, only by his raising his hat, and said she was. "Good, so am I. Let's go together," he said, and offered her his arm. "Life is very free and easy here," thought Sarah as she set out with him.

Down a grassy, rose-hedged lane which in Pretoria passed for a street they saw two fashionably dressed women on a verandah.

"Let's ask them," said Sarah's companion. "I don't think that would do at all," said Sarah, hastily, but her friend evidently imagined it would "do" as he mounted the stoep and, raising his hat with a broad sweep, asked if they had a room to let.

The women were kind and not in the least offended at being taken for lodging house keepers. They did not let rooms but invited them in. Her companion said he must be off but Sarah was tired and the offer of coffee tempting so she accepted, chatting with them till lunchtime.

"At least if I have nowhere to stay, this is the most remarkably friendly place, by daylight at any rate," she mused as she returned to the European. On the stoep after lunch she found a man she had met on the road from Heidelberg talking to the elderly gentleman of whom she had asked her way on the night of her arrival. Both greeted her as a long-lost friend and asked if they could do anything for her. She admitted she was having trouble finding somewhere to stay and added that she had letters of introduction to two ladies in Pretoria but did not like to present them as it would be tantamount to asking them to put her up.

One of the men said he knew both women. (Indeed, she soon discovered that everyone in Pretoria knew everyone else and their business as well.) He went off and reappeared shortly with a friend he introduced as Mr Farquharson, who was the husband of one of the women and son-in-law of the other. Mr Farquharson said his mother-in-law, Mrs Parker, had a room to spare and he would conduct her to the house – but the good lady was out and so it was back to the stable yard for another night.

Next morning she was woken by a servant from the European who shouted through the keyhole that the post cart from Newcastle was in and the rightful occupant of the room on her way back to it. Sarah was dressed and out in record time. However, her troubles were now over as Mr Farquharson appeared after breakfast and took her off to his own cottage at the upper end of the town.

"Oh, how nice it did seem, with its carpets, and sofas, and little nicknacks, and best of all, its pretty mistress, after travelling so long with rough men!"

After lunch she was escorted to Mrs Parker's cottage, a single-storeyed bungalow like all the rest, "a very gem of a cottage". In front was a small garden with so many flowers you could not put a finger between them. Behind were a well-stocked kitchen garden and an orchard bursting with fruit. The stoep was hung with flowering creepers and set about with ferns in pots, and comfortable cane chairs. There were two of the most diminutive housemaids she had ever seen, young Bushman sisters, still children, who tripped about the house in neat print dresses with bare feet.

Mrs Parker knew relatives of Sarah in England. Her house was a haven of refuge after months, years of travelling. Sarah relaxed and allowed herself to be petted and spoilt in a way she had not since childhood. Sitting on Mrs Parker's stoep, rocking in a cane chair, Sarah gossiped of family and "home" and felt comforted and restored. The brief interlude recharged her batteries and strengthened her to face the life she had mapped out for herself in the Transvaal.

9

A chapter of accidents

A week was spent in Pretoria, during which the party's belongings were unloaded from the wagons which had brought them up from Durban and repacked in the wagons taking them to Rustenburg, roughly 60 miles to the west of Pretoria. The men were to work on a farm there for a year, while Sarah was to live in the farmhouse and learn how to superintend a South African holding. She intended also to learn Afrikaans, which she calls the local Dutch patois, "with Kaffir, Hottentot and even English words mixed up with it so that a real Dutchman, or what they call here a Hollander, neither understands it nor is understood by the Boers".

Her heart sank when she saw the wagons. One was a buckwagon, with a bucksail to cover the goods. The other was a tent-wagon but as she could see daylight through the holes in the tent she believed it would not be much good if they were caught in a storm. When everything was in there was scarcely any room left under this canopy – about a foot and a half had been left at the back for dressing and undressing. To add to her woes her own tent had been lost in the mêlée. Both wagons looked rickety and the spans of oxen a poor lot. One was driven by a coloured man – South African term for half-caste – called William, the other by an African.

They left Pretoria about midday and were barely out of the town when, in crossing a small spruit, the *disselboom* – the pole to which the oxen were yoked – of the buckwagon broke. If the journey from Durban had had its unpleasant moments, the trek to Rustenburg swiftly degenerated into bad farce. The damage delayed them till the following afternoon.

They were at the start of the broad valley which lies south of the Magaliesberg. Though at their highest point the mountains reach a height of just over 6,000 feet above sea level they do not look impressive from the valley, which is nowhere more than 800 feet below. From a distance they seem featureless and uninteresting but on closer acquaintance the wooded kloofs, the wealth of flowers in the long grass and the crown, or *krans* – the rocky cliff that runs near the top of large parts of the range – surprise with their beauty.

Sarah's party were to cross the Magaliesberg by Silkaatsnek, or Mzilikazi's Pass, so called because it was the scene of Mzilikazi's defeat by the Boers in 1838. Mzilikazi had led the third group of Ndebele to leave Natal, crossing the Drakensberg in 1823, joined on his way by fugitive bands of Zulu warriors fleeing from Shaka. As he moved north, Mzilikazi burned the country behind him. This scorched-earth policy was a mark of Ndebele movement for some time to come. In the Transvaal Mzilikazi and his warriors attacked the Sotho people they found living there in settled villages, seizing the women and pressing the men into service in their army, which accordingly grew in number the further they went.

After his defeat Mzilikazi moved across the Limpopo River and built his "Great Place", Bulawayo, founding the Matabele nation of what became Rhodesia (now Zimbabwe). Having defeated him the Boers regarded themselves as rightful heirs by conquest to his Transvaal empire, which they construed as including everything between the Limpopo and the Vaal, to the north and south, and the Kalahari Desert and the Drakensberg Escarpment, west and east. They claimed to have liberated all the other Africans within these boundaries from Mzilikazi's tyrannies, but many of the tribes, notably the Ngwato, the Venda and the Pedi, had never been under his sway, or at worst only for a short time. They had either remained independent or freed themselves and saw no reason for becoming grateful vassals of the Boers. However, the Sotho and Venda tribes were split by personal feuds and rivalries between chiefs and these the Boers exploited. Their attitude to the indigenous inhabitants was made clear by Article 9 of the Transvaal Republican constitution. It states that, "The people (*het volk*) are not prepared to allow any equality of the non-white with the white inhabitants, either in Church or State."

How much of the history of the area Sarah knew as she strolled about, exploring and waiting for the wagon to be repaired, she did not say. She later became well versed in the history of the English settlers in the Transvaal but seems always to have remained largely out of sympathy with the Boers. She never allowed this, however, to overcome her innate sense of justice. There were times when she sprang to the Afrikaners' defence when she thought them maligned and she frequently commented on their fine qualities.

Their second night on the road was uncomfortable as the wagons became separated and the African driver missed the road. As all the food was in one wagon and all the bedding in the other neither half of the party was pleased. Next day they reassembled and were at the foot of the pass by midday. Sarah decided after lunch to walk ahead of the wagons, both to enjoy the beautiful scenery undisturbed and to avoid having to see the incessant flogging of the oxen which so upset her. Most drivers were adept with the enormously long leather whips and could flick a fly off the ear of the leading ox. They could produce deafening cracks of the whip a hair's breadth from the ox they wished to "speak to" and have the desired effect without actually touching it, so that sometimes Sarah may have been upsetting herself for nothing, but without doubt there was plenty of actual flogging too.

Sarah asked William, who spoke little English, which road she should take and was told to keep left. This being the general direction in which Rustenburg lay she took it as correct and set off. It was a delight to have a short space of solitude in such glorious surroundings and when she came to the top of the pass she gasped at the view suddenly spread out below her. She was looking down onto lush, park-like country, the beginning of the Bushveld, quite different in character to the south side of the mountains – stretching to the distant horizon with strange conical hills breaking the level lie of the land. A well-made road wound through clumps of trees and flowering shrubs, many hung with creepers and ferns. She started down, keeping to the left as instructed when she came to a fork, but had not gone far when one of the brief but devastating Transvaal thunderstorms came on. She was quickly soaked to the skin. She waited under thick bushes till it passed and then went back a bit to look for the wagons but there was no sign of them. However, she was sure she was on the right road so wandered on, savouring the lovely scenery, till she met a small cart with two men in it; one an old man with a long beard, the other "a sleek but dirty-looking fellow in black clothes with a sanctimonious look about him". She asked him if this was the way to Rustenburg, but was told she should have taken the other fork near the summit. Saluting her with his whip, he drove on.

It was nearly sunset but the sky ahead was clear and the rocky *krans* above her, reflecting the low light, looked magnificent. There were masses of tiny birds, brightly coloured with small crests, and she strolled on watching them. The wagons, she thought, would now be outspanned and she would soon find them when she returned to the fork. When she turned to go back she realised she had waited too long. The sky above the pass was inky black and lightning seared across the top of the mountain, heavy ominous drops of rain fell and there was a tremendous crash of thunder. By the time she reached the fork in the road it was pitch dark, she was drenched to the skin and by the flashes of lightning she could see clearly from the state of the dirt road that no wagon had passed recently. There was no choice but to climb back to the top of the pass and there she found the tent-wagon outspanned. There was no sign of the other with the food in it – it was stuck half way up. The rain was pouring down and there was nothing to eat. The men were swigging rum. Deciding it might keep the chill out, Sarah accepted some from the bottle, rolled herself in damp blankets (for the wagon-tent leaked just as she had expected), turned in for the night – and slept!

The weather was slow to clear the next morning and it was a late start. They got as far as the Crocodile River and there William made the mistake of outspanning before they had crossed.

Next morning Sarah was up early enjoying a cup of coffee long before any of the others were awake. The tent-wagon went down to the drift – as a ford is called in South Africa – and crossed with little difficulty, but the buck-wagon stuck fast in the middle of the river. Sarah wondered wearily when, if ever, South Africa would build bridges. There was much flogging and swearing and then the *disselboom* broke again. The oxen were taken out and attached to the back of the wagon so they could pull it to the bank whence it had started. The oxen were turned loose while the *disselboom* was repaired.

This took a long time, during which the oxen wandered off and were lost in the bush. By the time they had been rounded up and inspanned and the wagon was back at the drift it was late afternoon. After more flogging and cussing and swearing the wagon stuck again and the *disselboom* broke for the third time. William, who said that getting into the water made him ill, confined his efforts to dancing on the bank, shrieking at the African driver. It became dark and William decided to leave the wagon where it was in the middle of the stream until morning. No one raised any objection, though there was clearly another storm coming up and Sarah had already learnt that these downpours could turn an almost dry riverbed into a raging torrent in an hour or so.

Before going to sleep in the tented-wagon she "made sundry arrangements". She wore her mackintosh and had her waterproof sheet spread over her. A few things she prized she placed under her, put a fresh candle in her lantern and a box of matches in the mackintosh pocket, rolled herself in the still-damp blankets and waited for what the night would bring. "I was awakened by a rattling crash of thunder, followed by a series of explosions which seemed as if they must rend something in pieces. The lightning was terrific, the wind howled round and battered the wagon as if it would overturn it, the rain poured down in torrents and I could hear the rushing of the river. I lit my lantern, with difficulty, protecting the match under my mackintosh. The sight was absurd! The rain was coming into the wagon like a shower-bath." Before long it worked through the contents of the wagon and out at the bottom. She was amused at the sulphurous comments she heard from the men who were sleeping under it.

Next morning she applied her favourite adjective – "comical" – to the sight of the camp, festooned with damp clothing vainly trying to dry in a drizzle, while the owners wandered about looking disconsolate. The buckwagon was still in the river, which had risen almost to the top of it. Everything in it was soaked though luckily not washed away – only the tarpaulin had gone. It was early evening before the *disselboom* was again mended and the wagon dragged out. "Having now been three days without having been able to change my wet clothes and obliged to sleep in damp blankets, I was getting tired of it."

A local farmer rode up to the camp and asked if there was anything he could do for the travellers. Sarah begged him to find her a horse so that she could ride on to Rustenburg as she was quite sure there would be more upsets and disasters with the wagons before they got there. He replied that it was impossible. Horse sickness was bad north of the Magaliesberg and there was hardly a horse to be ridden – the one he had was borrowed. He promised, however, to find someone with a cart to drive her there and the following morning sent a "Kaffir boy" to the camp to fetch her. She had found a discreet dressing place among the trees and having carried a rubber bucket of water to it had been able to wash and change. Putting a few things into a valise she set off with the "boy" along a bridle path that led to the farm, where breakfast was ready for her. It was a small, thatched farmhouse on a grassy slope at the foot of the Magaliesberg, surrounded by a luxuriant orchard of orange, lemon, fig, peach, apricot and quince trees and a few coffee bushes which testified to the warm climate. It looked idyllic but inside the house was dark, bleak and comfortless. The lady of the house spoke no English but understood a little German so they "scraped along together".

Her husband told Sarah that he had had great difficulty in finding a cart to take her the rest of the journey. The only one available belonged to his neighbour, the sanctimonious-looking gentleman she had met when she had walked over the pass. The trouble was that he was a Dopper, member of "a very sanctified sect of the Dutch Church". "He had shuddered in holy horror at the idea of his committing the impropriety of driving alone with any woman not related to him, neither would his conscience allow him to hire out his vehicle so as to facilitate any such improper act on the part of his neighbour." However, his scruples had been overcome when Sarah's host had promised to make a third in the cart and act as chaperone.

They set off: the little Dopper dour and alone on the driving seat while Sarah and her chaperone sat together in the back. The Dopper said nothing at all, but the other was extremely chatty, which at first pleased Sarah until it dawned on her that he was completely mad. He was friendly and pleasant but so obviously unbalanced that Sarah became frightened of him and was thankful that the Dopper was doing the driving. They outspanned three times, twice at farms. At the first she was given a basket of superb fruit, at the second good coffee, milk and *boerbeskuit*. Her mad chaperone introduced her to the people as his second wife – that much she understood – but speaking no "Dutch" herself was embarrassed at not being able to put the people right and had to confine herself to shaking her head vigorously. Looking at them chatting together it occurred to her that "these Boers, if dressed up in antique fashion, would look like the models from which Rembrandt and others of the old masters painted".

The third stop was within sight of Rustenburg and was demanded by her fellow passenger. "We must outspan here," he said. "I must change my trousers before we get to Rustenburg. I know some people there." He disappeared into the bushes "in mufti, and reappeared in magnificence". They bowled into Rustenburg in fine style. The 60 miles from Pretoria had taken her five days to cover.

"The village of Rustenburg," Sarah wrote later, "from which one can see the last place inhabited by white people, and through whose streets numbers of Kaffirs and Kaffir women troop daily, dressed in skins, and adorned with barbaric ornaments, appeared to me to be a sort of Ultima Thule." It now lies close to the border of one of the most populous of the former "Bantu homelands", Bophuthatswana, and the city of Ga-Rankuwa. In January 1879 Rustenburg was a peaceful, small place with a few shops, a post office, a jail, a mill, a mission station and three churches. "Everything looked as if it was just winking between two sleeps," said Sarah.

There was an inn kept by an Englishman and his big, jolly Boer wife, "the cheeriest, heartiest, most kindhearted, and sturdiest of housewives". No being, whether it went on two legs or four, appealed to her in vain. Her livestock were glossy and sleek, her dogs and cats well fed. Two orphans she had taken in because their stepmothers ill-treated them adored her and she was talking of taking in a third. Sarah, tired, lame, a widow and a stranger, went straight to Mrs Brown's heart and was welcomed to the inn as into the bosom of the family.

The hotel was a farmhouse, with a few outside rooms tacked on to accommodate travellers, to one of which Sarah was shown. Everywhere was scrupulously clean and the meals were ample. A local doctor who was unmarried came in for his meals and Sarah was pleased to find that he knew friends of hers in England. Breakfast was served at eight, dinner at one and supper at six "and then a chat in the big sitting-room till we all went to bed". Friends of the Browns often dropped in and Sarah listened as they talked "Dutch", Mrs Brown not being fluent in English. She was delighted to hear that Sarah wanted to learn the language and offered to teach her, but Sarah soon grew wary of this as she found the jolly hostess a "dangerous preceptress". She would teach her phrases, assuring her of their meaning, only, when Sarah used them, to give away by her ringing laugh and nods and winks that they really meant something quite different.

There was a bevy of dogs in the house, including a small spaniel named Gip which Mrs Brown had rescued from a man who was maltreating him. Gip became so fond of Sarah that Mrs Brown made her a present of him.

The wagons and the rest of the party reached Rustenburg several days after Sarah. They quickly suspected that they had all been utterly deceived over the farm scheme. It was another week or so before the whole thing was shown up but it then became apparent that if there ever had been such a scheme, which was doubtful, it certainly no longer existed. There was neither work nor lodging for them. After the journey she had made and the money she had committed, this was a devastating shock for Sarah. She dismissed at once the idea of returning to England and admitting what had happened, but her money was running low and if she could not find a job which provided her with lodging, as the farm scheme would have done, she would be in trouble. Living in hotels and boarding houses in the Transvaal was relatively expensive in those days. It was already plain to her that she could not undertake any sort of farming, on which she had set her heart, until she had mastered the local Dutch patois, but how she was to live while she learnt it she simply did not know.

In this dilemma she saw one of the local clergymen, Mr Richardson, to whom she had a letter of introduction from the rector of Pretoria, to ask his advice. It turned out to be the best move she could have made. He asked if she would be willing to go as governess to a farmer's family who lived about 35 miles from Rustenburg on the other side of the Magaliesberg. The farmer's name was Jennings and he had two daughters he wished to have a good education. Sarah enquired in the town about Mr Jennings and heard everywhere that he and his family were well thought of and that his farmhouse was one of the finest in the Transvaal. Sarah returned to Mr Richardson and said she would go. Posts went out from Rustenburg only once a week so it was a while before a reply came to the clergyman's letter recommending Sarah. The heat, the monotony of routine at the hotel and the anxiety as to her future, combined to produce a terrible strain on Sarah. She passed the time by starting a novel. She sat up late to work on it and rose at dawn to continue, forgetting her own troubles by inventing others for her characters. Which of her books this was she did not say but it could well have been *Excelsior*, into which she poured so much of her own joys and woes and her love for Nathaniel.

One beautiful evening, at the end of a hot day, she came out onto the steps that led to her room and saw two grey horses grazing that she had not seen before. A handsome man, with a sunburnt face, blue eyes and a bushy, reddish-brown beard, wearing riding clothes and the inevitable wide-awake hat, came to her and said, "Mrs Heckford, I think. I'm Jennings. I came while you were out. Those are my horses." It was 11 February. She had not expected him so early though he had written to say he would fetch her as soon as he could. He had offered £5 a month, with washing, and had said she might take other pupils as well as his daughters at any terms she could make, and he would give such pupils their dinner. As they strolled over to his horses they quickly sized each other up and took an immediate liking to each other. "We settled everything in five minutes," Sarah recorded. She told him he could find out from Mr Richardson who she was and what her antecedents were but he brushed that aside, saying that he liked everything he had heard and seen of her, and was not bothered about references. How soon could she be ready to start? She agreed to go the next morning.

10
Surprise

Sarah was up early and soon had everything that would go into it packed into William Jennings's Cape cart. Her heavy luggage she left with Mrs Brown till a wagon could be sent for it. After breakfast and much handshaking all round she climbed into the cart. Gip was barking desperately to be taken too and when Mr Jennings agreed she tucked him joyfully under her arm. She was taking a leap in the dark and wondered nervously what sort of family she was going to.

"That asking whether I might take my dog seemed like the first plunge into a cold bath on a frosty morning. It was part of the role I had to play now, and I wondered how I should play it. I had always pitied governesses, and had also always objected to be an object of pity myself – even to myself." Bearing in mind her remarks about governesses in *The Life of Christ* it is not hard to appreciate how Sarah felt at being forced to surrender her independence and go as governess in a farmer's family. Having aspired to becoming a doctor, been mistress of her own comfortable home and matron of the East London Hospital, it was obviously galling to her. She probably saw no conflict between her feelings then and her published assertions that it was morally the best way to earn your living by working for others for wages "because it teaches us our relative value in this world". When she wrote that it is unlikely that she expected to find her own worth equated with that of the despised governess.

She need not have worried, however, because she was on the way to meet the family who – especially William's wife Mary – would become dear and trusted friends to the end of her life.

William Jennings's father, James Jennens, (as the name was then spelt) had been born in England, at Longbridge Deverill in Wiltshire, and had arrived at the Cape as a baby with his mother in sad circumstances. They were with a party led by Edward Ford, part of what came to be known as the "1820 Settlers". There was great distress in England at that time, particularly in the rural areas, and much unemployment, following the drastic drop in prices at the close of the Napoleonic Wars. At the same time the British Government was having difficulty in administering the troubled frontier districts of the eastern Cape where the white colonists had come into conflict with the Xhosas. They hit on the idea of bringing out British settlers and using them to create a belt of dense settlement to hold the frontier. A small fleet of ships was assembled to carry them. Promises were made of grants of fertile land but most of the men who went out had no knowledge of farming, let alone of frontier conditions in Africa.

James Jennens's father, another James, was 28, and his wife Mary 30, when they decided to join the emigrants with their year-old son. They boarded the *Weymouth*, a sailing vessel of about 400 tons, at Portsmouth on 21 December 1819. Some days later, when the ship had put out into Spithead, James Jennens was taken seriously ill and it was decided to put the family ashore. He was taken off by longboat and admitted to Haslar Hospital but before Mary and the baby could follow a gale blew up which made landing impossible. The *Weymouth* sailed for the Cape with them still aboard. It was only on her arrival in South Africa that Mary learnt her husband had died the day after entering hospital.

The voyage, which cost each member of the party £24/10/3 (approximately £1,750 at 2008 values) was a hard one with gales and icy weather for the first part of the way and several of the ships carrying the settlers were nearly wrecked. The emigrants were each issued with a blanket and a ration of oats, biscuits and meat. Water was rationed out at three quarts a day each for all purposes. The ships took them to Algoa Bay, where there were no proper landing facilities. They were rowed through the surf in the ships' longboats and soldiers and Africans waded out to help the women and children – there were a great many children, from babies to teenagers – onto the beach. Altogether 4,000 people were brought out in 1820 and settled in the Albany district west of the Fish River, and later in the valley of one of its tributaries, the Baviaans. Grahamstown developed as their centre – administrative, commercial and religious – and it was to the Grahamstown neighbourhood that Mary Jennens and young James finally came.

Each group had been allocated a separate site and they were taken to them in ox wagons by Afrikaner frontiersmen, who had been commandeered for the job by the Government. Friendly relations developed between the Dutch and English-speaking settlers, despite their very different backgrounds. They shared common problems and a common piety. Many of the settler parties were based on shared religious beliefs, such as a Wesleyan Methodist group, and religion was as vital to the new settlers as to the older Afrikaner colonists.

The 1820 Settlers met many difficulties. Grazing rather than cultivation was the profitable way to use the land on the frontier but their holdings had been made deliberately too small for them to be graziers because the politicians were aiming at a small, close-knit, settled community. Rust blighted their first wheat crops and the Xhosas raided their cattle. Full-scale war with the Xhosa broke out fourteen years after their arrival. Three times within thirty years (1834–5, 1846–7, 1850–1) their homesteads were burned, crops destroyed and cattle lifted. But many of them stayed on the frontier and made an important economic contribution in developing wool farming and trade. They had barely arrived before they set up schools, churches and libraries. For the next century they kept much closer to the mainstream of European culture than did the majority of the Afrikaners, but they and their descendants became South Africans, or, as Sarah Heckford called them, "English Africanders".

James Jennens grew up near Grahamstown and in 1837 married Sarah Saunders, of Port Elizabeth, who was only 15 at the time. By this time the name was being spelt "Jennings", as it is in the official list of the 1820 Settlers. They had a large family, of whom James William, always known as William to distinguish him from his father, was their second son, born on 13 September 1842. He was Sarah Heckford's new employer. James and Sarah Jennings trekked to the Transvaal in 1866, settling on the farm Blaauwbank, north of Krugersdorp. James was a famous hunter, who with his sons made expeditions into Matabeleland as far as the Zambesi valley. They went principally in search of ivory and became friendly with other hunters and explorers, such as Henry Hartley. The artist and traveller Thomas Baines described meeting Jennings in Matabeleland. William Jennings married Mary Reiken on 22 February 1866 at Molteno in the Cape and brought her to live at Blaauwbank with his family.

After a particularly profitable ivory-hunting trip in 1871 – though it was one on which the whole party suffered severely from "fever" (malaria) – William decided to buy a farm and set up a home of his own as he now had two daughters, Clifford Augusta and Sarah Hannah Maud. The farm he bought was Nooitgedacht – "Surprise" – and that was where he and Sarah Heckford were now bound, Augusta and Sarah her intended pupils.

It was late afternoon by the time they drove up the lane

between thorn trees and round the spur of a wooded hill to a solid, red-brick house with a long verandah or stoep, as such a feature is called in South Africa. It still stands now, more than a hundred years later, altered but still recognisably the house that Sarah describes. Behind it the Magaliesberg sweep up sharply to their highest point and in front one used to look out over rolling farmlands and orchards to the line of the Witwatersberg, but much has changed. It is still a beautiful setting and one of the family still lives in the house that Sarah knew. The long drive to it and the attractive front garden that were still there in the late 1960s have disappeared and the front of the house is now barricaded by a high fence. Part of the farm is in use producing day-old chicks for market, but most of it is divided into small plots with holiday cottages built on them. A recent visitor was told not to bother looking for the memorial to those killed in the Battle of Nooitgedacht, fought on the farm during the Anglo-Boer War, as it had been vandalised beyond recognition.

Mrs Jennings and the girls came out to meet the cart. They were wearing black in mourning for the youngest child, Edie, who had died of diphtheria at the age of two not long before. (In 1873 Mary and William's two baby sons had died of the same disease.)

Mary Jennings was tall and graceful, a handsome woman who moved well. Augusta, who was then eleven, was tall for her age, with brown, waist-length hair, dark-lashed blue eyes, a "peaches and cream" complexion and long slender hands. "I thought I had rarely seen such a lovely girl," said Sarah. Her sister, the nine-year-old Sarah, was in complete contrast, small for her age, bright, mischievous with sparkling eyes and a shock of unruly hair. "In some ways she reminded me of an unbroken Shetland pony and in my mind I installed her as my pet," wrote the new governess.

The family led her indoors. The house, which William Jennings had designed himself, had large, high, airy rooms. She was shown into a bedroom which led off the drawing room. It also had a door onto the stoep and a window that looked out towards a spur of the mountain and the wide valley towards Pretoria, which lay nearly sixty miles away to the east. After supper in the dining room they went into the attractively furnished drawing room, which contained a harmonium and a piano. The latter had been Augusta's eleventh birthday present from her father and the children played a duet for her. They could not yet read music but had picked it up by ear and kept perfect time together. The whole family were apparently musical, which was a relief to Sarah, who had agreed to provide music lessons.

It was then her turn to play. Her music was in her heavy luggage back at the inn and she had not touched a piano for months, or practised properly for years. However, it would have been churlish to have refused so she sat down rather anxiously and addressed herself to a piece called *The Battle of Waterloo* which the family wanted her to play. It was one of those pieces that sound more difficult than they are, and she read it easily enough. *Shells of Ocean* and a setting of *Home Sweet Home* followed. The piano was quite a good one and Sarah was beginning to enjoy herself. "It was very encouraging to hear that I gave great satisfaction – I was so dreadfully afraid I should not." Finally a battered piano score of the opera *Norma* was propped up in front of her. She was struck with the strangeness of playing those familiar tunes in that remote farmhouse on the Magaliesberg, where the voices and faces they recalled to her were unknown.

The music finished, the children kissed her affectionately, as if prepared to like her, and, saying goodnight to the family, she went to her room. Standing at the window she gazed unseeing at the outline of the mountain. The music of *Norma* had revived memories of all the things she had seen and done since she first heard *Casta Diva* sung. "Life is a wonderful romance for many of us," she wrote. "It never struck me more forcibly that it had been so, and was still so, for me than on that evening." The summer night chorus of frogs and cicadas barely impinged on her hearing as she stood in a reverie.

In the morning she woke early and went out for a walk with Gip. She strolled towards the dam – a good stream of water and a dam were the first things you looked for when buying a farm in this dry country, she said – and came upon an old thatched cottage used as a stable and store. This was the original farmhouse, one of the oldest in the Transvaal. It had been built by the Voortrekker and Transvaal pioneer Hermanus Potgieter, who was the first owner of the farm and had, in Sarah's succinct phrase, "been made mincemeat of by the Kaffirs in days not indeed far distant" – in 1854, actually.

The house had been the Jennings's first home when they came to Nooitgedacht in 1872. It had been in bad repair and Mary Jennings had often to rig up umbrellas to shelter the children when rain leaked through the roof. The mud walls had rhinoceros horns and the hoofs of buck built into them to act as clothes hangers. There were no windows, only holes in the walls closed by shutters in bad weather. This house finally collapsed many years ago and there is now no trace of it.

Near the old house was a large orchard where oranges, lemons, several varieties of peach, pear, apricots, figs, quince and pomegranate grew. Beyond it the lane crossed the wall of the dam and ran on through the fields of mealies (maize) into the valley.

Returning to the house, Sarah was met by the children and taken in to breakfast, where plans for lessons were discussed. William Jennings decided that as it was nearing the weekend, Sarah should have a short break to make herself at home. Lessons should begin on the Monday. A small room off the end of the stoep had been set aside as the classroom. William's parents, James, the old hunter, and Sarah Jennings, also lived on the farm in a small cottage on the portion called Groenfontein, with their two youngest daughters, Alice and Ada. These girls were to share the lessons with their nieces.

Alice, small, plump and pretty, was sixteen and already engaged to be married to a neighbouring farmer and trader. She was a reliable and conscientious girl and Sarah soon found she could be left in charge of the younger ones if necessary. Ada was thirteen, almost as tall as Augusta and with the same slender hands, an attractive child with a mass of thick, brown hair, slim and graceful. She "looked like a little princess in disguise", said Sarah, "except for when she went in for a romp, at which she excelled".

Sarah found she had to keep the lessons simple to start with. None of the girls had had any proper schooling before. Even Alice had to be taught to spell monosyllables and was flummoxed by the meaning of words which would have been familiar to children in England half her age. They made good pupils, however, and worked hard.

Life at Nooitgedacht was monotonous but pleasant. They breakfasted between seven and eight o'clock and began lessons immediately after. At one there was an hour's break for lunch and then more lessons till five and afternoon tea. After supper at seven there was "a chat or a little music" before an early bed.

It was a long day for Alice, who helped her mother with a number of tasks before walking with Ada across the farm to school – a distance of nearly a mile. Sarah grew fond of all the children. Little Sarah was her pet but she was strict with her as with the others, admitting to making her "cry about four days out of seven!"

Books were a problem. Everything had to be fetched from Pretoria and even there it was difficult to get what she wanted. She found it difficult to explain quite common things to children whose experience was so limited. She was at a loss to explain what a bridge was when the nearest they had seen to such a thing was a plank thrown across a spruit. To explain the idea of a steam engine or a steamboat taxed her to the limit, and she almost admitted defeat trying to convey an understanding of what a city was like to girls who thought Pretoria a vast metropolis. However, the children got on well and the parents were satisfied.

William Jennings sometimes let Sarah ride his favourite horse, Free State, and she began to long for one of her own. Once William took her to a small kraal on the property where she admired the neat, round, thatched huts. "The Kaffirs living in the kraal were what are called raw Kaffirs," she explained, "the men indeed being in some sort clothed in old European garments, but the women wearing skins and the children being naked." Mr Jennings, in return for allowing them to live on his property, could call on their services for getting in the crops without payment. At other times he had to pay them a shilling a day. He also had the right to call on the women to hoe the fields "or to scoffel, as it is called here". This is of course the Dutch word *schoffel*, which is also the root of the word scuffle when it is used in England in the sense of to hoe or weed. The women he would pay with a basket of fruit each. If there was no fruit available at the time he need not pay them at all.

Also living on the farm were several families of what Sarah calls "urlams, or civilised kaffirs". The word she was probably trying to transcribe is *oorlams* – clever, knowing, smart, shrewd, crafty or sly are some of the meanings the dictionary gives. "Cheeky kaffir" was a widely used approximation. These were Africans who had had the benefit of school at the mission station in Rustenburg where they had "learned a little reading and singing of hymns". They lived in square mud houses and ate European food, she noted, adding, "I don't think the schooling did them much good. I heard of one Kaffir woman saying that when she came back from school and had been made a Christian she would sit on a chair and eat with a knife and fork, and not let the raw Kaffirs eat with her, for then she would be better than they." At this time Sarah did not have a good opinion of the missionaries and their influence over the Africans. However, about fifteen years later, when she knew the country and its people better, she came to a grudging admission of the worth of the work the missionaries did. William Jennings was a kind and indulgent employer who could get African labour when his neighbours could not.

One Saturday when Sarah had been at the farm about a month she borrowed Free State to visit Alice and Ada's parents. She found that their cottage, on a picturesque spur of the mountain with a huge wild fig tree before it, was only a mud and stone cabin, with bare rafters and thatch overhead. This surprised her, but in the suburbs of Pretoria and Johannesburg there are still single-storeyed houses built without ceilings and open to the thatch. Such houses keep pleasantly cool in the hot weather though the thatch is a fire hazard in the dry season.

James and Sarah Jennings's cottage, however, was only one long room, divided by canvas screens, the walls bare, and planks supported on the rafters doing duty as shelves. There were no windows, but openings in the wall which had removable frames with calico stretched over them to close them against bad weather. The kitchen was outside in a round straw hut. "There was an old piano, however, in this funny little building, and on it Alice and Ada practised their music."

Sarah Jennings kept no servant. She and Alice did all the work, including washing in a washing machine. They also made the family's clothes. "Ada, the princess, did nothing, not even mend her own clothes," observed Sarah, adding, "How Alice managed to do the work she did and learn her lessons I don't know, but she did manage it." There were books in the house as well as the piano. James Jennings, she discovered, was "a thorough old gentleman in all his ways and thoughts, with a fund of queerly assorted information". He had always been a great reader and delighted in buying job lots of books in sales. Now bent and grey-bearded, he still had the keen eyes of the hunter and an easy seat in the saddle.

Mary Jennings, on the other hand, had help in the house but worked hard, for all that, and did much sewing. Augusta, like Ada, "did nothing but look ornamental", but small Sarah was already an industrious little housewife.

In this family Sarah was not treated like a governess but

as a welcome guest who was given the best of everything. Mary Jennings showed her true kindness when Gip was ill. She made no objection when Sarah left the classroom to attend to the dog and when it eventually died had a grave dug for it. Sarah missed the little creature badly – it had been fond of her when she was a stranger with no friend to turn to – and she appreciated the family's sympathy. Soon, however, she acquired a cross-bred terrier, Roughy.

All through the early months of 1879 the "Boer scare" went on with a continuous round of rumours. Gruesome stories of what the Boers meant to do to the English, and especially to families like the Jennings who were loyal to Britain, were being circulated. Sarah worried about George Warner. He was on a farm about thirty miles away and without a horse of her own she was concerned that she could not get over to see him.

One afternoon she was in the schoolroom with the children when one of them shouted, "There's Uncle Walter." There was a clamour to go outside to see their bachelor uncle from Marico. The children raced out and in a moment William came in and asked Sarah to meet his brother. She found a good-looking man – "what a handsome family they are", she thought to herself – standing by his horse with another on a leading rein.

"That's a nice little horse, what do you think of him?" asked William, indicating the led horse. "Not bad," said Sarah, not much taken with the lean and draggle-tailed animal. "Think he would suit you?" asked William. At that Sarah took a better look. It struck her as being good at all points and showing good blood. It had been ridden hard and was under-fed and dirty, but she believed time and her care would cure that. It was a roan, with white stockings and blaze and a chestnut mane and tail. It appeared mild and well-mannered.

"I think I might like it if the price isn't too high," she said. "Would twenty pounds be all right?" said William. She hesitated at the thought of the hole that would make in her budget but finally agreed. Walter assured her he had had the horse for some time and it was sound and fit for a lady to ride so the bargain was struck and Eclipse changed hands. They turned him out to graze and Walter rode off well pleased with the business. "I have my saddle and tack with me, as I thought I might buy a horse. If you could allow me forage and space in the stable with your three I will look after him entirely myself," said Sarah and that was readily agreed. They all went in to tea and shortly after a neighbour came in.

"Have you bought that horse off Walter Jennings?" he asked. "Yes, why?" asked Sarah. "Are you a good horsewoman?" "No." "Then take care – he'll break your neck. He bucked Walter Jennings off him and Walter Scrooby too. He nearly threw me but I jumped off. I never saw a horse buck as cleverly as he does," and so saying he went off, leaving Sarah in considerable dismay and the family embarrassed. However, the deal was done and she would have to make the best of it. The best turned out very good. He was troublesome to groom at first and was certainly lively but with Sarah on his back he never attempted more than a "playful little jump". Sarah was in fact an excellent horsewoman and had a way with animals. Soon Eclipse was docile in return for firm but kind handling. The local farmers, seeing her ride by, would exclaim at the change in him. There was not much time for riding but she felt happier now she could get hold of George if trouble really should threaten.

As far as religion was concerned, the Jennings family imagined that Sarah shared their own conventional Anglican beliefs. She observed a discreet silence about her unorthodox ideas. Had they read her book on Christ and communism they might have looked with fresh eyes at their governess. There was no church within reach of Nooitgedacht in the 1870s. Occasionally Mr Richardson rode over from Rustenburg, stayed a night or two at the farm and held a Sunday service in the drawing room. Sarah accompanied the hymns on the piano. They would have liked her to play the harmonium but with her lame leg she could not easily manage it. Relatives and friends came from a distance around to join the service.

At times Bishop Bousfield, the Anglican bishop of Pretoria, rode out to the valley to visit his flock and stayed a few days at Nooitgedacht. He was the first incumbent of the See and had arrived from England at the same time as Sarah. He was a powerful character with a highly developed sense of his own importance. When he and his large party had arrived outside Pretoria they outspanned for the night close to where the Pretoria Art Museum is now. Next morning Advocate Henry Cooper, with Judge John Kotze, Chief Justice of the Transvaal, with him, drove out to meet the bishop and escort him into the town in his four-seated American spider. As they crossed the Apies River by Meintjie's Drift, Advocate Cooper said, "Bishop, you are now within the town." In reply the bishop exclaimed, "Pretoria, henceforth thou art a city, for I am in thee!" Cooper and the judge were highly amused. "The above episcopal remark is a good index of Dr Bousfield, both as a bishop and as a man," the judge wrote in his memoirs. The bishop was unpopular in many quarters but he did a great deal of good work in difficult pioneering days. He rode enormous distances visiting his scattered diocese. It was in May 1879 that Sarah met the tall and handsome bishop when he came to Nooitgedacht for the first confirmation service ever held in the valley. The candidates were old James and Sarah Jennings, their daughters Alice and Ada and their granddaughter Augusta. Watching the scene from her seat at the piano Sarah was moved almost to tears.

Augusta had a pet rock rabbit (dassie), a plump and mischievous little animal with sharp teeth. On the night of the confirmation the bishop retired to bed to find that the dassie had taken possession. Being new to the country the bishop was afraid to touch him and Augusta had to be called to remove him from the bishop's bed, much to

Sarah's amusement. The sight of a six-foot-two-inch bishop cowering before a rock rabbit really tickled her sense of humour.

William Jennings was away at the time on a trading trip to Natal with a neighbour, George Rex, who farmed towards Rustenburg. They had left in early April and Sarah had been envious as she watched them leave. Her energetic soul was already fretting at the quiet and dependent life she was leading. At the end of April the remainder of her luggage arrived from Rustenburg. Mary Jennings had sent a wagon for it. With the wagon came George Warner, amidst a flurry of excitement from the girls. It would be pleasant to know what they made of the English boy and he of them. It had been arranged that George should go to the Scroobies at Skeerpoort, "where he could learn and make himself useful in return for his board and lodging". It was a relief to Sarah to have him closer at hand and with friends. Mrs Scrooby was a sister of William Jennings.

The schoolroom routine was broken by outings. She rode with Augusta to see Mrs Rex soon after William and her husband had left, as Augusta reported in a letter to her father on 20 April, adding, "Mrs Heckford cleaned her horse every day as usual." She told her father that Mrs Heckford and "Aunt Alice" had also ridden to Skeerpoort to see "Aunt Mary". Doubtless Sarah went to see how George was settling down. The Scrooby family, like the Jenningses a large one, became lifelong friends of Sarah's.

She visited the original Jennings farm at Blaauwbank and here she saw gold mining in its most primitive form and first tried her hand at panning gold. Alluvial gold had been found on the farm in 1874 and it became well known in the early days of the Transvaal gold rush. William's brothers Jeremiah and John Jennings worked the farm in partnership after their father retired to Groenfontein. The alluvial gold soon ran out but there was rich quartz with visible gold. A company called the Nil Desperandum Co-operative Quartz Mining Company was formed to work the gold, with that delightful character, the Pretoria trader and versifier Albert Brodrick, as chairman. It is thought to be the first company to have carried out systematic gold exploration in South Africa. A tunnel was driven and machinery brought in 1876; a shaft was sunk in 1878. The quartz, however, was tremendously hard and the machinery then available could not crush it properly. After the Main Reef Conglomerates – the softer "banket" – were discovered on the other (southern) side of the Witwatersrand in 1886 Blaauwbank gradually went out of production.

"Boer scares" continued and Mary Jennings and Sarah debated what they should do if Boer insurgents came to Nooitgedacht. They decided they would lock the two girls in one of the rooms and would tell the invaders to take anything they wanted, but they would defend the girls with pistols and knives. Mary Jennings said she had heard that the Boers did not kill the women of their enemies but would strip them and make laughing stocks of them. The children quite enjoyed the scare and Ada made a game of it. Putting on her governess's mackintosh, she girded herself with a knife and pistol, blackened her eyebrows and drew a moustache with burnt cork. Sarah and Mary Jennings were still sitting over the tea table while Ada was preparing this game. "We heard a violent knocking at the kitchen door. Sannie, the maid, opened it reluctantly, being dreadfully afraid of the Boers. A gruff voice exclaimed, 'Waar is Bill Jennings?' and presented a pistol in her face. Sannie and two little Kaffir children uttered a succession of unearthly yells, and rushed into the dining-room, where they clung to Mrs Jennings' dress, hiding their faces, whilst the 'Boer' dashed past, pistol in hand, to search the rooms. We had a good laugh and Ada was delighted at her success."

It was winter by the time William Jennings returned from Natal in June. Grass fires flared as local farmers burnt off the dry brown grass and trekked to the Bushveld with their stock. This annual migration fascinated Sarah. She was sure that cattle could be kept on the Highveld through the winter if only the farmers would grow fodder and provide shelter for their animals. The nights were bitterly cold but the days pleasant and at least one did not have to worry about the horse sickness for a few months. The extended picnic when tents were pitched in the balmy climate of the Bushveld, however, was thoroughly enjoyed by most families, who would have been reluctant to give it up in return for anything so tedious and akin to hard work as growing winter fodder when the Bushveld grass was green and there for the taking. They left the burnt Highveld fallow till spring brought the new grass through. One result of this method of farming was that milk and butter were almost unprocurable on the Highveld in winter. Sarah was shocked to find that "a shilling a bottle was willingly given" for milk in Pretoria, and that butter reached the terrible price of four or even five shillings a pound.

William Jennings was himself doubtful of the value of sending cattle to the Bushveld – the long journey meant they often returned in poor condition and while there they had to be watched carefully in case they ate the *gijblaar*, a weed that was fatally poisonous to them. However, he did as everyone else did and the cattle went off in the charge of the Nel family, who were *bywoners* (people farming on someone else's land, enjoying certain privileges in return for their services) on the farm. William's parents were also going down, leaving Alice and Ada to continue their lessons at Nooitgedacht. The schoolroom was bitterly cold. Mary Jennings would give them dishes of hot embers to warm their toes and they wrapped up in jackets and shawls. The drawing room was cosy in the evenings with a big fire.

August 15 was little Sarah's tenth birthday and a family expedition was arranged to the farm of William's brother, at Vaalplaas, about twelve miles away. The four girls, escorted by one of Walter Scrooby's younger brothers and Alice's "intended", set off in great excitement, taking their cousin Harriet Scrooby with them. Around lunchtime the next day they were startled when the cart returned without either Augusta or Sarah. There was a note of terror in Mary Jennings's voice as she called out, "Where are my children?" Sarah, it appeared, was seriously ill with a sore throat and Augusta was ill too. Mary Jennings went white and Sarah remembered that diphtheria had killed her three youngest children. "Come with me. I must go at once and there is no doctor anywhere near. Please help me," Mary pleaded. They set off immediately and reached Vaalplaas just before dark. The house was crowded and there was only one small room to nurse the two girls in. Augusta merely had a bad cold, but her sister had a high fever and was delirious.

"There, for the first time, did I see the misery of illness in this country," wrote Sarah in her account of this time. Augusta was recovered enough to be sent home the next day, but young Sarah's throat had ulcerated and she was extremely ill for a day or two. As soon as she showed signs of mending, Sarah returned to Nooitgedacht to look after the other girls, and it was then that she realised just how fond she had become of the whole family and especially of her small namesake. "I could have cried for joy the day she was brought home."

11
Green springs

There were changes in the air. Sarah was becoming restless. She had only intended remaining a governess for a year at the most and now her class was about to be reduced by half. Old James Jennings, who suffered badly from bronchitis, was finding Groenfontein too much for him. He and his wife, taking Alice and Ada with them, were moving to Pretoria, to be near another of their daughters, Emma, who was married to Walter Scrooby's brother, Alginy.

Sarah reckoned that she had now learned as much as she could from observing the farming methods of William Jennings and his neighbours. She had learned enough of the "Taal" to get by and began to look about for a farm of her own. There were some interesting advertisements in the *Volkstem* and *Argus* papers, so when she heard that Walter Scrooby and his wife were visiting Pretoria at the beginning of September for the races, taking George Warner with them, she asked if she might go too. They were taking their wagon so she would be able to send a change of clothes instead of having to stay in her riding habit all the time as she would if she rode there alone. William Jennings was also going to the races and when he heard Sarah wanted to go he said Mary and the girls should join the party. There were tremendous preparations and packing up of food, for they were to live in the wagons in Pretoria.

The children were gleeful at the prospect and when the morning came for the wagons to be loaded they were beside themselves with excitement. Sarah felt her spirits rise with theirs. Mrs Jennings and the children went off in the wagon to join the Scroobies. Giving them a fair start, William, with Sarah on Eclipse, rode after them. They caught up with them outspanned halfway to Grootplaats, the Scrooby farm at Skeerpoort, had a meal with them and rode on ahead.

Beyond Skeerpoort they called at a farm that greatly interested Sarah because it was run by a woman. They stopped to exchange greetings and a tall, gaunt widow congratulated Sarah on her attempts at speaking "Dutch". "This old lady was a remarkable woman," said Sarah. "Hospitable and free-handed to all, of whatever nation they might be, she was yet a frugal manager. She and her first husband (she was the widow of three) had started life with a wagon and a span of oxen. I don't know what sort of man he was but she was a host in herself. If her oxen stuck in a difficult drift she would tuck up her petticoats, pull off her boots, and leaping from the wagon, take the whip from her Kaffir and drive the team through herself. If labour was scarce at harvest time or when water had to be led on the lands she thought nothing of doing the necessary work, but she attended to her household duties withal. She had never allowed her children to take any part in politics and I don't think anyone exactly knew what she thought of British rule. Like all Boer women and men, she regarded husbands as articles so necessary to household comfort that no time must be lost in replacing them when they died. Still, she was of opinion that there was some limitation as to age in the matter." She had apparently given short shrift not long before to a would-be suitor less than half her age who had ridden to pay court with barely half an eye to her charms and more than the rest to her broad acres.

As they rode on again Sarah was deep in thought. If this

woman could do so much, both in farming and in transport, why couldn't she? That the other had been born to the country, was not handicapped by lameness and had a large family of sons and sons-in-law helping her did not seem to occur to Sarah.

They were to stay the night at the farm owned by Alice's future husband. They found there not only the Scrooby wagon, but old Mr Jennings as well. Alice and Ada had persuaded him to take them to the races. As most of the large Scrooby clan were already in Pretoria it looked like being a good party. Mooiplaats lived up to its name – "pretty farm". Sarah thought it more like an English holding than any she had seen so far and was amused to see that the dining room had been papered with pictures from *The Illustrated London News*. Many of them recalled to her the ghosts of former days.

It was barely light next morning when a cavalcade of wagons set out on the road to Pretoria. Walter Scrooby, William Jennings and Sarah watched them go and went back to the farmhouse for coffee before saddling up and riding after them. They joined the wagons where they had outspanned after crossing the Crocodile River. Campfires were already alight and breakfast cooking. Sarah sat on the bank of the river and looked up the wooded gorge through which the Crocodile ran at that point. In the morning light, with the river flowing swiftly, it looked the most beautiful picnic spot she had seen.

That evening the wagons outspanned on the north side of Daspoort, a low, rocky ridge to the west of Pretoria, about two miles from the centre. Next morning they started early to get to the marketplace in good time. This journey, from Hekpoort to Pretoria, with two nights on the road, can now easily be covered by car in little over an hour.

Pretoria had grown since Sarah had last seen it nine months before and much building was going on. They set up their camp and made arrangements for her, Mary Jennings and the two children to sleep in the wagon. Sannie, the maid, was to sleep on the wagon box at the front, "from which she had a tendency to roll down on my head in the night. Our washing arrangements were limited, and camp life, though jolly in its proper place, is a bore on the outskirts of a village, particularly when the village calls itself a city".

The next morning Sarah visited her Pretoria acquaintances and rode with William to see the races. "The scene was characteristic of South Africa – the ox wagon element predominating, but there were also traps of various kinds drawn up in line, a grandstand, with the ring close to it, and two women besides myself," Sarah noted. Both horses and jockeys were good and she enjoyed the meeting. During the course of the day she was hugely amused to be told by a lordly gentleman that "he was glad to see the Boers doing this sort of thing as it approached to civilisation", only to be told afterwards that this man was himself a Boer, the son of a trekker.

One of her male acquaintances invited her to lunch at the Edinburgh Hotel. She was now sufficiently used to the free and easy colonial manners to accept with alacrity. By the end of the day most men in Pretoria were drunk and fights were frequent. Thinking that "the surroundings of the course would be too lively", she did not go to the second day of the race meeting. She was annoyed to find that she could do no business because the whole town was shut up for the races. The next morning the wagons set off for home while Sarah remained behind. An hour or two sufficed for her to realise there were no good farms for sale and she caught up with the party at their midday outspan.

When they reached Nooitgedacht they were shocked to find that a huge grass fire had got out of hand and swept almost up to the house itself. The farm was a waste of black, flecked with white ash. Sarah's dog, Roughy, had run away in fright, but he returned a day or two later. They were also disturbed to hear that a neighbour, a brother of Paul Kruger, had been hit on the head with a knobkerrie by an

Sarah in 1861 at the age of 21

Sarah's sister Annie Goff

A sketched portrait of Nathaniel Heckford

This drawing of one of the wards at the East London Hospital in Butcher Row appeared in *The Illustrated London News* of 27 April 1872.

The original East London Hospital in Butcher Row, Ratcliff.

Pretoria from Meintjies Kop, where the Union Buildings now stand, painted by Thomas Baines in 1872. The view is towards the west. The road from Natal comes in on the left and approaches the village between the double row of poplar trees. Note the wagons outspanned in the bottom left-hand corner of the picture.

Nooitgedacht farm in the 1970s.

William Jennings, 'Mr Higgins' of *A Lady Trader in the Transvaal*, and his wife Mary.

Augusta & Sarah Jennings

Marian Matthews as a young girl.

Marian Longobardi, née Matthews, adopted daughter of Sarah Heckford, in Naples shortly after her marriage.

Sarah Heckford as a young married woman in about 1870.

George Warner, 'Jimmy' of *A Lady Trader in the Transvaal*, in 1879.

Sarah Heckford in Johannesburg in 1892.

The original homestead on Ravenshill.

Dora Scrimgeour in the doorway of 'the romantic abode' during her visit to Ravenshill in 1895.

The house built for Augusta and Harry Hinds on the section of Nooitgedacht called Fountains. It was full of mementos of Sarah Heckford.

The wagon camp in the Siege of Pretoria.

Sarah Eland sitting on the *disselboom* of Mrs Heckford's wagon at Ravenshill, 1894.

One of George Heys' mail coaches on the Great North Road in the 1890s carrying passengers for Pietersburg, Mashonaland and the Klein Letaba goldfields. It was in one of these that Sarah Heckford travelled to Pretoria in 1895. (Painted E. Castres)

George & Sarah Hinds at Nooitgedacht.

Fountains on the Nooitgedacht estate in 2008.

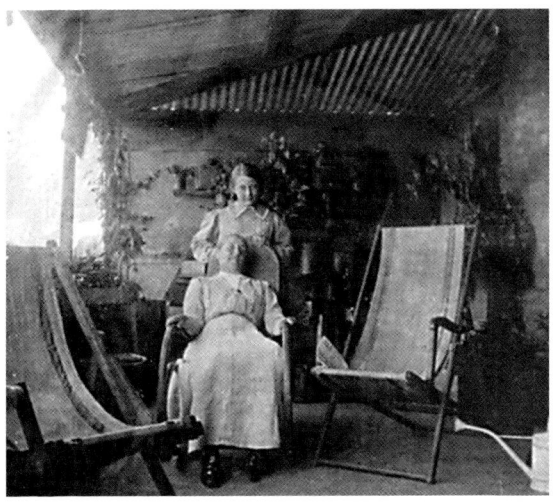
Dora Scrimgeour and Sarah Eland at Ravenshill.

Dora Scrimgeour's wagon and donkeys ready for the trek from Johannesburg to the Northern Transvaal in 1895. Dora is mounted, on the left of the picture. Sarah Heckford stands behind the donkeys, holding her horse, on the right.

Sarah Heckford in October 1902, drawn by Lady Sarah Nicholson.

Sarah's grave in Pretoria West cemetery as in the early 1970s.

African on his farm with whom he had had an argument, and had died of the injury.

The routine of lessons was resumed, broken only by Sarah's constant enquiries for a farm. No one in the vicinity was prepared to sell except at an exorbitant price. William worried that she might be trying to take on more than she could cope with, especially if she moved to a district where she knew nobody. He offered her a conditional sale of the portion of his farm his father had occupied, including the cottage by the fig tree. The condition was that she should not pay for it or take transfer for six months or more. If she could not make a go of it then she would be free to leave without any obligations. Her first inclination was to refuse, not wishing to be beholden to this good friend, but after thinking it over she accepted.

While she was preparing to move to Groenfontein she was called out to doctor the wife of a neighbouring farmer. On the way home she called at Grootplaats to see George Warner, who was to live with her and help with the work. She found Mrs Scrooby distressed over the baby, which seemed extremely ill. She diagnosed pneumonia. It was a small house and the one bedroom was stiflingly hot.

For two days Sarah did not leave the child. After that, though still ill, it was out of danger, but Sarah herself felt a bad bout of malaria coming on. Alice Jennings came over to nurse the baby and Sarah, leaving strict instructions for its care, just managed to get to Nooitgedacht before she was prostrated with fever. "I had to lie by for a day or two, and even then I felt weak."

It was 19 November of that year – 1879 – that Sarah moved into the cottage on Groenfontein. She had some stock as she had bought James's flock of sheep and Mrs Jennings's fowls and two pigs. Ada had left her two cats – to her great sorrow and for the simple reason that they had refused to be put into the wagon when the time came to leave for Pretoria. One "was an ancient specimen of the feline race, with a crooked eye, and the most surprising voice a cat was ever gifted with".

The cottage was sparsely furnished. A bed lent by Mrs Jennings, an old chair, and a washstand and dressing table contrived from packing cases equipped the bedroom. A deal table, three more old upright chairs and a broken square piano she used as a table, adorned the sitting room. Nathaniel's photograph hung in pride of place. Planks across the rafters did for shelves and nails on the walls, with lines of string, enabled her to hang up her clothes and other articles. The third section of the cottage, behind a canvas partition, doubled as storeroom and as a bedroom for a young Englishman who had come to Nooitgedacht asking for work. She had taken him on despite being sure he was a deserter. George slept sometimes in the storeroom, sometimes in the sitting room – presumably on the floor. Goat and sheepskins did duty for carpets. The skins of wild cats killed on Nooitgedacht festooned a broken old folding chair and gave the place, Sarah thought, something of the air of Robinson Crusoe's cabin.

"After experience of the same, I think a Robinson Crusoe cabin is nicer to read about than to live in," said Sarah. "And yet sometimes of an evening, with the light of a dip made from the fat of my own sheep lighting up the motley ornaments of bridles, saddles, bits, firearms, tools of various sorts hanging on the walls and faintly showing the dogs crouching on the floor and the cats' heads peering from the rafters overhead, I used to think it made not a bad picture of an African squatter's interior."

Outside, the farm was as beautiful as she could wish, lying in a small upland valley along the side of the Magaliesberg and bounded by wooded ravines where ferns and rare flowers grew by the rocky streams. There was a small plateau, ringed by rocks near the tiny dam James Jennings had made, which she earmarked as the site of the house she intended to build. From there on a clear day she could see eastwards up the valley as far as Daspoort Ridge, with a glimpse of white where the Mooiplaats farmhouse stood. In the other direction she looked over rolling ground for almost the same distance. On fine evenings she would stand there planning how the place would look when she had everything ready for visitors. The road from Pretoria crossed the lower portion of the property and she daydreamed how, as she drove her guests, she would say at that bend in the road, "Look, you can see the house now."

Meanwhile it was hard going with so little help. She was up before dawn each day, calling the small African herdboy who slept in the kitchen to light the fire, and waking George and Barry, the "deserter". She herself cleaned the stable and groomed Eclipse, tended sheep that were ill or lame, often skinning and cutting up one that had been killed for the table, and did much of the work about the house as the African servant she had engaged "frequently gave herself a holiday". Then there were the hens to be fed. These creatures were determined to share the house with them and if food was left unwatched on the table or dough put to rise without being properly covered they were on it in a moment. George called them "insulting creatures" and threw broom handles, brushes and boots after them.

As it was summer the biggest job was dealing with the enormous crops of fruit that grew on the farm. African girls arrived from kraals as far as 30 miles away, bringing conical baskets on their heads which they expected to fill once for themselves in payment for helping with the harvest. They came walking gracefully in single file, arms and legs heavily ornamented with beadwork, heads bound with bright handkerchiefs and with skins or blankets draped round their shoulders. The fruit was cut up or peeled and spread out on frames of wood and reeds, called *stellasies*, to dry in the sun. If rain threatened they had to be brought into the house, and a running war was fought with the hens who thought the entire operation was for their benefit. It was hard work but dried fruit sold well, apart from being useful for her own larder. One method of preserving which Sarah learnt from the Africans was to take peaches or apricots which had become too ripe for drying and squeeze them to a pulp in the hands. The skin and the pips were discarded and the pulp spread on a greased board. When it was dry it could be peeled off and rolled like thick paper. Sarah was surprised to find how good it tasted.

Itinerant labourers called at the farm and when she had enough help she started work on a larger dam and the house she had planned. But the labour was unreliable, costs higher than she had reckoned and returns on her produce lower than she had been led to expect. She had serious misgivings about the whole project. Brick-making for the house continued, however, as she desperately wanted a home of her own and a base from which to operate the projects that were forming in her mind.

At the end of 1879 there was a renewal of the "Boer scare", but Sarah was too busy to take much notice. Her sheep were badly affected by ticks and there was "sheep fever", as she called it, which was killing many of the animals in the valley. She worked long hours in the sheep kraal and lost hardly any. "I became quite an expert sheep doctor and could throw a good-sized lamb alone," she remarked with understandable pride. She was called out from time to time to attend sick children of friends and found this a relief from the monotonous and gruelling work of Groenfontein.

As the new year came in the Jennings planned a visit to Mary's family in the Cape. The weather was intensely hot and Sarah felt malaria taking a grip of her again. George was laid up with a mild attack and then William rode over to say Augusta was ailing. She found the child was not just ailing but seriously ill and she and her mother sat up all night with her.

William set off to see his brother at Marico but returned unexpectedly. "Now the Boers have really broken out," he told them. "One of their people, Pretorius, has been arrested and many of the Boers are riding to Potchefstroom. There is to be an uprising to free him from the British." William wanted to put the family in the wagon and start for the Cape at once but Augusta was dangerously ill and there was no question of moving her. Next morning she was slightly better and Sarah rode back to Groenfontein. There was much talk in the valley of the gathering at Potchefstroom and those who did not have horses were speaking of "acquiring" them. Sarah feared that Eclipse might be "jumped", the local euphemism for stolen, and slept in his stable with her revolver beside her for several nights, until things calmed down again.

About this time her suspicions about Barry were confirmed. An officer arrived with a small company of troops and arrested him as a deserter. The passage of this company down the valley frightened the Boers, who were sure they were to be arrested for insurrection. It was said that one man spent the night in a sluit and another up a tree to escape.

Being now a woman of property Sarah decided she had better make a new will. It was signed on 26 February 1880, and gave her address as the East London Hospital. The executors were her old friend Ashton Warner and a London solicitor, Francis Claughton Matthews. Whether he was a relative of Marian's or the name is merely a coincidence is not known. Apart from a few minor bequests, including one to George Brunton Warner of her "one hundred pound share in the Transvaal Farming Trading and Mining Association", everything was left to her adopted daughter – the name is written as Mary Ann Longobardi. A trust was to be set up and administered for her sole benefit – nothing was to go to Longobardi "or to any second or subsequent husband".

When Augusta finally recovered all was set for the family's trip to the Cape. Sarah was to oversee Nooitgedacht while they were away. During discussions about this William offered her his span of black oxen and a wagon. The span was reduced from its original 18 to 12 but all the animals were salted and had twice been down the road to Natal. The price was £12 each, but Sarah knew they were well worth it and clinched the bargain in considerable excitement.

In the first few days of February final preparations were made for the family to leave. Sarah was to ride with them as far as the Jennings's place at Vaalbank, so slept at Nooitgedacht the night before their departure. She felt ill but could not make out whether it was the fever coming on or just nervousness at the thought of being left on her own for two months. "I knew how I depended on William Jennings," she wrote. "I knew I should never really succeed till I was completely self-dependent and by the time they came back I would be."

When they got to Vaalbank Sarah was aching in every bone and lay down on her bed for the afternoon. Next morning she was on the stoep having coffee before riding back to Groenfontein and feeling rather ill, when she suddenly fainted dead away. "I know of no more annoying thing than to faint in another person's house, particularly when the performance is followed by such prostration that one has to be supported to bed," she wrote. Mary was so worried that she said they would put off their trip and take her back to Nooitgedacht, but Sarah knew what a disappointment that would be and begged them to start as planned.

When, still feeling weak, she finally got back to Groenfontein, things were in a bad state and she felt too ill to cope, with "fever sores" all over her body. "My hands, my legs and feet were particularly affected by them and the pain almost crippled me. There was no use lying by, however, and I began my usual routine next day."

Labour troubles pursued her and the day came when George announced he was seeking his fortune elsewhere and departed, with his saddlebag slung over his shoulder, by a path that led over the mountain to Rustenburg. She could not blame the lad and felt guilty about him.

These troubles were largely of her own making, though she could not see it that way. She may have escaped from

Belgravia but she took with her the Victorian obsession with the niceties of social distinction, which bedevilled the British administration of their Indian and African empire and laid up trouble for the future. Sarah had observed and to some extent adapted to the "free and easy" colonial manners of the Transvaal, yet complained of the difficulties of "maintaining the proper relationship of master and servant". By this she meant the relationship between white employer and employee. The solution in future, she thought, would be to employ only Africans, who would remain in the posture of servants. She added that there were a good many "half-castes", the inevitable concomitant of colonial development, and these, called "bastards" locally, she had heard made excellent servants.

Sarah had written – and doubtless spoken – many times of her belief in the good that resided in everyone, of the worth of the poor and the value of working for one's living, yet she apparently saw no contradiction in eating her meals by herself in her bedroom rather than in the sitting room with the white men who worked with her.

Trouble had come to a head when she had several men in her employ, one of whom was "a gentleman born" though down on his uppers. The others were a German and an Englishman, of working class origins, and two Indians – she called them "coolies". She treated them all alike at work, but after work she had Egerton, the gentleman, to eat meals with her and to sit with her of an evening. They played chess together and talked about books and music and painting. When she insisted that the other men address Egerton as "Mr" the fat was really in the fire. She had already commented that in the Transvaal "Mr" was rarely used, people addressing others or referring to them merely by the surname or the Christian name and surname together, but she still tried to insist on this inappropriate usage. George seemed to find it reasonable that he should address an older man as Mr, especially when he was a "gentleman's prodigal son", but the others refused, saying that

Egerton had brought himself down to their level and had forfeited all claim to social superiority. The Indians also refused, which particularly annoyed Sarah "as I knew what they were in their own country and they knew that I knew because I spoke to them in Hindustani".

The upshot of this was that she was finally left with only Egerton, who was unused to farming and could not handle oxen, and her African labourers. A week or two earlier she had ridden to Pretoria to check the estimates she had been given for materials and labour for the house and outbuildings she felt were necessary for the proper working of Groenfontein. She found that it was going to cost her far more than she could afford. The trouble over Egerton was the last straw and when the Jennings family returned from the Cape at the end of March she told William that she could not go on. Where to go and what to do to make enough money to buy a farm that would suit her better and be more profitable she did not know.

12

A lady trader

Before she could leave Groenfontein there was much to do. She sold her wool clip and was then able to pay William the compensation he demanded. She was surprised and hurt that he asked for it, thinking that the improvements she had made to the farm and the stack of bricks she was leaving were worth a good deal.

Winter was approaching and the annual trek to the Bushveld about to begin. Sarah made a plan. She first cabled Coutts, her London bankers, asking for her balance to be sure she had sufficient capital. The answer was about £600. She planned to take her newly acquired wagon and span, with two of her African labourers as driver and *voorloper* (literally, forerunner – he leads the front pair of oxen). She would go first to Pretoria, where she was expecting goods she had ordered some time before from England, make up the load with trading goods from one of the wholesalers, and trek to the Bushveld to trade with the Boers at their winter camps and with the Africans. If she was lucky and got rid of her stock quickly for cash, she would leave the wagon in the Bushveld, where the grass would be green, and ride back with the proceeds to Pretoria. There she would see about buying a farm. If things did not go so well, or, as was likely, she had to accept barter, then she would remain with the wagon. The Boers often preferred barter. Hides and skins, biltong, ostrich feathers and ivory were the commonest barter goods, offered in return for tea, sugar, pins and needles, dress materials, crockery, saucepans and similar goods.

The smous, as such an itinerant trader or pedlar was called, was a familiar figure in the Transvaal, but a woman smous was unknown, inconceivable. That a widow of 40, small and slight, lame into the bargain, subject to severe attacks of malaria and probably tubercular as well, should even contemplate such a project astounded everyone. Sarah not only contemplated it, she set about carrying it out. William agreed to run her sheep with his until she had somewhere for them. George came over from Vaalplaas, where he was now working in the store, to help her pack up and begged to go with her to the Bushveld, but she felt the whole scheme was too risky for her to take him.

She killed one of her pigs and sold the other, loaded her fowls, forage, seed oats and pumpkins into the wagon to sell on the Pretoria market and prepared to set out. Egerton was to go with her, riding Dandy, the pony she had bought at an auction "Under the Oaks" on her previous visit to Pretoria. Saying goodbye to the Jennings family and to George was hard. She looked around homely, friendly Nooitgedacht and pretty Groenfontein and tried to comfort Roughy who, as if with a presentiment of evil, yelped miserably with drooping tail and had to be coaxed to go with them. Suddenly she hated to leave the farms. "I could have cried as I turned my back on them, if crying had been of any use."

As they rode off she looked at the wagon with its indifferent driver and untutored *voorloper*, at Egerton "who knew as little about oxen and wagons as I did", and at her splendid span of oxen, and for a moment her heart quailed. However, it was a bright afternoon and if there was a risk in what she was about to do there was also the excitement that went with the taking of risks. Excitement was something Sarah had always craved and on which she throve. During the monotonous weeks at Groenfontein while the Jennings were away she had thought that if she did not soon have some excitement she would be ill or go mad. Here was the excitement and before they had ridden far she cheered up and thought the whole thing really enjoyable.

Arrived in Pretoria she chose a good pitch at the market and sat on her horse beside the wagon waiting for customers. She was startled to find how many people knew her and spoke to her by name when she did not know them at all: she was a celebrity as a rich and enterprising farmer. "I knew, of course, that there were unexpressed additions to these two adjectives, namely 'inexperienced', 'green' and 'fair game'." However, she stuck out for good prices for her produce and when a Mr Veldman was introduced to her as being able to help her find a farm she was immediately on her guard, though she accepted an invitation to visit his wife.

Not that she had time for social calls. Her goods from England had arrived. They had to be unpacked, priced and loaded on her wagon. Then she had to select other merchandise to make up her stock-in-trade. This took a week, during which time they camped on a farm close to Pretoria and slept in the open. She bought a third horse as a pack animal. It was a big, bony, half-broken colt for which she paid £15. It had a fiddle head so she called it Violin. She found time to have her photograph taken for Mary Jennings, as she had promised. She was not much pleased with the result. "The individual represented in it struck me, as I looked at her, to be absurdly unfitted for a 'smous'." No one could have disagreed with that judgement.

They were ready to start when her driver and voorloper announced that they would not leave Pretoria without a big pay rise. This, she declared, was blackmail. They had waited till the last minute, knowing that all available drivers were engaged. She told them to go and rode to Pretoria to look for replacements, leaving Egerton in charge of the loaded wagon. For two weeks she searched, visiting kraals and going daily to Pretoria. The weather became bitterly cold. Every morning the grass was white with hoar frost and so were their blankets. Sarah became ill and was soon choked with bronchitis, but would not give up. She could have gone to a friend's house but felt that as Egerton had to remain to guard the wagon she should rough it with him. Possibly he would have been happier if she had put up in the town. As it was he was kindness itself, getting up when he heard her coughing to see what he could do to help her. "How jolly he was over it all, as if it was the pleasantest thing in the world to turn out of his bed and walk about in a bitter cold night. He did all this in such a perfectly natural and unaffected way, so that it seemed as if it were an everyday occurrence for him to have to act nurse to a bronchitic lady in the open veld."

After a fortnight of this she decided that perhaps they had better move into Pretoria. Mr and Mrs Veldman, despite her earlier wariness of them, rallied round with help and let them bring the wagon, oxen and horses onto their large erf on the outskirts of the village. Their house was chock-full but there was a small, damp outhouse with a fireplace which they let her use. There was no furniture and Sarah slept on the floor – Egerton slept outside.

There was still no driver to be had and Sarah began to worry as other traders were ahead of her on the road. There were no farms to buy, either, and in despair she looked for a house in Pretoria, one that had a stable. Prices were high – nearly £1,000 for a cottage of five or six rooms. One good one, in a large productive garden, fetched the quite outrageous price of £2,500. At last she found one to suit her and the same day someone recommended a driver, "a bastard or half-caste". His name was Hendrik, and he spoke English. She engaged him at half a crown a day. He brought with him a Khoikhoi named Hans whom he begged her to take as voorloper. "I was obliged to pay him one and sixpence a day." That was not the end of it for Hans had in tow a small boy, another Hendrik, for whom he was responsible and Sarah had to take him on as well, ten shillings a month being finally agreed. The cavalcade was about to leave when word came of a good farm close to Pretoria to rent at 16 shillings a month. There was some legal snag as the rent had been mortgaged. She was anxious to get the wagon out of Pretoria "as drivers and voorlopers have a nasty habit of getting drunk all the time there", so she said she would take the wagon a day's trek and then ride back.

It was the end of June when they left Pretoria by the road to the east, more than a month later than she had intended. The first night they outspanned "about three miles out of town" – somewhere in what are today the eastern suburbs of Pretoria. After an early start next morning they outspanned for breakfast at Derdepoort, a pass through the Magaliesberg where the road turns north. Two men riding back to Pretoria from the Waterberg with wagons loaded with leather stopped to buy pipes and sugar – her first customers. A good day's trek brought them to a mission station, on a slope near a small river. There was no shelter from the bitter wind but it seemed the best place to stop.

It was three o'clock the next morning when she started back to Pretoria, taking Hendrik as escort and leaving Egerton in charge of the wagon. During the ride her watch chain broke and she lost some trinkets attached to it, of sentimental value, and felt it an ill omen. She was half frozen when they reached the Veldmans at breakfast time and coffee, bacon and eggs were more than welcome.

The ride had been in vain, however. The deal over the farm had fallen through and the cottage she wanted had been snapped up by someone else. She told Mr Veldman that if he could find another he could offer £400 on her behalf. It was late afternoon before she was ready to leave and half past nine that night before she got back to the wagon. Egerton had shot a hare and made soup.

A short trek the next day – the horses must have been tired if Sarah was not – took them to an outspan at a bend in the Apies River. Sitting at the campfire they were startled when a man suddenly loomed out of the pitch blackness and, in a strong Irish accent, asked where he could find water. He told them that he and his two companions were prospectors and veterans of the Australian gold diggings. They were bound for the northern Transvaal to try their luck in the Soutpansberg – the "Salt Pan Mountains" – travelling on foot with a couple of donkeys to carry their packs.

Next morning, heading north-east, they crossed the Pienaars River and made for the Elands River which they reached in the early afternoon, well ahead of the wagon. It was bleak, flat, monotonous country dotted with thorn bushes, the grass dry. A woodcutter told them there were three other traders ahead of them on the road and trade in the Bushveld was slack.

They chose their outspan and Egerton went off to shoot for the pot. Sarah lay in the grass, half dozing in the warm sun. It was late when the wagon emerged from the bush. "This meant dinner, whereat my heart rejoiced."

Next morning she rode to a nearby Boer camp. At the first tent, though the people were agog with curiosity over the extraordinary spectacle of a woman smous on a horse, they were not disposed either to talk or to buy. At the next tent it was different. Two women were on their own there, their menfolk away in Pretoria. They gave her coffee and overwhelmed her with questions. Why had she come to this country? Was she married? Had she children with her? Had she ever had any children? And who was the white man with her?

Many people had been speculating about Mr Egerton. That Sarah was by this time a little in love with him is likely. That they were lovers is possible – there was plenty of opportunity. What is certain is that some people suspected they were. She was only 40 and a passionate and romantically-minded woman, but she had been ecstatically happy with Nathaniel and remained devotedly loyal to his memory for the rest of her life. She frequently comments on the way Boer men and women remarried almost immediately after bereavement as if this was something peculiar. She never contemplated remarriage herself.

The likely explanation of her association with the mysterious Mr Egerton – which was not his real name – is that he was down and out and she wanted to help him. His problem was drink, as it was with so many of the young men who went to seek their fortune in the Transvaal in the 19th century. The reason, as Sarah saw for herself, was that there was nothing in Pretoria to do but drink. Boarding houses did not exist, lodgings with a family were hard to find, while hotels had no reading rooms or lounges. There was nowhere to sit of an evening. No wonder the warmth and companionship of the many bars and canteens drew the lonely stranger.

Sarah shrewdly observed that the sons of gentlemen, unused to roughing it, were apt to go downhill quicker than the robuster sons of the working class. Egerton, as she was at pains to point out, was a gentleman. Helping the weak and unfortunate was the mainspring of her life. She was genuinely determined to help Egerton rehabilitate himself and when Sarah was determined on a course of action she neither counted the cost nor thought how it might appear to others. It took quite a while for it to dawn on her that her relationship with Egerton was being misconstrued.

She was undoubtedly fond of him. The descriptions of domestic bliss – games of chess at Groenfontein, playing the piano to him at Nooitgedacht when the Jennings family was away and she had the key to the house, his nursing of her when she was down with bronchitis, the evenings she spent lying on her bed in the hut at the Veldmans, watching him by the light of the fire as he cooked their supper – all give her away. But it was not till the Boer women in their tent cross-examined her that it began to occur to her that her behaviour was being commented upon unfavourably. Gossip might have been the explanation of George's abrupt departure from Groenfontein, coupled with his later return and plea to be the one to be taken to the Bushveld, of her troubles with the other workmen, even of William Jennings's treatment of her – more harsh than she had expected – when she left Groenfontein. William and Mary might well have been disconcerted on their return from the Cape to find what was being said in the neighbourhood about Sarah and Egerton, though knowing and liking her as they did they would have given her the benefit of the doubt.

Sarah was not discountenanced by this cross-questioning in the Bushveld. Rather the other way about. She was pleased that she had sufficiently mastered "the Boer lingo" to make herself understood and to understand the two women at least moderately well. She tells us that she was anxious to learn the language not only because she needed to if she was to succeed in her trading venture but because she wanted to know the Boers and to understand them. She had seen that many of them lived "in a state of dirt and disorder that reminds one of an Irish hovel". She knew that they held beliefs – such as that the earth was flat – which other people would regard as "absurdly ignorant". Many of her English-speaking friends had regaled her with stories of the brutalities of "Paul Kruger and his men" towards the "Kaffirs", stories of slaughter and slavery. She knew that some of these stories would have been embellished in the telling but that some had a basis in truth. She had met Boers who were as civilised and as cleanly as she was herself and whose homes were models of neatness, if not comfort. Then again she had "heard that the Boers were a treacherous, lying, hypocritical people, with all the faults but none of the virtues supposed to belong to a rough peasant". Sarah, however, was not prepared to judge and condemn on hearsay. "I thought I would now begin to learn a little of them from my own observation."

On the next day's trek they came to a kraal. Sarah sent Hendrik to ask if she could buy mealies for the horses.

He returned surrounded by a troop of whooping, yelling, naked children, followed by women dressed mostly in beads, and men in an assortment of cast-off, tattered European clothing. They brought mealies and pumpkins and swarmed over the wagon to examine the African goods she had. It looked to Sarah like a grotesque caricature of sale time at a popular department store in London's Oxford Street.

They kept along the Elands River for a few days but trade was poor and Sarah turned due north to the Waterberg. This took them through an area of deep sand where the going was hard and the wagon in constant danger of sticking. They passed a hill known as Maroelakop, because of its crown of marula trees. There was a strong spring at its foot and nearby an encampment of Boers. The people greeted her civilly and bought a number of things. One of them brought her a glass of wine. Later she found he was the leader of the dissidents who opposed British rule.

At the Waterberg Sarah went to the German Mission. The missionary and his wife were hospitable and welcoming although they were still mourning the death of their youngest child from fever a short while before. The death rate in the Transvaal in the 1870s was high. Malaria, typhoid, diphtheria, enteric fever and pneumonia were common, and then there were the hazards of snakebite and encounters with wild animals. Added to these was the toll of accidents, and there were no hospitals and few doctors.

They stayed at the mission for some days as Africans poured in from the surrounding areas at news of a *smous*. Then they moved on, trading at kraals across the Nylstroom (the Nile River, named by the first Trekkers who thought they had discovered the source of the Nile) until all the African goods were gone. Sarah was a great success with the Africans; they found "the pretty missis on the horse" irresistible.

They turned south again, passing Makapansgat where she fell in with a man who wanted to buy Eclipse. She refused to part with him but agreed to sell him Dandy for £30 in gold sovereigns, a healthy profit on the £15 she had paid for him a few months before.

Near the mission station they were joined by another trader going their way. On the road back to Maroelakop they spotted a large herd of wildebeest and Sarah and her fellow trader raced after it. "They were a magnificent sight, bounding through the bush with their tails flying, the bulls tossing their long black manes." In the excitement she did not notice which way they had turned. Eclipse put his foot in a hole and when she pulled him up her companion was out of sight. She turned back to where she thought the road was but she was lost in the featureless bush. They had been told at the mission that there were lions in the area: it was not a comfortable thought. She looked back at the line of hills they had crossed and using them as a guide set off through the bush to where she guessed Maroelakop must be. When she got there she found the other trader had arrived and was conferring with the "Dissident Boers" as to how much longer they should wait before they started a search.

There were no further incidents on the return to Pretoria. Mr Veldman had found her a house but had let it, not expecting her back so soon. He invited her to outspan on his erf.

Back in Pretoria it was finally borne in on Sarah that her relationship with Egerton was being talked about to the detriment of them both. She reluctantly decided they would have to part company. She feared he would be back on the bottle again before long but there seemed nothing more she could do for him. To keep him with her would be likely to affect her trading chances. Many of the Boers were strait-laced in the extreme and would refuse to do business with someone they suspected of blatantly immoral behaviour. This small-mindedness and slavery to convention angered her. She had written in her book on *Christ and Communism* that it was the duty of those who could to give employment to those who needed it, but if keeping

Egerton ruined her business venture she would not be able to pay him. After a battle with herself she admitted defeat and sadly told him he must find other work.

She felt more confident now of her ability to manage the wagon and to trade on her own. Money was tight because not only had she bought the cottage in Pretoria but also a small farm roughly 30 miles south-east of the town. It had grazing rights on the larger farm of which it had formerly been a part. As it lay on the breezy uplands on the edge of the Witwatersrand it was healthy for horses and sheep and she reckoned it would be a good site for a store. She had got Jackalsfontein cheap but she needed to husband her resources.

She was going to miss Egerton badly but the break had to be made. He found a labouring job and she gave him the key to the storeroom on the Veldmans' erf to save him the cost of a hotel room. She wondered how long she herself would resist the lure of the canteens if she had to return each evening to that dismal hut, cook a meal on a wood fire and then afterwards have nothing to do but sit on a box and read by the light of a single candle, or go to sleep.

She was determined to get back to the Bushveld as soon as possible. This time she loaded up almost entirely with African goods as she found "Kaffir trading" paid the best. She also took out a bottle licence from the magistrate and bought a keg of Cape brandy. The storeman who sold it to her and who had previously given her useful tips on trading, beckoned her aside when the keg had been loaded on the wagon. "When you get well out from amongst the Boers," he said, "for I understand you are going right in amongst the Kaffirs this time, just top up the cask with water. The Kaffirs won't notice. I wouldn't advise you to put tobacco in it, like some traders do. That I don't think is right. Just fill it up with water. It won't pay well enough if you don't."

She was now ready to leave again. She had had to dismiss Hans, the *voorloper*, because of his fondness for dagga (cannabis). He had once or twice become violent after smoking it and she dared not risk taking him again. Little Hendrik had become afraid of his "protector" and pleaded to stay with Sarah. She was glad to keep him, finding him lively and intelligent. In Hans's place she engaged a big Zulu, Piet.

They left this time by a wooded ravine through the Magaliesberg, full of chattering monkeys. Once through the mountain, they outspanned on the farm of an elderly Hollander who was greatly in favour of British rule. From there Sarah pressed on as fast as she could to Maroelakop, where she found the Engelsbergs – the "Dissident Boers" – who seemed pleased to see her. Two other men she knew, Du Plessis (who had bought Dandy) and De Klerk, were also there and after supper they sat round the fire. The talk was of the Boer gathering which had been held to discuss starting Boer-run stores, the goods to be imported direct so as to oust the English traders, on whom the Boers were then totally dependent, from the Transvaal. The men did not realise she could understand them. She was intrigued to hear Barend Engelsberg say he had subscribed £100 to the scheme and name other Boers who had contributed. There was debate as to whether they should import from America or Germany, both countries having made liberal offers.

At this point Sarah, mustering her best "Dutch", joined in. "I think the plan you propose is a good one and I dare say you will get your goods cheaper than you do now. But I think you should avoid dealing with the Americans. They are first-rate men of business but they would be too sharp for you. It would be safer for you to deal with the Germans."

There was a staggered silence while they took in not only what she had said but that she had said it in their language. "Are you born English?" asked De Klerk after a while. "Well, yes, at least I am an English subject," said Sarah. "But I was born in Ireland and both my parents were Irish." "Ah," said De Klerk, as if that explained everything, and the conversation turned to the favourite subject of horses. Eclipse was admired and soon the mutual interest "established a freemasonry between us, the men being ready to listen to all I had to tell of my horses, and to recount long tales of their past and present horses in return". All this time the women had been sitting apart talking about babies and cooking (in a way not unknown today) but Sarah preferred to talk about horses with the men.

At the Waterberg mission station she learnt that her German friend had resigned. Piet, the Zulu, distinguished himself by getting hopelessly drunk on sorghum beer. All next day he sat under the wagon deploring his headache and the disgrace Sarah kept him in. Moving on again she passed the warm springs near Naboomspruit and went on towards the Makapansberg. She reached the camp of young Du Plessis and De Klerk and was delighted to see Dandy looking well cared for. He knew her and wanted to follow her wagon. Boer families who had been camped further up were moving back towards the Highveld now that it was well into August. She heard many well-authenticated accounts of lions having killed in the neighbourhood so kept fires going all night and she and the men slept in a circle round the horses.

Trade was good and she stayed near the Du Plessis for several days. She was astonished when a Mrs Nel asked her why she was trading when she had so much money in her London bank. Telegrams, it seemed, were public property in the Transvaal.

She began to regret having brought the brandy. The Boers would ask for a tot, which she said she could not sell as she had only a bottle licence. Then they would club together and buy a bottle between two or three of them which they would drink in a remarkably short time and return for another. Du Plessis sold her beautiful ostrich feathers and it was only after the deal that she found it was the closed season for shooting ostriches. She and the man would be liable for a fine of £500 if they were discovered. Du Plessis, however, was far more afraid of his father-in-law, who had promised to shoot the cock bird for another trader, law or no law.

De Klerk was an older man who told her he believed the Transvaal was far better off under English rule than it had been under Boer management. All the same, if war came everything he had would be thrown on the side of his own people, even if he thought they were wrong. "You will go with your nation and I with mine," he said, in sombre foreshadowing of events.

Before she left she bought Dandy back, giving Violin and £5 in exchange. Du Plessis was reluctant but needed the money. Sarah was pleased as Dandy was certainly salted while she did not think that Violin was.

She now entered country that was new to her. She rode through a deep, wooded valley. The bush took on a tropical look, with enormous cactus trees. Where the valley broadened into a wonderful spread of green she passed the last white camp, the Makapansberg showing blue and misty away to her right, between modern Mokopane (Potgietersrus) and Polokwane (Pietersburg).

When she reached Makapanspoort she outspanned and sent Hendrik with a bottle of brandy as a present to the chief, with a request for permission to trade with his people. Makapan in return sent his thanks, said she would be welcome and that he would protect her. She would have to trade for corn and mealies. The people were due to pay taxes to the government and if they did not have the cash would have to pay in cattle at a very poor rate of exchange. If she insisted on cash she would do little business and corn would fetch a good price in Pretoria. The Africans came to the wagons in swarms, the men in front, unburdened, and the women behind with baskets of corn and mealies on their heads. It was exhausting work, as the corn had to be examined carefully and weighed. From seven in the morning until seven that night she measured corn into sacks, Piet with a whip trying to keep control of the milling crowd. At the end of the day she was tired out and nearly mad with the non-stop shouting and general din. This went on for several days. "It was amusing however, and I had a good opportunity of observing the Kaffir in his natural state."

By this time her supplies of coffee and meat were low and she decided to return to Pretoria. It was extremely hot and ticks and other insects were trying. For once she found it difficult to sleep. Before she could start out Makapan visited her and invited her to a feast he was giving the next day to "make rain". As rains were due fairly soon Sarah thought he could hardly fail. Next morning when she woke, groups of young warriors in their best finery were passing on their way to the chief's kraal. As soon as she had dressed she started off with an interpreter she had brought from the German mission, climbing the precipitous hill to the kraal. Makapan met her and led her to his house, offering her coffee. The kraal was a labyrinth of huts, each with an enclosed yard, and there was a huge stockade in the centre. Makapan said he would kill an ox that day and send her meat. He asked her several times if she were not surprised at the vast size of his kraal and its impregnability.

It had been impregnable once but when his father, also Makapan (Mokopane), one of the Sotho chiefs, had been the first seriously to challenge encroaching white settlement in the northern Transvaal by massacring a hunting expedition, the Boers had retaliated by blockading about 3,000 of his followers in a cave and slaughtering them. The first Makapan had died in about 1860. In 1867 his son, Sarah's host, had seen the chance of revenge when the Venda tribe in the Soutpansberg had risen against the Boers. Paul Kruger, at the head of a commando 400 strong, had been forced to withdraw, the white settlers had followed and the collapse had spread as far as Nylstroom. Makapan II and the other Sotho chiefs had joined the rebellion and had been subdued again only a few years before Sarah ventured into his kraal.

The dance began in the stockade at noon. The young

warriors wore leather girdles fringed with wild cats' tails, with rosettes and tassels in their hair, "war horns" of brass, copper or tin hung round their necks and buckskin covering their legs. Each carried an assegai and some had rifles, which they discharged in the air as they entered the stockade. A dense mass of women and children, laughing, singing, yelling and clapping their hands, lined the way as Makapan led Sarah to a seat of honour beside his throne. Many, she noted, had scabies. Some of the men were painted as skeletons, others daubed with red mud. Singly, or in small groups, the men rushed into the arena with a yell to execute a war dance, perhaps assegaing an imaginary foe with a savage exultation that made Sarah's blood run cold.

At one point one of the men made up as a skeleton rushed at Sarah, ending with his assegai an inch from her nose. "I think he was disappointed I did not scream," she remarked laconically. The climax came when Makapan led his warriors into the arena. "Fine looking Kaffirs, all be-cat-tailed, they advanced armed to the teeth, their long shields slung on their arms, dancing their slow war dance, singing the accompanying war song and rattling their assegais on their shields. The dancers moved very slightly, their song a chant more than singing. It looked like the movement of men held in a leash, impatient for it to be slipped. It sounded so threatening, like the muttering of a storm, one could imagine the yell that would burst forth if the leash were slipped."

Makapan himself, in an astonishing get-up of "a gentleman's morning wrapper with the girdle tied at the back and a white hat with narrow brim and three ostrich feathers in it", did a solo dance and then it was all over, as she thought, and she started down the hill in the stifling heat. She was pursued and told that the pièce de résistance was yet to come, the ox was to be killed by a lingering and revolting torture in the arena – but she politely declined to go back and witness something so horrific.

She told Hendrik that if Makapan sent meat from the ox he was to say she did not eat the flesh of animals which had been tortured and was to send it back. Word reached Makapan and he sent her goat's meat, which she let the "boys" eat.

13

Return to Pretoria and war

It had been a most successful expedition. She had traded far more corn than she could carry in one wagon. It was late in the season – nearing the end of September – and the rains would start within the next few weeks. She needed to set out for Pretoria at once. The Africans sold her intricately woven baskets to store the grain she could not carry away and Makapan promised to guard it for her.

Before she left he visited her with a fellow chief, Mapela. Sarah described the latter as "big, sensual and violent looking", dressed in a dandified European fashion. He wanted to buy Eclipse and through the interpreter offered £100 for him. Sarah declined, saying she would not sell the horse at any price. "At that moment I admitted distinctly to myself that trading was not my forte. Fancy a smous refusing to make eighty pounds clear profit!" Later she heard this had become a standing joke among the Boers, and given her a reputation for being very rich.

As she headed south Sarah found the Bushveld deserted, the Boers having trekked back to their farms. It was getting too hot to trek in the middle of the day, which slowed her up. She had no food left, except rice and lard, and nothing to drink but milkless, sugarless tea. She was glad to meet the trader with whom she had chased the wildebeest, who gave her a little sugar, and further on a Boer going up to the Woodbush, who gave her *boerbeskuit* in exchange for lard.

She called at the Waterberg mission, and while camped there began to have serious trouble with Piet, the Zulu *voorloper*. She suspected he was stealing from the wagon and selling on his own account. When this proved true and she also found that the key to the tap of the brandy keg was missing, she had no option but to hand him over to the *landdrost* (magistrate) at Nylstroom, who came to her wagon. The magistrate, a German, asked Piet if he had any complaint against his employer. "No, never have I had such a good mistress," said the Zulu. "I eat the same food as she does, and the other day she gave up some of her own dinner to me because she thought I had not had enough."

Evidence was given that Piet had been in a neighbouring kraal and had pulled a knife to resist arrest. By this time a crowd of local Boers had gathered. "Twenty-five lashes," said the magistrate and there was an eager movement among them. Jan Steyn, a man with a crumpled face, bristling black hair and beady eyes, looking like a weasel that has caught sight of a rat, grabbed at Piet. "De Klerk also had a bloodthirsty look about him, and gloated hungrily on Piet," wrote Sarah. "Even Willem du Plessis looked excited."

Piet screamed that he would pay a fine and the magistrate ordered Steyn to let go of him. "I will pay three pounds," said Piet. "Don't let him off! Flog him!" snarled the group of Boers. "I'm sure he can't pay – he hasn't any money," said Sarah, doubtfully. "Well, if he can pay three pounds then the law says he need not be flogged," said the magistrate.

Uproar broke out with the Boers furious and the Africans shouting. Sarah had a job to make herself heard but finally managed to say that as his employer she thought Piet should be flogged at once without any more argument and allowed to go. "Well, you have the right to choose whether he be flogged or fined," said the magistrate, "and flogging will be the best course. Twenty-five lashes."

Sarah was shocked at the way the Boers, and Hendrik, her coloured driver, were on the Zulu in a second, "like hounds on a fox". The spectacle shocked and disgusted her. Seeing the viciousness in their faces she understood for the first time that the stories she had heard of Boer cruelty to the natives could well be true. She saw also that it was a cruelty born mostly of fear, but also of suppressed guilt, and typical of the frontier mentality the world over.

Then anger boiled up in her. She pushed into the mob of men who towered over her and, threatening them with her riding whip, she shouted, "Look here, if you don't leave that man alone I'll send every one of you away from my wagon. He is to be punished, not tortured. Stand back all of you." And they stood back, muttering angrily.

Sarah took up her stance in front of Piet as he was tied to the *disselboom* to receive his punishment. She had never seen a man flogged before and did not relish seeing it now. She was sickened by the whole business, but thought that if she moved away Piet would be lynched, not justly punished for theft. It was not a severe beating, she believed, and he took it well, though when he got up she could see he was in a rage. She paid him his wages and told him to go.

The Boers were not satisfied, however, and when they learnt that Piet had been selling brandy to their "kraal Kaffirs", their fury was terrible. The law that intoxicating liquor might not be sold to an African without the permission of his master was broken daily in Pretoria, but *landdrosts* in the country were stricter. Jan Steyn and De Klerk thundered against the "kraal Kaffirs" and said that if such villainy continued the Africans might rise and murder all the whites in their beds and an example must be made. Piet was again arrested just as Sarah was leaving and she was told she must await his trial.

This took place in the *landdrost*'s office, one of the four tumble-down wood and iron buildings that made up what Sarah described as "the imaginary town of Nylstroom". The proceedings had something in common with the trial of the Knave of Hearts. Everybody talked at once and the magistrate's frequent appeals for order met little response. Piet called De Klerk "Oom" (uncle – a usual form of address among Afrikaners) and De Klerk shouted angrily that he was not his uncle. Hendrik, who was chief witness, set up a loud banter with a friend among the spectators. Piet became bored and sat down on a chair and was immediately shouted at to stand up or else squat. As the day grew hotter the crowded court room became steadily more foetid and unpleasant.

Eventually Piet was sentenced to six months in prison and was led away to the crazy little jail. He escaped a few days later and disappeared so his punishment in the end was not severe.

Sarah got out her account books and did some stock-taking, which showed that Piet had robbed her of £50. This was bad enough but the delay was almost as serious. She had thought she might find a wagon at Waterberg to send up for the balance of the corn but there was none to be had. She would have to go on to Pretoria and return to Makapanspoort when she had sold what she was carrying, but storms were already threatening. It was obvious the rains would break soon, making the going heavy and the rivers impassable for days at a time.

In the heat she felt a dose of fever coming on. Ahead lay a stretch of "turf country" which the heavily laden wagon would not be able to pass if it rained. In addition there was no room for her to shelter under the wagon tent. Then Du Plessis offered to sell her a wagon and she divided her span, to which she had added several oxen taken in trade, and split the load.

It was hot, with a strong wind blowing, when the work was done. At the wagon that evening Sarah noted a fever sore on her hand and knew she "was in for it". She trekked that night feeling extremely ill. It was blisteringly hot with little water to be found and many springs dry. The fever came on with a vengeance and sores broke out all over her body, making riding painful.

As they came to the Pienaars River the sun had a brassy heat and storm clouds were rising. Riding through the drift the water was barely up to the horses' knees. She took them onto a rise beyond the river and flung herself in the grass, too shaky with fever to move. It was late when the wagons caught up with her, the oxen weak from lack of water. By the time they and the horses had been fed, watered and tied up for the night the first ominous drops had fallen. Sarah crawled under the wagon tent as the downpour began. Next morning when she looked out she saw "an enormous lake stretching far and wide, with the tops of trees showing like islands here and there". This was the start of what was to prove one of the wettest summers ever.

It rained for three days while Sarah lay in the wagon, too weak to sit a horse. Five days later she rode into Pretoria in pouring rain, still burning and shivering with fever, there being no one but herself to take charge of the horses. She found that the Basotho War had broken out and grain was fetching high prices. "So far my speculation in trading grain had turned out a success."

She went to the Veldmans, where she was offered the use of the stables and a room adjoining them and invited to have her meals with the family. Going out in the dark the first evening to see to the oxen she "tumbled against Mr Egerton". She had not expected to find him still there and was at a loss what to say to him. Soon afterwards he went off as a volunteer for the Basotho War and she never saw him again.

Her loads of grain sold well but she was too ill to ride far. Hendrik had proved trustworthy so she engaged another coloured driver and sent the two of them off with the wagons, and a few goods to trade on the way, to fetch the rest of the grain from Makapanspoort.

As soon as Sarah felt better she thought she would go to her new farm to put it in order. She bought a wagon cheap and a span of salted oxen. The atmosphere in Pretoria by the beginning of November was electric, with rumours flying and a general feeling of apprehension. Sarah was sure war was coming and the Boers would fight. Lord Carnarvon had resigned in January 1879, but his successor as Colonial Secretary, Sir Michael Hicks-Beach, was also an imperialist and determined on federation. His instrument was the High Commissioner, Sir Bartle Frere. However, British mismanagement, coupled with the military ineptitude shown up by the disaster of Isandhlwana, had stiffened the Boer opposition to British plans.

Shepstone had promised that the Transvaal would "remain a separate government, with its own laws and legislature" and had then proceeded to rule it as a strict Crown colony. When he was replaced as Administrator by Sir Owen Lanyon matters went from bad to worse. Lanyon has been described as "a timorous despot". He was remote from the people he governed, dependent on small military garrisons in the towns and obsessed with making ends meet by rigidly enforcing the unpopular tax laws. To the Boers all direct taxes were an iniquity, and to pay them to the British was taken as recognising the interlopers in Pretoria.

At the same time Afrikaner nationalism was beginning to appear as a cohesive force. Before 1870 the Boers had been thinly scattered over four provinces, divided between three different churches and without common institutions to focus their loyalty. In addition the Boers in the Republics were increasingly unable to understand English or to express themselves freely in Dutch, but the language they did speak – the patois that was beginning to be called Afrikaans – had no literature. Carnarvon's interventions in the Cape, the Free State and the Transvaal had aroused anxieties and the Keate Award of 1871, which had given the diamond fields to the Cape, had also given the Boers in the Republics that potent tool for the building of nationalism, a common sense of grievance.

Between 1875 and 1877 a group of Afrikaner intellectuals in Paarl, near Cape Town, led by a predikant, S.J. du Toit, founded the "Genootskap van Regte Afrikaners" (Society of True Afrikaners). They launched a newspaper, *Die Afrikaanse Patriot*, and published *Die Geskiedenis van ons Land in die Taal van ons Volk* (The History of our Country in the Language of our People). The circulation of both was small but the ideas they set out and repeatedly hammered home spread quickly. The central theme was that the Afrikaners were a distinct people or nation, occupying a distinct fatherland, South Africa, speaking a distinct language, Afrikaans, and endowed by God with the destiny to rule South Africa and civilise its heathen people. It was a heady brew, with especially potent effects on the rural Afrikaner of the Transvaal. Sarah had encountered the feelings it inspired on her trading trips. The negative aspects of this burgeoning Afrikaner nationalism were opposition to the English and rejection of the Africans.

Sarah's certainty that war was near was based on a conversation with De Klerk on the way back from Makapanspoort. He had asked if she thought the Americans or any of the European powers would support the Boers against the British, but before she could answer had said, "But in any case we shall fight." After a pause he had continued, "I will tell you our plans. I don't count you as an enemy. This is what you will hear. Some man will refuse to pay his taxes and then your Government will seize property to the amount of what is due. And then we shall rise. We shall take that property out of the hand of the authorities, and if they interfere with us we shall fight. But until then we have done with talking." (This was a reference to Paul Kruger and Piet Joubert's visit to London in 1878 when they had presented a petition signed by 6,591 Transvaalers opposed to the Annexation. Hicks-Beach had refused to reopen the question.)

"I'd be sorry if you did that," Sarah had replied. "We haven't many troops in the country now, but for you to go to war with the English nation is like a little child going to fight a man."

De Klerk had agreed but had told her that the Boers were not afraid of British cannon. "We don't fight as you do," he had said. "What is the use of cannon against men who scurry round singly on horseback, and who shoot at you from behind stones and trees without your seeing them? We shan't meet your troops in the open Highveld, don't you believe it. We shall go into Natal to meet you."

His words had so impressed her that back in Pretoria she wondered if she ought not to tell Sir Owen Lanyon what she had heard, and from whom. But De Klerk had spoken to her in confidence. As she had allowed him to speak she felt she should not break it. Had she gone to Sir Owen it is unlikely that it would have done any good as that gentleman refused absolutely to believe the reports he heard and right up to the last moment thought the Boers would not rise.

Sarah was about to leave for Jackalsfontein when she heard of the affair of Bezuidenhout's wagon. Piet Bezuidenhout, of Potchefstroom, had refused to pay his taxes. The magistrate had attached his wagon under a court order and a party of 300 armed Boers led by Commandant Piet Cronje had seized it back. It was clear to Sarah that the programme De Klerk had outlined to her was being put into action.

Her wagon was ready to start when a bad storm broke. By the time the weather cleared the driver and *voorloper* were too hopelessly drunk to go. Next morning when she set out the driver proved incompetent and the *voorloper* recalcitrant. She had to put her horse at him and threaten him with her whip to get him to his feet and at the team's head. It took five hours to reach the Six Mile Spruit – so called because it was that distance from Pretoria. In the drift the wagon stuck. The bad driver only made matters worse and Sarah had to appeal to a nearby farmer to tow her out. Furious, she told the driver to take his blanket and rode with him back to Pretoria.

She sacked him and engaged another. She was about to

return to the wagon when she met George, looking doleful as his employer had laid him off. He had left the Jennings's store to work for a Pretoria surveyor. Everything in the town was at a standstill with the threat of war and he could not get work. Sarah said he had better come along and help her, an offer he jumped at.

The new man, Andries, proved a better driver but they had only gone a few miles when yet another storm broke. "I was afraid the horses would get alarmed and stood by them until the fury of the storm abated, which was not for some hours," wrote Sarah, as if standing for hours deafened with thunder and soaked to the skin holding two terrified horses were as unremarkable as we might find catching a bus. It was a miserable journey, not made any easier when they found the Jukskei in flood. George was taken ill soon after they passed it.

She put him in the wagon and led his horse. That night they outspanned on the farm of a man named Williams, whose wife gave them freshly baked bread, milk and eggs, which were some consolation on a night of howling wind and rain. Mr Williams had a newspaper which reported that the storm had been widespread "and the public buildings in Nylstroom had been blown down by a hurricane", which made Sarah laugh as she remembered the flimsy jail from which Piet had escaped, and the ramshackle courtroom.

They reached Jackalsfontein in a storm and found the cottage there had suffered the same fate as the "public buildings" at Nylstroom and there was no shelter for them. However, she was able to rent a room in the house of a Boer family whose farm adjoined hers. Their name was Du Plessis, but they were no relation of her Waterberg friend.

Jackalsfontein was just a bare, windswept grassy upland with no natural trees for miles around, though a few had been planted. But as a farm it was a better prospect than Groenfontein. Neither sheep nor horses were plagued there by the ailments that attacked them in the Magaliesberg and the pasture was excellent, with none of the poisonous herbs so common in some parts of the Transvaal. The soil was good and so was the water supply and Sarah reckoned a store would do well. There were no kraals anywhere around and so no African labour, but there were many small farms run by Boers with large families who were glad if their younger members could earn a bit extra.

She pitched her tent on Jackalsfontein for George and found shelter for her horses in a deserted, tumbledown house. The servants and driver slept in the wagon.

The family with whom she lodged had several young sons who helped her with ploughing and sowing, for which she was grateful. They were kind and hospitable but the women were trying, "an entanglement of slatternly women with loud voices". She wondered why so many Boer peasant women looked dull and depressed, when the peasants of southern Italy, equally poor and tied to a life of incessant toil, did not. The answer, she thought, was "look at the men". Most of them were big, rough-handed, rough-voiced and grimy-looking, a kindly people though "in many ways cunning". Their conversation among themselves she found "coarse and impertinent", but they treated her civilly. She had to accept that what she found offensive was not meant to be so but was considered by her hosts as proof of friendly feeling and "a source of innocent amusement". The men would smoke even when women were present, she commented, and both men and women would "spit on the ground in a manner trying to weak nerves".

All her new neighbours received her with friendliness and much encouragement for her plans to start a store. In response to her questions they professed to know nothing of the affair of Bezuidenhout's wagon and developments at Potchefstroom. However, Sarah was quite sure that they did know and that De Klerk's plan was in full operation.

The weather continued stormy but she had to get back to Pretoria to meet her wagons due in from Waterberg. Because of the weather it was ten at night when she rode into Pretoria with Andries, whom she had taken as escort.

The Veldmans were asleep so she went supperless to bed in the room by their stables. Next day Andries "went on the spree" and disappeared so she had both horses to look after.

The tenant of her house had become nervous and left Pretoria so she moved into it herself, with the barest minimum of furniture. Daily more alarming rumours reached the town. Before she left Jackalsfontein a neighbour had ridden over to tell her that Paul Kruger and M.W. Pretorius had sent out messages that every man ought, in the name of God, to attend a meeting which was to be held at Paardekraal just north of present-day Krugersdorp. All the young men were going and she had been urged to load her wagon with food and supplies as she could be sure of trade at the huge gathering. "I had no doubt it would be a good speculation," she wrote, "but I finally abandoned it, as I thought it would hardly be an honourable position for me to accept."

She now heard that the Jennings family and many of her Magaliesberg friends had come into Pretoria as their Boer neighbours had uttered threats against them such that they feared for their lives. That day and the next the whole village of Pretoria was in a state of agitation. There was a huge demand for wagons from people who thought they would be safer out of the place and wanted to trek to Natal. Sarah thought she could sell her old wagon and one of her spans.

On Monday, 13 December 1879 she started for Jackalsfontein, as the Boers in their thousands assembled at Paardekraal, within a day's ride of the farm. Near the Jukskei she met a Boer who told her it was in flood. She would never be able to cross it with the horses, let alone bring a wagon back through it, even if it did not rain again. Reluctantly she turned back towards Pretoria.

As she was passing the house of a "well known Boer" the owner came out and asked her where she was going. "If you mean to get into Pretoria," he said, "you had better push on. The Paardekraal meeting has broken up and the commando rides today for Pretoria." "Does it?" said Sarah. "Then I'm in luck – I'd like to see it." The old man looked at her oddly, not quite knowing what to make of that. He had not met her before but, with "that habit of hospitality which has become second nature to the Boer, he said, 'Won't you off-saddle? Although perhaps you had better push on if your horses are not tired.'" At that moment the post cart from Potchefstroom came in sight – the house was a post station. Thinking she might hear some real news at last Sarah accepted the invitation. She found the passengers were her friend Advocate Cooper and Judge de Wet. They all went into the house for coffee while the fresh horses were being put to the cart.

De Wet told them the commando was not to ride till the Thursday to give the British time to reply to their ultimatum. The old Volksraad had sat and decreed the restoration of the Republic. The Paardekraal meeting had elected a triumvirate to take charge. It consisted of Paul Kruger, who had emerged as the leader of the more conservative of the Transvaal Afrikaners, Pretorius and Commandant-General Joubert. A messenger had been despatched to Pretoria demanding that the Government offices be handed over to the Republic. If not the commandos would ride to seize them on Thursday. The meeting had apparently gone much further than Kruger, by nature cautious, had intended, but he and the other leaders had been carried along by the general feeling. Piet Cronje had set off to Potchefstroom to have the proclamation restoring the Republic printed, another party had moved off to hold the Lydenburg-Pretoria road to prevent reinforcements reaching the Pretoria garrison from that direction, and the main body had marched off to Heidelberg to hoist the Vierkleur – the old Republican flag.

De Wet, who had met the Boer leaders, still thought things might be patched up with a bit of tact, but Sarah believed that if things had come to such a pass war was inevitable. She was confirmed in this when their host said vehemently that the Boers would accept no compromise that did not restore their independence completely.

The post cart soon departed but Sarah remained as she wanted to hear what her host said when the others were out of the way. "It has always been my opinion," she wrote in *A Lady Trader*, "that although the English Government were perfectly justified in annexing the Transvaal, the manner in which it was annexed was not only an unjustifiable blunder but an unjust act." Her reasons for thinking the annexation justified were based on general principles which she found impossible to explain to her Boer friends, particularly with her still limited command of their language, but they grasped at once that she thought they had been badly treated. She tried to make clear to them that if war came she would side with England because she thought the British were right on general principles but this was a subtlety the Boers did not seem able to grasp. They assured her they understood she "must go with her nation". She wanted to explain that in certain circumstances if she thought her nation wrong she would not "go with it", but this she could not get across to them.

Sarah was confidently told that if the British did not hand over the government on the coming Thursday then even the presence of women and children would not prevent the Boers from storming Pretoria and fighting from street to street till they had taken it. Innocent blood would be on the heads of the English.

Having heard as much as she needed she decided that rain or no rain she must get to Jackalsfontein to give George the choice of staying on the farm or riding back with her to the uncertain safety of Pretoria. She took a different route to a drift on the Jukskei that was usually shallower than the one on the direct road and reached the farm after dark.

As soon as the neighbours heard of her arrival they all converged on the Du Plessis house and she had to tell and retell the news. There was excited discussion and it was late before she could get a word with George on his own. She told him of an encounter she had had with a farmer named Joubert near the Jukskei. Joubert had asked what news there was from Pretoria, and whether the English would hand over the country. When Sarah had said she thought not he had glared at her and, quivering with passion, said, "Then you don't think they will give us our country back? Then we shall fight. We will drive you from the country. Not one of your nation will remain alive – we will kill you all – all of you! Where are your troops? Sent to fight the Russians, the Irish, the Americans." Sarah had told him he was wrong, at which he had gone scarlet with rage and shouted, "Now I know you lie. There is your path. Go!" Sarah had stood her ground and said, "I won't go like this. I wish the Boers no harm. Give me your hand before I go." Joubert had hesitated, then given her his hand and a civil good-bye, but the encounter had shaken her.

She told George everything and said he must make his decision. He opted to stay on the farm and she could not help thinking he might be safer there, which was her main concern. The Du Plessis family said they would give him his meals and protect him if she were detained in Pretoria.

After a sleepless night Sarah was up at four to call her people and span in the wagon. Dawn was just breaking as she mounted Dandy and took up Eclipse's leading rein. George looked forlorn as he stood watching in the cold, faint light with Roughy in his arms. "Are you sure you don't want to come? There's still time to change your mind," asked Sarah, but he shook his head and turning Dandy towards the Jukskei she set out.

That night, the Tuesday, they outspanned three miles from Red House, crossed the Six Mile Spruit safely by moonlight before dawn and were in Pretoria at seven on the Wednesday morning. She was dismayed to find her Waterberg wagons were not in. She left the wagon at the auctioneer's but was told the sale she had counted on had been cancelled. The town was in a state of suppressed panic, with most shops and businesses closed.

Sarah opened up her cottage and sent for a carpenter to make shutters for the windows, as she had goods stored there. Tension rose when Thursday 16 December – Dingane's Day – dawned but it passed without event in Pretoria, despite frequent rumours that the Boers were riding through the hills above the town. Elsewhere, however, the action had begun. The Vierkleur was raised that day in Heidelberg as a rallying point for the commandoes and the first shots of the *Vryheidsoorlog* (Freedom War) were fired by Cronje at Potchefstroom.

At the time there were only 3,500 British troops in the whole of South Africa and their reputation was low. The Boers knew them to be badly disciplined, weakened by desertion and poor shots. On the other hand, the Boers were not highly regarded either. Even some of their own leaders feared they would cut and run at the first check or encounter with the English, as they had in former years run on several occasions from African tribes who stood up to them. They had no cannon, so that they could not easily reduce a siege. They did, however, have one great advantage: they were magnificent shots and they had the Wesley-Richards rifle which could kill at 600 yards. This was a factor that was grossly underrated by both Lanyon and Sir George Colley, the British commander in Natal.

During the night of Wednesday 15 December, the Boers cut the telegraph wire which had been opened only the previous year and which formed a tenuous but vital link with Durban. On the night of 17 December the Boer emissary Hendrik Schoeman had arrived in Pretoria demanding that the town be handed over, but as Colonel Bellairs was expecting reinforcements within a day or two the ultimatum was rejected.

On Monday 18 December, the last post cart from Natal arrived. The Boers had seized the mailbags but had allowed the passengers through unmolested. One of them, a young Miss Clarke, had managed to abstract some despatches for Sir Owen Lanyon from the mailbags before the Boers saw them and had smuggled them past the commando by hiding them in the bodice of her dress, though for the sake of modesty she transferred them to her hat before arriving at Lanyon's residence. From then on all communications with Natal were cut.

Late on the 18th, Sarah's wagons finally arrived from the north, but Hendrik brought bad news. The grain she had left at Makapanspoort had been badly damaged by rain. He had traded for grain and cattle but on reaching the Pienaars River had found it in flood. He had outspanned, waiting for it to go down, but after two days Boers nearby had told him that if he did not trek they would seize the oxen and the wagons. The river had been still too high to cross with a full load and the unyoked cattle. He had left some of the goods and the extra oxen at an African kraal and had swum the spans across, the loads remaining in the wagons getting wet in the process. It was a desperate disappointment but at least she had the wagons and the oxen were in splendid condition.

On the Sunday evening she was writing letters in her cottage, which was on the western outskirts of the village, near the military camp, when Hendrik rushed in, wild with excitement. The Boers were coming, he shouted. The Market Square was being fortified, rifles given out, everyone would be massacred, "half-castes" and "Kaffirs" were in even more danger than whites, he must have a gun. Sarah's breath was taken away. She saw he had been drinking but he was "not absolutely drunk". She thought she had better see what was happening and told him to saddle her horse. Riding down to the Market Square she found Hendrik had been right. Africans, superintended by an engineer officer, were hastily throwing up earthworks round the church. An excited crowd was crushed round a cart laden with rifles which were being handed out, but she was told there would be none for coloureds until all white men had been armed.

Seeing an officer she asked what arrangements were being made for the safe keeping of the many oxen and horses in the town. He asked her where she was going herself for refuge. She said she did not know, she supposed she would remain at her house near the camp common. "In that case you have been assigned to the convent laager and you had better go there," he said.

"But what about my wagons and oxen?" she asked. "I have three valuable spans and I don't want to lose them."

At this the officer showed interest. "We need wagons badly for barricading the streets," he said. "You had better bring them to me and then just turn your oxen loose in the square here."

"Between the earthworks and the barricades?" asked Sarah in astonishment, looking to where the streets leading to the square were being blocked with wagons, including the one she had left with the auctioneer. "Just let them go loose?" "Yes," was the reply. Sarah thanked him politely and rode off, thinking to herself "how singularly beneficial to all parties it would be to have thirty-eight oxen, maddened with fear, rushing about a small square that was being desperately defended – unless one looked upon the arrangement from the Boer point of view".

She went up to the camp to look for Lieutenant-Colonel Gildea, the commander of the detachment of the Royal Scots Fusiliers which garrisoned Pretoria, to ask his advice but he was not there so she formed her own plan. She brought all the oxen onto her own erf, barricading the entrance with two of the wagons and telling the drivers they must sleep near the animals that night.

By this time the streets were crowded with people heading for various places of refuge, and men with rifles slung over their shoulders were going off on patrol. A body of local volunteers, the 60-strong Pretoria Rifles, had been formed, while a few with good horses had formed a cavalry corps, the Pretoria Carbineers or D'Arcy's Horse. Ten extra horses had been bought to increase the strength of the mounted police under Captain Henry Nourse, a body affectionately known as "Nourse's 'Orses". The fact that the military garrison could be so strongly reinforced testifies to the size of the English population of the town.

There were also of course a good many Boer families, often with relatives among the rebel forces, whose presence worried Colonel Bellairs, commanding officer, Pretoria District. "Spy fever" took hold of Pretoria and some Boers were arrested on the flimsiest of evidence.

The situation looked bad but the authorities were not unduly worried, although 160 men had been sent to Potchefstroom. The garrison had been further depleted by allowing volunteers to go off to the Basotho War, while Sir George Colley was tied up in Pondoland and could not spare reinforcements for the Transvaal.

Belatedly orders were sent to Lieutenant-Colonel Anstruther, commanding a detachment of the 94th Regiment garrisoning Lydenburg, roughly 180 miles away in the eastern Transvaal, to make the long march back into Pretoria.

The night of Sunday the 19th was quiet and no attack materialised, though Sarah sat up near the stable most of the time. Next day came the news that the 94th had been massacred in a narrow pass at Bronkhorstspruit, about 30 miles out of Pretoria. Two injured survivors had been allowed by the Boers to go on into the town for medical help. News of the disaster shattered and unnerved the townspeople and managed to shake even Sir Owen Lanyon.

Though Anstruther had been ordered to take special precautions the long column, slowed by too much baggage, had been allowed to become strung out along the road. Few scouts had been posted with the result that the 94th had walked straight into a trap with the band playing and with soldiers carrying only 30 rounds of ammunition each. A small number of Boers hidden behind rocks and bushes above the road had shot the column to pieces. Two hundred and sixty-three officers and men were eliminated from the fighting, and all their supplies and equipment captured. Now the only possible reinforcements were Colley's troops in Natal.

Sarah went in search of guns for her men and saw the commissariat officers superintending the movement of stores into the camp. It was obvious that a siege was near. The town was in an uproar with all coloured men seen on the streets being seized for service and horses, wagons and oxen being commandeered. Women were packing up belongings ready for the order to go into laager and farmers from near the town were arriving with their families to add to the confusion. Sarah decided that she ought to offer her wagons and horses to the government. They were accepted with alacrity.

On the morning of Tuesday 21 December, martial law was proclaimed in the town. Everyone assembled in the market square and the Colonial Secretary, Mr George Hudson, read the proclamation, watched by Lanyon, Bellairs and Gildea. Then Major Le Mesurier explained that the town was too spread out for easy defence and street fighting might lead to tragic accidents and mistakes. Everyone must go into camp. Four long huts at the military camp were being set aside for women and children, while some were directed to the Loreto Convent, a daughter house of the Institute of the Blessed Virgin Mary, which had been opened in 1878. Behind it was the town gaol and a sandbag wall had been built joining the two to create the Convent Laager. The convent's main building was one of the few two-storeyed structures and as it stood on a rise on the western side of the town it commanded a good view of it. The unfortunate nuns were ousted and left with only their small chapel. The main building was sandbagged, loopholed and manned by the Pretoria Rifles. A further "wagon laager" was established to the west of the military camp.

Sarah decided that to be cooped up in a hut with dozens of other women and their possibly squalling infants was not to her liking. She went in search of Major Walton, the transport officer, to whom she had handed over her wagons. She explained to him that if she could have her largest tent-wagon back she could live in that and free a bed in the huts for someone who had no wagon. He agreed and gave her an order for it, telling her to return the oxen when she had got her wagon into camp.

She loaded up everything she had with her. Just as they had the team inspanned they heard the sound of cannon. Terror struck her African "boys" and the coloured men, who screamed that the Boers were on them and they would all be killed. Roads to the camp were crowded with people on foot, or in wagons and carts piled with mattresses and household effects. A storm broke and through heavy rain they all toiled to the camp to be told there had been a mistake, it was not ready for them and they should come back the next day.

"That evening," wrote Sarah, "I, having little to move, a horse to ride and last but not least no little children, wet, cold and tired, to console and feed, was probably the happiest person in Pretoria."

14
Pretoria besieged

The next day, 22 December 1880, everything was ready for them, the little town was abandoned and the whole population took up its abode in the various sections of the laager. It was no mean feat of organisation on the part of the British authorities. There were 3,700 civilians to be housed, 975 men and 676 women. There were 718 children, and the faintly surprising number of 1,331 African servants, who were sent to a site above the military camp. Sarah remarked that it was well placed for any African to slip out at night and carry information to the enemy. By the end of the siege she was quite sure this had often happened.

Sarah found a place for her wagon at the end of a line, facing the main road through the camp. This turned out to be a good choice as she was not so bothered by noise or campfire smoke as some people were. Also in the camp was Charles Du Val, an entertainer and journalist who had arrived in South Africa some months before to tour the country with his one-man show, "Odds and Ends". He had reached Pretoria in the middle of November and, being caught there by the war, had joined the Carbineers and somehow got himself onto Colonel Gildea's staff as Information Officer. The proprietor and editor of the *Transvaal Argus*, Charles Deecker, had brought its printing press into the camp and he and Du Val produced *The News of the*

Camp, published thrice weekly throughout the siege. The first number appeared on Christmas Day 1880, and reported: "Situation in the Camp: wet!"

This entertaining sheet met with the approval of the authorities, who found it useful for publishing official notices, in particular those concerning the sanitary arrangements. Nobody was to wash, or graze horses and cattle, above the camp near the sluits that provided water. Everyone living in huts or tents had to be out of them by 6.30 a.m. each morning and remain out till 9 a.m., during which time they would be inspected. There was a running battle between the camp orderlies and women who threw out slops and rubbish round their tents or wagons. There was much grumbling but orders were enforced and as a result, Sarah wrote, "the camp was well managed as far as the comfort and health of its inmates were concerned".

Even so there were some deaths from sickness and Sarah paints a pathetic picture of small coffins with a handful of flowers thrown on them being carried to the burial ground. Several babies and children died, and so did the French-born Mother Superior of the convent, Mother Margaret Mary, aged 34, who died of typhoid. There were births as well as deaths, and a great deal of flirting.

There were regular patrols and some skirmishes with the Boers. At Swartkoppies, east of the town, the Boers were defeated and prisoners taken, but at the Red House, near the Six Mile Spruit, the Boers triumphed and killed a number of Englishmen, including the much-liked Captain Sanctuary.

Despite the weather and a plague of fleas it was not all grim. Every evening the band of the Royal Fusiliers played on the parade ground and occasional concerts were given. On a fine evening, according to Sarah, it was an attractive picture "when all the various habitations were alight, and one caught glimpses of illuminated interiors, with dashes of bright colour in them, arranged in long vistas. The campfires burnt cheerily and one heard nothing but merry voices and laughter, snatches of song, and even, in one bungalow, the sound of a piano". All this and more was reported in *The News of the Camp*.

"Of course," said Sarah, "there was an unlimited amount of scandal and gossip of all sorts, and there was also an unlimited amount of squabbling, varying from the quarrel between Mrs A and Mrs B, which raged femininely and furiously, but nonetheless privately, to the noisy vociferation between another pair of ladies, which woke the neighbours from their slumbers for some fifty yards around the scene of warfare." Sometimes Captain Heygate, the camp Quartermaster, would be called to adjudicate. His must have been a thankless task but he had a quiet sense of humour which frequently saved the day. He was a languid young man who, while working hard, never seemed in a hurry, and gave Sarah the impression of wearing pale kid gloves – though she never saw him actually doing so.

After a week or so the authorities allowed people out of the camp for a few hours a day to inspect their deserted houses. The gardens were running wild and grass was growing in the streets. Wagons were run between the camp and the market square.

Sarah rose at dawn every day, saw her horses fed and checked her oxen, which were kept with their own drivers and *voorlopers*. After early coffee she fetched her rations. The camp was divided into wards, each in the charge of a wardmaster, who distributed the rations daily. She breakfasted before riding down to her cottage where she worked on her book, *A Lady Trader in the Transvaal*, which she began during the siege to pass the time. There were doctors and a hospital in the camp so her medical skills were not called on as they had been in the country. She returned "home" for dinner at about five, and after the meal "looked to the horses being settled for the night, inspected the oxen, and then paid visits".

William and Mary Jennings had their wagon near hers, as did his parents. Alice had married Thomas Hinds not long before and had been at Potchefstroom with her parents-in-law when the trouble started. They were relieved to hear she had escaped to her relatives in the Cape. Another friend, R.T.N. James, who farmed outside Pretoria, was one of the officials looking after her ward.

Sometimes the days were enlivened by distant shots and everyone would scurry back to the camp for safety, but after Christmas the authorities reopened the schools and the children were taken to them in wagons for an hour or two a day. Before that an elderly schoolmaster had set up a school of sorts in a tent but it blew down in a storm on top of him and the pupils so the authorities closed it.

The many African servants in the camp caused problems. Orders went out that passes to the white sections of the camp would be given for only one servant to each family and there were the strictest orders against ill-treatment of Africans. The camp newspaper repeatedly published an official notice reading: "Any Soldier, Volunteer or Civilian found ill-treating or threatening any Native will be immediately arrested and handed over to the Provost-Marshal, and be dealt with accordingly." This matter of the treatment of Africans was fundamental to the quarrel between the Boers and the English.

While Sarah held no brief for cruelty or unjust treatment she had realised from experience with her own workpeople that the untutored Africans respected those who dealt with them fairly but firmly. The result of the order about ill-treatment was that people were afraid to reprimand their servants "and the upshot of this was that they became very insolent". Sarah openly punished one of her leaders for neglecting her oxen one day and no action was taken against her. She remarked that her servants were the best behaved, but that she was sure some influence was at work to suborn the Africans against the British. There was much drunkenness among them, though white civilians could buy wine or spirits only on a special order from the Provost-Marshal or from a doctor and the sale of liquor to an African was forbidden except by permit.

One of her drivers told her one day that a friend of his had come into the camp from Waterberg. He brought news that Mapela had "broken out" and driven off Boer cattle. Mapela had captured Boer women and children and had put them in a laager, saying that he would show his respect for the English by taking good care of them, but a man he had found hiding among them he had had dragged out and killed. "It seemed odd to me to think of this selfsame Mapela sitting by my wagon in his smart dress a short time previously."

All through January and February the people in the camp were borne up by hopes that Sir George Colley would soon arrive from Natal to raise the siege. "We were counting the days until we should see him ride through Baviaanspoort at the head of a victorious column," she wrote. "Some said one day, some said another, would be the likely one for the welcome sight to greet our eyes, but none doubted that we should see him." *The News of the Camp* ran a sweepstake on the date.

This faith was misplaced. While 600 Boers cooped up a much larger number of British troops in Pretoria, 2,000 more occupied Laing's Nek, the pass through the Drakensberg that controlled the road to Natal where there were 1,200 British soldiers. At their head was Colley, now High Commissioner for South-East Africa, who proceeded to make a series of blunders comparable with those which had led to the disaster of Isandhlwana only two years before. He tried to storm the Boer positions at Laing's Nek and was repulsed. He was defeated again at Ingogo. Reinforcements were on the way to him but instead of waiting for them he occupied Majuba Mountain, overlooking the Boer position, in a brilliant night march. His men scaled the steep escarpment and were exhausted when they reached the top. Colley, who had not realised that the Transvaal side of the mountain had a relatively gentle and short slope, neglected to secure his position. The next day, 27 February 1881, the Boers were able to storm the summit in broad daylight and virtually annihilate the whole force, killing, wounding or capturing 200 British soldiers. Colley himself was among the dead.

It was some time before the news reached the beleaguered garrison and townspeople in Pretoria. Moves had already been made towards an armistice. The British Government had promised a settlement if the Boers would lay down their arms, but the message reached Joubert just after his first defeat of Colley when he was not in a receptive mood. Colley had sent word to Kruger demanding an answer within 48 hours, but it reached him only after the sender had been killed.

Majuba was a totally unnecessary military disaster for Britain. Fearing an uprising in the Orange Free State and possibly in the Cape as well, and with the Zulus restive at the British defeats, the London government had been anxiously looking for a way out of the entanglement almost from the start of hostilities. Colley, it is said, had pushed on without waiting for help because he had heard that women and children were starving in Pretoria. In fact, Colonel Bellairs had proved an excellent administrator and supplies were holding out.

The first rumours of the disaster reached Pretoria on 15 March 1881. "Many would not, could not, believe it," wrote Sarah. "It seemed too dreadful, too incredible to believe." Everyone was put on half rations and confirmation of the news, with a report on Colley's three engagements and his death, arrived on 23 March and was printed in *The News of the Camp*. Four days later a fresh blow was dealt the English when they heard the terms of the armistice: the Transvaal was to be handed back to Boer rule.

The shock was tremendous. People had built their lives and businesses on the assurance that the Transvaal would remain British. In siding with their countrymen many had alienated Boers who had previously been their friends. Worst of all, those who had lost relatives in the fighting felt that it had all been for nothing.

Sarah was stunned and incredulous. "It was not for myself that I felt the bitter ache at my heart, it was for the honour of England, a thousand times worse than any pain caused by personal loss: the one I could retrieve by courage and steadiness, but it made me feel almost mad to think that I was powerless to move as much as a feather's weight to retrieve the other."

She knew she was luckier than most: she had her wagons and most of her oxen had survived, also her horses. Others had lost everything they had. She went to see William and Mary, who were sitting in their wagon crushed with the news. "They knew they were ruined. They tried to take it bravely but you saw that the knowledge struck home."

The injustice of the treatment of the English-speaking Transvaalers by the English government, as she saw it, roused Sarah to a wrath that lasted for years and she lost no opportunity to tell the British public of the perfidy of their leaders. Though the people who suffered most were Boers who had sided with the British.

Everywhere in the camp there were similar stories. The thought of ruin, Sarah told her readers, was stoically borne but the disgrace they felt had been thrust upon them made them angry.

"Look at those fellows," shouted one old man as two officers rode past. "Look at them with their well-groomed horses and their dandy airs! It's all they're good for to look pretty. We wouldn't have disgraced ourselves."

Amid such bitter feelings the camp broke up. Something had been attained by the holding of Pretoria. Had it fallen to the Boers the position of the English would undoubtedly have been even worse.

There was tremendous excitement when the first group of Boers rode into town. Hendrik Schoeman, Henning Pretorius (who had distinguished himself in the Elandsfontein engagement) and Piet Joubert went through the camp greeting old acquaintances on their way to headquarters. Sarah thought how proud they must be to have forced these "handsomely dressed military gentlemen" to acknowledge as conquerors the men whom they had termed rebels. "We had found them a harder nut to crack than we had expected and the Government at home had considered the game not worth playing out… It was not a pleasant sight to see men who had truckled to the English now truckling to the Boers."

In the Market Square Boer wagons had come into town laden with produce. Sarah saw Hendrik Schoeman with a group of his friends and as she knew him she spoke to him. "I'm sorry for the peace," she said. "It is a disgrace to my country, but as far as my feelings towards you are concerned I heartily congratulate you. You have fought well and have earned your reward." Schoeman shook her hand warmly and said, "What you say is true and I thank you." His friends grunted their assent.

It was this generous and fair-minded attitude of Sarah's which gained for her a reputation which lasts to this day for being "pro-Boer". In point of fact she did not much like the Boers in general, though she had good friends among them, and was as ready to criticise them when she thought it justified as she was to praise when praise was due.

The town was in turmoil. The canteens were reopened "and the streets were full of howling, reeling wretches. All order seemed gone". Those of the English who could leave sold their homes at giveaway prices and left during April and May. Many of them were people who had come in since the annexation and who had relatives, possibly homes, to return to in England. They may have lost financially but their position was easy compared to others who had been born in the country, Boers who had accepted British rule and had been loyal citizens, and Cape-born English like William Jennings. They had no other country, no place to go. Many of them had no ties left with Europe and no choice but to stay where they were and make the best of things.

Business in the Transvaal collapsed. Banks called in all loans and moved out. Durban and Cape Town firms closed their Transvaal branches. The stagecoaches which had carried mails and passengers and which operated from

Natal and the Cape had lost all their horses and mules and withdrew their services from the Transvaal. Within a short time the Boer government was bankrupt and was kept afloat only by loans from some of the English who did stay and carry on their businesses. For some of these the rewards were great a few years later when the main gold reef on the Witwatersrand was discovered and Johannesburg sprang from the bare veld.

Meanwhile losses had to be assessed and compensation claimed where possible. This did not amount to much, as Sarah pointed out. Losses which had impoverished so many were largely not through looting. Crops and livestock had been pillaged but for the most part houses had been left untouched. It was the collapse of trade and property values that did the most damage and no compensation was payable for that. Sarah's cottage and the farm, which she had worked so hard to buy, were now worthless and unsaleable. Her stock of trading goods could be sold only at a huge loss and more merchandise, which she had ordered earlier and had paid for in good money, was now on its way from Natal, to be sold for bad – and little of that. She could see only one way out of her problems. There was a big demand for transport to Natal and she still had her wagons and spans. But winter was near and her oxen in poor shape. Though it was still April the grazing round the town had been eaten bare during the siege. If she could have set out at once all might have been well, but the authorities repeatedly delayed decisions about compensation due to her and told her she could not leave until it was settled.

The peace terms were still being haggled over – the Convention of Pretoria was not signed until the following August – and this meant uncertainty and some fear that war might break out again. Boer friends told her they thought renewed fighting likely and that the forts around Pretoria were being strengthened. This news convinced her that she must start for Natal at once.

"Auctions were crowded with articles for sale but there

were no buyers for there was no money... The whole village was in a state of demoralisation ... the Africans were as a rule either half or quite drunk – thieving was going on to a great extent for once out of the village the thief could defy the law."

William Jennings, who had taken his family back to Nooitgedacht, rode in to tell her all his sheep had been stolen. He looked pinched and ill. Most of her best sheep had gone too, but a few remained. She asked if he would like to buy them cheap but he replied sadly that he had no money. The Nel family – the *bywoners* who had originally moved uninvited into a shack on the farm and had stayed there during the siege – had helped themselves freely and now jeered at and tormented the Jenningses. On top of this William had received notice from neighbouring Boers that his standing crops, and indeed everything he had, were confiscated to the new Boer government. He showed her the letter which stated that he would be held personally responsible for everything on the farm to be surrendered as soon as the peace conference was over. Sarah took him to Hendrik Schoeman who told him that the letter was completely unauthorised and the seizure of his sheep and crops illegal. But meanwhile she and William were sufferers with no hope of redress. As William said goodbye and rode away Sarah did not realise she would not see him again. He set about rebuilding his ravaged farm, but his health had been undermined by fever on hunting trips to Mashonaland. The worry and strain of the days of the "Retrocession" told on him. He had severe sunstroke on a trading trip taking ivory down to Durban and died on 13 March 1882, aged 39. When the news reached Sarah she angrily blamed the British government for his death because of their betrayal of "loyal Africanders". She sent a wagon to Jackalsfontein to fetch George, who arrived safe and sound with Roughy.

Rumours reached Pretoria of disaffection among Africans in the northern Transvaal, who were threatening to rise if handed over to Boer rule. There was still no word about compensation and Sarah chafed at the delay. She had contracted to take loads to Natal and there was little time to reach the Drakensberg before the worst of the winter set in. She had been working hard at loading the wagons and felt ill again. She struggled on but finally collapsed and was in bed for three weeks. She had barely regained her feet when word came from the Attorney-General: no compensation was to be paid to her at all. "It was a terrible blow and the delay in giving me the answer fatal."

She was still weak and shaky when there was trouble with her "boys" and her trusted Hendrik bolted. Her goods from Natal had not arrived and she was not really fit enough to travel – but dared not stay longer. As soon as she had found another driver she set out, taking George with her.

"It was a terrible trek. I rode by the side of the oxen to see they were tenderly treated and not over-driven. I saw them blanketed every night before lying down and often I got up of a cold night to see that they were covered. I watched them as if they were children, but all was in vain, one by one they drooped, and lay down and died." It broke her heart. Of an evening round the campfire the great beasts would nuzzle her and take bread or mealies from her hand. When her favourite ox was dying it lay with its muzzle on her lap and she cried. Roughy was bitten by a snake and died. Her other dog, Prince, was shot by a Boer whose house they were passing. At Harrismith she gave in. There was a farmer with fodder who was prepared to buy her remaining oxen. She saw it would be cruel to force her diminishing spans across the Berg in the bitter cold. The dry season was well under way and there was no grazing.

She arranged for her loads to be taken on later by someone else and determined to go on down into Natal, hoping for work as a governess at least for the rest of the winter. Trade was bad and she could get only a poor price for her wagons before she left Harrismith.

As she and George crossed the Drakensberg on Eclipse and Dandy her heart was bitter but she still had some hope left. However, Natal turned out barren. It was full of emigrants from the Transvaal seeking work. The slump in the north had depressed trade in Natal as well. She was relieved when George found a good job in Durban but no one wanted or had money for a governess. Sadly and reluctantly she took ship for England.

15

Friends and spirits

During the voyage home Sarah completed the manuscript of *A Lady Trader in the Transvaal*. On reaching London she found a publisher and it was brought out early in 1882 by Sampson Low & Co. It competed for attention with Charles Du Val's book, *With a Show Through Southern Africa*, which appeared at about the same time and was the more successful of the two. This was partly because Du Val was well known in London as an entertainer and also because it was written in a bright and breezy style.

Sarah's book is a revealing self-portrait and gives a more detailed view of life in the Transvaal because she was there longer and knew more people, but it is not as well written. The style is earnest, the narrative sometimes involved and she has a distressing fondness for the words "pretty", "very", "tiny" and "nice". However, the book did have a measure of success, becoming quite well known. She followed it with her novel *Excelsior*, referred to earlier, which, though undated, seems to have been published in 1883 or 1884. She wrote another novel, *The White House*, of which no copy has yet come to light and it may be that this was also written during the years back in England following the Transvaal War.

She kept up a busy correspondence with the friends she had left in South Africa, particularly Mary Jennings.

R.T.N. James and his wife wrote to her, James having said he would keep an eye on Jackalsfontein for her. (James, a farmer and speculator, built up a large estate at Silverton, about eight miles east of Pretoria. He was later president of the Transvaal Agricultural Society and a leading figure in Pretoria but he died insolvent in 1920 with all his properties heavily mortgaged.) Friends like these kept Sarah well informed of developments in the Transvaal.

During the 1880s Sarah's name appears in the list of governors of the East London Hospital but she played no active part in its affairs. However, when money was needed to enlarge the building the committee turned to her for help. The result was *The Story of the East London Hospital*, which formed part of a book called *Voluntaries for an East London Hospital*, to which leading writers of the day contributed stories and poems. The proceeds of its sale went to the hospital building fund.

No detailed account remains of Sarah's life between the end of 1881 and 1887, though there are some clues. She busied herself with philanthropic work in the East End of London and started a co-operative store at Woolwich, basing it on the idealised communism of her book of 1873.

Her sister, Annie, was living in Upper Norwood, in south-east London. The sisters had drifted apart and quarrelled at some stage. They had a cousin, Sarah Eland, (born Fetherstonehaugh), whose husband had deserted her, leaving her with a small son. She came to London with him and was living with Annie Goff when Sarah returned from the Transvaal.

Among the old friends Sarah went to see on her return to England was Illa Keightley. Illa's sister, Sarah, had married Sir Charles Nicholson and they had a large house, The Grange, at Totteridge, just north of London. He was much older than his wife – he was 57 when they married. Born in 1808 he had qualified as a doctor in 1833 and had then gone out to Australia, spending a short time at the Cape on the way, so was interested in everything Sarah could tell about South Africa. In Australia he had been Speaker of the Legislative Council of New South Wales and the first Chancellor of the University of Sydney, which he had helped to found. He was knighted in 1852 and created a baronet in 1859. In 1856 he had gone to Egypt where for two years he carried out excavations at Memphis. He translated and published the funeral hieroglyphics he found. He also discovered a papyrus containing the mysterious religious writings known as *The Book of the Dead*.

Sir Charles and his wife shared Sarah's interest in Eastern religions and mysticism. Lady Sarah was a distinguished artist – she had a large studio at The Grange. She and her sister Illa were fascinated by the supernatural. A friendship sprang up between the two Sarahs and they made some occult experiments. Notes have survived in Lady Sarah's handwriting headed "Recollections of automatic writings given through Sarah Heckford, about 1882 to 1884."

There was at this time a ferment of speculation about Spiritualism and the occult. The Society for Psychical Research was founded in 1882 and Sir William Crookes's *Researches in Spiritual Phenomena* had been published in 1874. Many sincere Christians tried to reconcile belief in the occult with orthodox religion. Sarah had had "second sight" all her life. Some years after Nathaniel's death, while staying with relatives of his, she told them she had seen her hostess's brother standing at the foot of her bed covered in seaweed. It was only later they learnt he had been drowned.

From Lady Nicholson's notes it seems that there were numerous séances at which Sarah's "spirit guide" was asked questions to which it replied through her automatic writing. One section read: "Creative forces called Ongars work the chief part in the creation of mankind." It called human beings "demons", saying that they were good or bad or a mixture of both, these being "indifferent demons".

Once the spirit guide was asked about the divinity of Christ, which is of interest when one remembers Sarah's connection with the Unitarian Church and her book on Christ and Communism. Sarah, in a trance state, wrote: "Our Lord entered into our human condition as far as feeling our infirmities and temptations as human beings, but there was always in Him more contact and affinity with the spiritual life than could ever be approached by any mortal." "He spoke of Him as the Thought of God," said Lady Nicholson, "and when we asked if we might say 'The Word' instead of 'The Thought' he replied, 'Yes, if the Word is but the expression of the Thought.'"

She mentioned that her sister, Illa, disagreed with some of the conclusions they had drawn from the automatic writings and was sending a book Sarah would find interesting. Lady Nicholson said she was "so glad to see you and your sister together once again", indicating that the breach between Annie and Sarah had been healed.

Lady Nicholson introduced a girl named Dora Scrimgeour to Sarah. Dora, who was about 20, was anxious to find charitable work to do and Sarah enlisted her help with the Woolwich Co-op. Dora, who was one of six sisters brought up in a large house in Highgate, came completely under Sarah's sway and developed a "crush" on her. The two became devoted friends, despite nearly 25 years' difference in age. There were strong lesbian overtones in their relationship over the next 14 years of which neither was likely to have been aware.

News of the discovery of gold on the Witwatersrand and the proclamation of the new township of Johannesburg in August 1886 reached London immediately, but the true nature and extent of the new goldfields were not at first appreciated. During the course of the following year, however, more and more information reached Sarah about the tracing of the Main Reef and developments in the area. She began to wonder if there was gold on Jackalsfontein. R.T.N. James, who had made successful speculations, urged her to return. She could not afford to speculate herself but perhaps she could sell her farm profitably and start again.

Like so many who go to Africa, on her return to Europe it haunted her and she longed to go back. She was sure of a welcome from her many friends and it did seem that now it might again be possible to support herself. Her missionary zeal for "uplifting" the people around her which had first found expression in her work for the East London Hospital she now felt could be exercised in Africa, where she had already seen the crying need for better education. The vague notion of combining farming, schooling and medical care which she had outlined to Nathaniel in their midnight talks in the old cholera hospital 20 years before was beginning to crystallise. She saw that the Transvaal might be the field where she was ultimately called upon to deploy her "diminutive efforts".

Once her mind was made up she set out for Pretoria with all speed. This time she landed at Cape Town and took the train which now ran as far as Kimberley. There she transferred to one of the coaches which carried passengers and mail on to the Transvaal. Early in 1882 the Transvaal government had sought tenders for services to replace the ones withdrawn by Cape-based firms in the depression. The Zeederberg brothers and George Heys had stepped in to fill the breach and had been well placed to take advantage of the bonanza presented by the proclamation of the Witwatersrand goldfields. George Heys had altered his route from Kimberley almost within hours to run through the mining camp, setting up an office in a tent.

When Sarah reached Johannesburg – The Camp, as the inhabitants called it – at the beginning of May 1888, she was astonished to see that where two years before there had been almost empty grassy uplands there were now streets laid out. The first crop of wood and corrugated iron houses were already being replaced by respectable buildings of brick, many of two storeys.

After an overnight stop she continued to Pretoria. The 36-mile journey took about five hours. There was a stop soon after the crossing of the Jukskei River for lunch at the Halfway House Hotel, a flourishing new development which was no great distance from Jackalsfontein. By the time she reached Pretoria she was excited and hopeful. The coach pulled up at the spanking new Post Office in what was now known as Church Square – the market having been moved to the old outspan, the site of the present-day State Opera House on Church Street East between Van der Walt and Du Toit streets. She was agog to see what other changes had taken place.

The first she noted was an improvement in the hotels, and calling on old friends, she noted imposing new houses. It was almost unbelievable that the shabby village full of people bewailing their ruin she had left seven years before should be this prosperous town of thriving merchants which even boasted gentlemen's clubs on the lines of the famous clubs of London's West End.

At Nooitgedacht the welcome she received almost reduced her to tears. Mary Jennings had soldiered on and with the help of her husband's family and loyal African employees had rebuilt the farm into a flourishing concern. Augusta and Sarah had grown into good-looking women and Sarah, now 19, was already married to George Hinds, a younger brother of her Aunt Alice's husband, Thomas. George and Sarah had settled at Nooitgedacht, and their first baby, named William after his grandfather, was born on 10 June 1888.

With the house full and the new baby to be considered, Sarah accepted the Jameses' invitation to stay with them for a while at Silverton. Before she left London she had asked an agent who dealt in Transvaal properties to find a buyer for Jackalsfontein. He had told her that as soon as she reached Pretoria she should have a survey done of the farm. She had engaged a surveyor named Knox and had sent his report off post-haste to London, but post-haste in those days was not remarkably fast.

By July Sarah was fretting and anxious, when on the 5th she received a letter from Dora Scrimgeour written on

31 May. She sat down at once to reply to "My Dear little Dora" (who was all of 26 at the time) detailing the delays and irritations she was meeting. In the same mail came a letter dated 7 June from Mr Semple, her London solicitor. He had found a possible buyer for Jackalsfontein who had postponed his decision until he had seen the surveyor's report. Semple, Sarah told Dora, was "chafing a good deal against the jog-trottishness of his life". She went on: "It is a great pity when people who have a capacity for going at a rattling pace can't get out of a jog-trotting life; it seems as great a shame as to put a high-bred horse to turn a mill... People who, to use his own beautiful illustration, 'paw the air like a deer' ought to be put to something different if the world were ordered aright."

She had heard that Dora had met her cousin, Sarah Eland. "I am so glad you and she like each other." Dora was living in Sussex with her widowed mother who had bought a country estate, Wispers, and was farming it. Dora found it hard to get on with her mother and was impatient – as Sarah had been so long before – for useful work. She was missing the "inspiration" of Sarah's presence. No appeal to Sarah ever went unanswered and she responded to this plea in two ways. First she told Dora in some detail the story of her own childhood and youth, her storming of the barricades of "young-lady-dom" and her marriage, because it "may be of some little help to you in comparing your difficulties with mine". Her own were perhaps greater than Dora's and yet she had been able to transcend them so Dora must not be despondent about her own life. Then she turned to a practical suggestion as to what Dora might do. Why not, she asked, invest some of her allowance in breeding stock, such as a good cow, a few sheep, hens, perhaps bees, and farm in a small way on her own account, paying her mother for grazing, fodder or the use of farm buildings or implements that she needed? She would then be taking decisions of her own and bearing the consequences. Well-managed stock would soon multiply and she might be able to contract to supply the Woolwich Co-operative, "which would put you in touch with the real world of bread-winners".

On the 11th she added a further page, beginning "agony of agonies! One horse's head is not well and the other is lame, so Mr James can't go to Pretoria at all this week and I am stuck". She was impatient to get to Pretoria to begin her next project, in anticipation of the sale of Jackalsfontein bringing in some working capital, but "now I am stuck for another week! Oh dear! This is sticking with a vengeance! I hope you are keeping up your spirits – I have to be after mine with all sorts of expedients to keep them on their legs at all". By way of a postscript she added a story which had greatly amused her. "A wretched man tried the experiment of selling photographs of pictures and statues by the old masters in the streets of Pretoria the other day. The Landdrost had him up for selling 'immoral pictures', said he had caught him at it – had the photograph – shocking picture – three naked women – bought it of him. The picture was produced in court. It was 'The Three Graces!' Wretched man's counsel explained it was a photograph of a work of art – an old statue – but the Virtuous Boer was obdurate, said it would corrupt the virtues of the nation to see such things and was with difficulty restrained from punishing the offender."

Sarah and Dora kept up a voluminous correspondence, mostly in the form of "diaries" which they posted off to each other monthly. Only a small part has survived, but what has gives a vivid picture of Sarah's life in the Transvaal from this time on.

The business of Jackalsfontein dragged on for several months. The holders of the bond that she had taken over with the property threatened to sue her for the amount owing as she had not been able to keep up the payments, but she still had no buyer. Many years later the ground became extremely valuable as the northern suburbs of Johannesburg spread and eventually engulfed it, but that was far in the unforeseeable future. For the time being the farm was a liability rather than an asset.

From Silverton Sarah went on a round of visits to members of the Jennings family, unable to go ahead with her trading project. Failing to sell the farm on the London market she put it in the hands of a Johannesburg agent, Isaac Lithauer. She had done business with him in Pretoria in 1880, where he advertised as "The People's Auctioneer". By the end of November matters were coming to a head. Sarah was staying with Alfred and Ida Jennings at Hekpoort when she heard from the bond holders' attorney, Charles Leonard, that they intended to foreclose.

She left Hekpoort on Sunday 2 December for Johannesburg, where she arrived on the Tuesday and went straight to see Lithauer. He had had no offers for the property so she went to see Leonard to ask for an extension of time. He would agree only to one week. When the time was up and there was still no buyer she went back to Leonard, offering to give transfer of the farm to the bondholders to have done with the business.

Leonard was doubtful. "I'm afraid my clients don't want the ground. They want the full amount of the bond," he told her.

"Jackalsfontein is my only asset," she replied. "I have tried both here and in London to sell it but in six months there has been no firm offer. There is no way I can meet my obligations except by transferring the farm to the bondholders."

"If you cannot sell it, the bondholders are not likely to be able to either," Leonard told her. "You will have to find the money somehow."

In this impasse Sarah hurried to Lithauer. "Do the best you can, and whatever you get for the property above £1,200 we will share equally, but watch the bondholders carefully and don't let them get up to any tricks." She could not remain longer in Johannesburg because she was going to Blaauwbank, presumably as a governess, where she was to be paid £100 a year. Lithauer had advised her that under Transvaal law no creditor could sue and attach a person's "means of livelihood". A teacher or doctor, for example, could not be deprived of fees earned unless they were invested in a business venture.

She was glad to get out of Johannesburg, where the dust and wind and discomforts of the house she was staying in tried her, but there were some aspects of life there she enjoyed, particularly "the meeting of people I know, and the sight of the morning markets and Saturday auctions, at both of which you see enormous squares literally crammed with oxen and wagons, horses, men, articles of all sorts".

On arrival at Blaauwbank, however, she found there had been some unlooked-for domestic upheavals and the post she had been expecting would not be forthcoming after all. It was a Saturday and after a pleasant weekend she drove to Hekpoort with a shooting party to collect her dog, which she had left there. On the way over she had stopped at Hartley's Hotel at Vaalbank, booked a room and left a case there. The shooting party dropped her off on the way back. Fred Hartley, the proprietor, was a brother of the famous explorer and hunter Henry Hartley.

The next day, 20 December, Sarah settled down on the stoep to write a long letter to Dora. She described the problem of Jackalsfontein but felt confident she could trust Lithauer to look after the business for her as "he is as sharp as a needle, an American of Hebrew extraction and an old Transvaalite". She had still not heard if the bondholders would accept transfer of the farm instead of cash and thought they were waiting to see if she started a business before they sued her. "They will rue it if they do," she said cheerfully. She had found out (and it is a fair guess that Lithauer had told her) that if she went into business on her own she could be sued for the bond, but if she could get someone to give her their power of attorney, she could trade or hold property in that person's name and not be touched. She had written to Semple asking him for his power of attorney, to trade as his agent. "I don't like fighting like this," she told Dora. "It is using means that are in themselves crooked, which no one who had fairly incurred a debt ought to use." If the bondholders sued her, however, an irregularity in the bond would come to light and their case against her might collapse. "If they force me into a corner ... then I shall consider myself right in fighting them with their own weapons. And do you know (I don't think it is creditable to me – but it is a fact) I shall be glad in a sort of way."

With this comment – one can almost hear the chuckle as she wrote it – she turned from business to a description of the hotel which she said was quite the best she had come across in South Africa. Everything was clean and orderly, and the stabling for her horse was good. "You may judge that we are pretty well fed here when I tell you our bill of fare yesterday. Breakfast – porridge and milk, chops, eggs and tea. Lunch – cold mutton, salmi of fish, hot rolls, cheese, fresh butter, plum tartlets and tea. Dinner – soup, chicken pie, roast mutton, vegetables and rice pudding. All well done." She had decided to stay for a month, for which she would pay £7/10s – with washing!

"I am tired of being a guest, and tired too of not knowing what I am going to do, so for the next month or two I mean to be quite independent and do my best to map out a future."

The letter ended with a reference to a manuscript that she had sent to Dora, asking her to find a publisher for it. Dora appears to have had trouble placing it as Sarah suggested that she might write out a resume of the plot to show the publishers, and added, "Perhaps Mr Philip could advise." George Philip had published *Excelsior*, which had not done well, and he was evidently wary of another flop. The previous September, while at Nooitgedacht, Sarah had painted a watercolour that was evidently intended as the title page of this book. In the centre is the portrait of a young woman, for which Augusta Jennings had modelled.

Beneath it is the title "A Romance of the Raand [sic]. A Tale of the Wilderness. By Mrs Heckford." Around it is a border showing a bridle, a saddlebag, a riding crop, a pestle and mortar, and at the bottom a scene of a man and a woman riding pell-mell across the veld. As this painting was found among Mary Jennings's papers after her death it seems unlikely that Sarah ever did find a publisher for her romance.

16

Back in business

By the time her month of rest and reflection at Hartley's Hotel was up Sarah had made a plan and charted her immediate future. In January of 1889 she rented a two-room shanty – one room for her, one for her horse – in Booysens, on the southern side of Johannesburg. She acquired a diminutive office in the business centre of the town and set up as a share broker's agent, selling mining shares.

There were many speculative businesses in those days and records were not as accurately kept then as they are now so it is not surprising that Sarah's small concern has disappeared without trace, though she soon became well known in Johannesburg. She was now nearly 50. She had cut her hair short in an "Eton crop" which was streaked with grey. The small, determined figure with the limp and the brave carriage of the head was pointed out to newcomers as one of the acknowledged characters of The Camp.

Sarah moved to Johannesburg on the crest of the boom and wrote enthusiastically to her friends and relatives in England. She sold shares to Dora and probably other friends as well. She urged her cousin Sarah Eland to come out and join her as soon as her son Frank finished school.

Her timing, however, was as disastrous as it had proved in 1880. In March of 1889 the mines began to strike pyrites. This meant that the yield of gold from a ton of ore was greatly reduced and the cost of extracting it much higher. The boom collapsed almost overnight and shares on the Rand became worth at best about a tenth of their quoted prices. Many of the mines were no longer payable and the biggest slump in Johannesburg's history began. The share market collapsed and the end of gold-mining on the Rand was forecast. About 8,000 of the 25,000 white inhabitants packed and left. Before long the discovery of the cyanide process for extracting gold from pyritic ore not only restored the profitability of the mines but made the Rand more prosperous than before, but by then many of the early pioneers had been ruined and Sarah's agency wrecked.

She kept her head down and weathered the storm. In the nick of time Lithauer's efforts had paid off and he had managed to sell Jackalsfontein. She was now clear of debt with a small amount in hand. She could and did take whatever knocks came her way with what she would have called "steadiness" and shook off setbacks like a dog emerging from a pond. She was distressed, however, that she had been the cause of Dora's losing money and determined to make it good.

The effect of the Johannesburg episode was to convince her that the only really sound investment was in land and that her original scheme of ten years before of combining farming and trading had been sound. She would ride transport again and buy Dora a farm to recoup her losses. Farms in the Transvaal could often be bought then for less than £50 if they were in the outlying areas, but the term farm did not mean what it did in England. Sarah bought one near Middelburg, about 100 miles east of Pretoria on the road to Mozambique, and went out to have a look at it.

She found there was nothing there, just an area of coarse grass, rock and thorn scrub between four beacons. There were no buildings, there was no water and no attempt had been made to develop it since it had first been allocated as a "burgher right". Under this system the son of a burgher

(Transvaal citizen), when he reached 18, was entitled to a "farm" contained between beacons which marked how far a man could ride to the four points of the compass in a day. Many of the Boers who acquired land in this way lived in Pretoria and never visited or developed their property. They were often willing to sell it for the proverbial song.

Sarah reckoned that £1,000 would be needed to make anything of the Middelburg farm and wrote to Dora asking her to send the money. Dora replied that she could not afford to, so Sarah sold it and looked for something that would need less capital to work. Meanwhile she invested in two wagons and spans of oxen and set out to rebuild her fortunes by riding transport to the Bushveld, taking the Great North Road she had first travelled ten years before.

It was on this road that she later found the ideal farm for Dora, Tobias-zyn-loop, near Naboomspruit. The soil was good, there was a primitive house on it, African labour was available and there was a good water supply – the name means "Tobias's stream". This investment turned out well, as a few years later the railway to Pietersburg was built over the farm and Dora was bought out at a good price. The railway siding named Tobias marked the site.

The transport business throve and Dora took shares in it, giving Sarah the capital she needed for trading goods. The northern Transvaal, after many setbacks, was developing and there had been exciting finds of gold in the Soutpansberg, along the Klein Letaba River. In addition the area was densely populated by Africans, which made "Kaffir trading" profitable. The low ground was still unhealthy – it was not until the 1940s that malaria was controlled and even now it is wise to take anti-malaria pills if visiting it in the summer – but the prospectors and diggers thought of nothing but the gold to be found and did not leave at the end of winter as the Boer farmers from the Highveld had done, so that trading became a year-round proposition.

Sarah Eland sailed from England on 26 November 1890, taking Frank, 17 and fresh out of school, with her.

They joined Sarah in Johannesburg at Christmas and Frank found a job with the Standard Bank. He worked there diligently enough for a year or so but was not the sort to take kindly to the life of a bank clerk on a high stool. It was too much for him to see Sarah go off with the wagons while he stayed at home with his mother and eventually he threw up his bank job and went transport riding as well.

At what stage the three of them, the two Sarahs and Frank, moved permanently to the northern Transvaal, is not clear. In the 1890s it was rough, tough pioneering country, teeming with game, with the few white inhabitants thinly scattered and with the lure of gold. In the winter of 1891 Sarah Heckford spent several months on the Klein Letaba goldfields, combining trading with prospecting, painting and writing. This resulted in a series of stories entitled *True Transvaal Tales*, of which the manuscript survives though there is no record of its having been published. In it she described in detail the method of panning gold and said she found it difficult to learn "the trick of correctly agitating the pan".

She set out from Pietersburg with her wagons down the track that ran for about 90 miles over the mountains to the Letaba River, carrying the kind of stores and supplies the diggers needed and for which they would pay in gold. She was bound for the Birthday Mine. There are differing versions of how it got its name. As Sarah tells the story, a Boer on a hunting expedition was resting on a boulder. He knocked his pipe out against it and noticed something glittering. Scratching at the rock with his pocketknife he dug out a piece of yellow stuff. Thinking it might be precious metal he took it to a prospector who was working nearby, who confirmed that it was indeed gold. As it was the Boer's birthday the prospector promptly named the find "The Birthday Reef". It is still marked on maps today as "Birthday".

Sarah included this story in *The Lost Reef on the Tsama*, the second of her *True Transvaal Tales*. It is corroborated by G.G. Munnik, who was a government official in the area at the time, in *Kronieke van Noordelike Transvaal* (Chronicles of the Northern Transvaal), which he wrote in 1890. He names the Boer as Cornelis Grobler. Other writers much later attribute the discovery to the brothers Duncan and Malcolm Clark, but though they were among the early exploiters of the reef it must be accepted that they were not the original discoverers. Grobler, like so many early finders of gold, did not make much money out of it but the Birthday Mine yielded respectable fortunes for some astute operators and in its heyday the shares rocketed from £1 to around £34.

Sarah greatly enjoyed meeting and talking to "the motley crew of gold-seekers". One of these was a character known as "Solo" Smith – "the sobriquet suited him well, for he habitually monopolised conversation". Solo caught up with Sarah as she was beginning the steep descent from the Buffelsberg. "Hallo," she called out, "I didn't know you were on your way to the Birthday." "No more I am," said Solo, doffing his slouch hat, and with a knowing wink added, "I've got something quite different on. Grand thing! Nobody knows about it but me. Birthday will be nothing to it, but mum's the word! I'll tell you about it when we outspan for I can trust you."

At the outspan Sarah was intrigued by Solo's two-wheeled cart. She had never seen anything like it before and her account of it reads like Lewis Carroll's description of the White Knight's horse, hung about with impedimenta. There were small bins all round the outside, with locks and compartments for things Solo often needed on the road. Inside the tent which covered it the cart was ingeniously fitted up and festooned with articles, such as a hurricane lamp, family photographs "and several canvas bags, neatly made by Solo himself, of suitable shapes to contain his toilette and other necessaries, his diary, which he kept minutely, and his Prayer Book".

"Wonderful fellow, old David," Solo said that evening. "Always find consolation in the psalms. Many a time when I've been downright broken-hearted or as savage as a bear

– can't find the reef – boys won't work – everything goes wrong – turn up the psalms, and there you are! Old David knew all about it, felt just the same, tells you all about it. Never miss reading him every night."

At the drift on the Klein Letaba they parted company, Solo swearing Sarah to secrecy. "Don't mention me if you can help it but if anyone asks where I turned off tell them you can't describe the place," were his parting words.

Solo was heading for the Tsama River (spelled Nsama on modern maps) to follow up rumours that a prospector named Pigott had made a big find. As the Tsama was even more unhealthy than the Letaba and the bush more dense not many people ventured to it. Solo had the reputation of being fonder of spying out the finds of others than of working hard on his own discoveries and Pigott, on his rare appearances in the bars of Pietersburg when he came to sell his gold, told everyone, "If I find that prowling hawk anywhere near me I'll put a bullet into him that'll stop him."

One of these visits ended disastrously. A canteen keeper thought he could worm the secret of the Tsama reef out of Pigott by keeping him drunk, but only succeeded in getting him into a mad fury in which he shot the canteen keeper dead. Pigott was arrested and tried to bribe the warder to let him go free by giving him a rough map of the find. The warder took the map but gave Pigott no chance to escape. He was taken to Pretoria and sentenced to ten years in gaol. Solo claimed to have seen the map and swore he knew the place. A few days after Sarah had parted with him he turned up at the Birthday in a towering rage. He had located the spot shown on the map but when he had dug all he had found were Pigott's pick and shovel. But the gold was there, all right, and was later worked as the famous Louis Moore Mine.

Sarah was given a warm welcome when she reached the Birthday Mine. "The rough track to the mine," she wrote, "ended abruptly in a small clearing in the forest, and a row of the most picturesque abodes imaginable, called rondavels. They were circular, built of rough timber plastered with mud, and had conical, thatched roofs with overhanging eaves. In these the staff of the Birthday Mining Company lived. Close by were the workings, not as yet sufficiently advanced as to disfigure the scene... No battery as yet obtruded its ugly shape to shock the eye, or its deafening din to distract the ear. It seemed an ideal mining camp, standing alone in the midst of the vast forest, with its background of low wooded hills, and with the solitary Mangombe Mountain rising abruptly from the otherwise unbroken level of tree tops to the north-west."

She chose a spot at the edge of the clearing for her camp and began business right away. She was carrying shirts, hats, boots, shovels, diggers' supplies of all sorts, and the usual beads, mirrors, coils of shiny wire, blankets and brightly coloured cloth the Africans loved to buy.

She remained based at the Birthday but travelled round the scattered prospectors and the other mines in the area. And she panned £40 worth of gold on her own account. By the time she had disposed of all her goods and started on the long trek south again her immediate financial problems were over.

She returned to the Letaba goldfields often during the next few years but the Birthday Mine lost its charm once the battery was installed and after that she camped some distance away in the forest. It had lost its charm, she remarked, for wild animals as well. "Previously they had made themselves a little inconveniently at home there, in as much as a lion had taken the liberty of killing a horse and two oxen not far from my camp, and a wolf, by imprudently giving vent to his feelings by a prolonged howl, whilst sitting one moonlight night contemplating my donkey, robbed himself of the chance of having a supper off it."

Sarah kept an eye out on her trading trips for a farm suitable for the next stage of her plan. In 1893 she rented a portion of the farm Platland, on the banks of the Brandboontjies River, near Mooketsi. (Brandboontjies means "burning beans". This is a rank weed common in the area. It bears seeds covered with hairs which are intensely irritating to the skin, producing red weals like a burn.) Platland belonged to a Daniel Erasmus, who had a fondness for drink which cost him his life when he mistook a bottle of acid for brandy.

At the same time Sarah bought a small farm, Boschluishoek, which she called Elandshoek, nearby and a mile or two off the road to Pietersburg, but she never lived on it, working it from Platland. Between farming, trading and riding transport to the Birthday Mine she and the Elands could, she thought, make a reasonable living. The Brandboontjies valley, however, was not a good choice from the health point of view. It was almost on the Tropic of Capricorn and fever was bad there. They were all affected, Sarah worst of all, and she looked around for a farm on one of the surrounding hills.

She found what she wanted on the ridge called Malematsa, 4,500 feet up and overlooking the Brandboontjies valley. On 11 November 1893 she wrote out and signed a description of the farm, evidently for her trustees in England. It is headed: "Description of Sterkwater which I propose registering as 'Ravenshill', there being about 100 'Sterkwaters' and the name being ugly." Sterkwater meant "strong water" and was so named by the original owner who was said to have bought it for a bottle of whisky. Sarah paid £47 for it. The farm covered about 1,000 acres on the western edge of the Woodbush Mountains and was an "occupation farm". This meant that it had been awarded under an Act of the Transvaal Republican Government of 1886: "The Occupation Law for Government Lands situated in the district of Soutpansberg and part of the Waterberg."

This Act, passed fairly soon after the amendment to the Pretoria Convention which removed the British Government veto on legislation affecting Africans, was part of the Kruger policy for subduing the African population. The "occupation farms" were much smaller than the old Voortrekker farms and the area was unhealthy. However, they were productive and could be bought for the cost of the survey and drawing up of the *grondbrief* (title deeds), say £8 to £10, so were eagerly taken up. To keep out land speculators the Act laid down that each person might only have one farm and the owner had to live on it permanently and build a house. Government inspectors went round to see that these regulations were obeyed. Failure to observe them would mean the loss of the farm. For this reason Sarah registered Ravenshill in Frank Eland's name as he was to live there and work it, while she would be away some of the time attending to the trading and transport side of her business, and visiting England. "The value of land in Soutpansberg is rising," she told the trustees, "and when the 'occupation law' is repealed, as is at present being agitated for, the value of farms will increase suddenly and greatly." The Act was slightly amended in 1894 but was not in fact repealed until after Sarah's death.

Unlike the windy uplands of the Highveld with their cold winters the northern Transvaal had a large African population, divided into several tribes. The anger of the Africans was roused when whites moved in and occupied land which the tribes regarded as theirs and where some of them had lived for more than 300 years. Tribal boundaries were violated by whites who grazed cattle wherever they liked and hunted in traditional African hunting grounds. Few thought of paying a courtesy call on the local chiefs and "asking for the road". When government officials arrived from Pretoria and blandly told the tribes their boundaries had been redrawn and they were allocated to "homelands" which were often less than half the size of territories they had previously occupied, African anger boiled over. They burned the whites' houses and crops and hamstrung or drove off their cattle. The whites howled to Pretoria for the protection they had been promised and in 1890 General Piet Joubert rode against the tribes. When Sarah bought

Ravenshill the Soutpansberg was outwardly calm but below the surface it was seething. Captain Adolf Schiel, a German and the Native Commissioner for Soutpansberg, believed that "guns speak louder than words", which did not make for peace.

Twenty acres on Ravenshill had been cleared for cultivation, the rest was mostly covered by indigenous mist-belt forest. There was a strong stream with a furrow already made but no house, and the road to it was bad even by the standards of the Transvaal in the 1890s. To the northwest the ground falls steeply to the Brandboontjies and one looks out on range upon range of mountains. On the other side of the ridge the land slopes more gently.

"Its shape is triangular," Sarah wrote, "its longest side being adjacent to the location assigned to the great Kaffir Chieftainess Modjadje [sic], which renders it a valuable trading station."

Modjadji, the Rain Queen, ruled the Lobedu tribe and was the original of Rider Haggard's *She*. Traditionally a peaceable, good-natured people, the Lobedu none the less dominated the surrounding tribes by their prestige as children of the Rain Queen and their skill as metal workers. They had come from the north, where one of Monomotapa's sons quarrelled with his father and broke away to found his own kingdom. He initiated the tradition that when the chief became old he would take poison, after which his spirit would appoint his successor from among his sons. One of his daughters was seduced by a brother and bore a son. Rather than say who was responsible she ran away with the baby and a small band of followers, taking the tribe's sacred beads, the secret of the rain-making charms. They crossed the Limpopo and the Lowveld, settling on the slopes of the Drakensberg where the moisture-laden clouds from the Indian Ocean drop their rain. This was in the 1650s, about the time the first white men settled at the Cape.

In the early days there were fights between the sons of the chief, and Chief Mugudo decided the only way to save the tribe was for all future chiefs to be women. One of his daughters had to commit incest with him and bear a daughter who would be his descendant as well as hers. His favourite daughter recoiled in horror but her ambitious sister Modjadji agreed. Her first baby was a boy and was strangled at birth, and when Mugudo's wife took too close an interest she too was murdered. Then Modjadji had a girl, her father took the ritual poison and she succeeded him. Despite this bloodstained start her reign was peaceful and prosperous. The tribe reached its apogee under her daughter/sister Modjadji II, who was the ruler Sarah described as "the great Kaffir Chieftainess".

The Lobedu are still there on their mountain near Duiwelskloof, and when the towering thunderclouds begin to grow the Africans look up and say "Modjadji is making rain."

Modjadji lived in seclusion, designed to heighten the mystery surrounding the rain charms. Other chiefs sent their daughters to her court as her "wives", the Batanoni, asking that she make rain fall on their lands and not on those of their enemies. These "wives" were offered to important visitors and any children they bore were regarded as Modjadji's. Her consort "disappeared" as soon as he had fathered a daughter – any boy baby was strangled. Nowadays the tribe has evolved a more acceptable and politically sophisticated method of arranging the succession.

Few whites ever saw Modjadji. When Joubert commanded her to appear and pay taxes in person he thought he had humbled her in forcing her to leave her kraal, but in fact she was impersonated by her sister. Sarah Heckford met her. She got to know the formidable chieftainess well and became her friend and adviser. The Boers were furious and called Sarah "Modjadje's lawyer". Modjadji II was an old woman when Sarah came to Ravenshill and she took the ritual poison in 1896. Her daughter, however, when her turn came declined to keep up the tradition and lived to a ripe old age.

17

Ravenshill

On the same day that Sarah wrote her description of Ravenshill, Saturday 11 November 1893, she commenced a new section of the diary she still sent regularly to Dora Scrimgeour. A large part of it chronicles the minutiae of work on the farms. It gives a good picture of the hardworking life of the pioneering farmer in the Lowveld and provides interesting sidelights on political events of the day.

Frank and Mrs Eland were to remain at Platland while Sarah went to Ravenshill. She intended to camp in her wagon while supervising the building of a house, putting the neglected farm in order and setting up the trading post she planned. It was a beautiful morning – 15 November – as she set out up the rough, steep track that led first to the Medingen Mission, where she outspanned and roasted mealies for breakfast. She called on the German missionary's wife, Mrs Reuter, who gave her cocoa without milk and "was friendly as usual".

Dr Fritz Reuter was a Prussian who had qualified in Berlin. He joined the Berlin Missionary Society at the time a wealthy widow, the Baronin von Meding, gave a large sum of money for a mission in Africa at a place where no missionary had been before. The Society sent Reuter out to the Soutpansberg in 1880. He found the Lobedu and won Modjadji's confidence. She granted him land for a mission, church, school and clinic. It was named the Medingen Mission and the way to Ravenshill is over its land.

Fritz Reuter worked for the rest of his life at Medingen and died there in 1941 at the age of 93. He and his wife are buried beside the large, austere and impressive church he built. It was the Reuters who finally changed Sarah's opinion about the value of the work of the missionaries in Africa.

Over the cocoa Mrs Reuter told Sarah that the Dicke brothers, Germans who had farmed near Medingen since the early 1880s, had lately started a trading post on their farm. They were not doing any trade, however, "owing to their having burnt down the hut of one of their Kaffirs, the kraal Captain, for insubordination". What worried Sarah was not the thought of competition but the swarms of locusts which "have eaten every blade of grass".

At Ravenshill she camped at the edge of the forest. Every green thing had been eaten and the Africans living on the farm had lost all their crops in three days. The outlook for trading with them was bad in consequence. That evening the kraal head, Malata, came to see her. He was one of Modjadji's "sons". "He said he was glad an English person had bought the farm, as the Boers tormented the Kaffirs and made them work for nothing. I gave him a 2/- shirt (which he appeared to be in need of) and he rejoiced when I explained that I should expect every hut on Ravenshill to pay me 10/- a year rent, so that if a man had two wives he must pay 20/-, but that I should pay every man employed. He said it was good, that the Kaffirs would be glad."

The next day's diary has a sad entry: "Martin [her African driver] says that he can see that Frank is ploughing at Platland." Sarah's sight was failing and she was going blind in her left eye. Platland lies directly below Ravenshill and on a clear day anyone with normal sight could easily see a plough and oxen moving across it.

Despite the locusts trade began to look up and she moved the wagon to a spot near her boundary where it could more easily be found. By the 22nd it was raining but trade was "fair – all in mealies and principally for salt". The next day she sent a note to Mrs Eland asking if she could spare Frank for a few days to help her. It was late when the messenger returned saying Frank, who had harvested the beans, finished the ploughing and sown pumpkins and melons, would come in a day or two. As more rain threatened she moved herself and the sacks of mealies she had traded into a leaky, abandoned rondavel.

On 25 November she had a sinister visitor, "a most forbidding looking Kaffir", who sat engrossed in conversation with Malata. Eventually he came to tell her about a row the previous day between the Dicke brothers and the Africans who worked on their farm. She had difficulty in understanding him but managed to make out that Modjadji wished her to write a report to Pretoria about it, complaining that the Dickes had shot one of her – Modjadji's – people. While Sarah was not clear exactly what had happened she was sure "this will stop trade for the present, alas!".

That night there was heavy rain and a high wind. "The music of the forest was grand – just like a distant organ pealing with orchestral accompaniment – some wild theme. I had to have a basin on my pillow to catch the drip that came in and bring the foal into the rondavel with me to give it shelter." The entry ends with "I find that my Kaffir name here is Mamusagiana." This is made up of two words, the first meaning "mother of kindness", the second "to dance". It can be translated as "the kind woman who dances around" or "who has quick movements".

Frank arrived and on 28 November they set about building a wooden shack, using materials from a ruined house formerly owned by a woodcutter. Frank brought further news of the Dicke affair. The Lobedu had driven off some of the Dickes' cattle. The brothers and another German named Kurtzhahn had pursued the Lobedu and fired a kraal on neighbouring land. In return the Lobedu had fired Johann Dicke's rondavel and "in defence Dicke and his companions fired, each shot hitting its man". Daniel Erasmus had been involved in the fracas "and had made things straight for Dicke with the Veld Cornet who would doubtless send in a favourable report". From this it was clear why Modjadji was anxious Sarah should make a report to Pretoria.

The rain continued, hampering the house building. Sarah still had the foal in her rondavel at night "which is not very pleasant". She sent to Platland for rum and Mrs Eland sent up venison as well, which cheered them. "Everything is in a state of drip, drop or stickiness from the rain. Even when it stops there is a thick Scotch mist." No possible further escape from young-lady-dom than this – sharing a leaking shed with a foal on an African hillside with a tot of rum to keep the weather out.

A note from Mrs Eland arrived saying that the veld cornet had, surprisingly, put in a report that was unfavourable to the Dicke brothers. None of the Africans they had shot was dead "but we are in danger. Dicke's escapade has, as was to be expected, stopped trade for the present". Soon they heard that one of the wounded Africans had died and alarm spread among the local whites. Many packed up and trekked to Haenertsburg, in the Woodbush, for safety. Sarah, confident of her friendship with Modjadji and sure the Africans would not harm her, refused to be panicked.

She decided to visit Pietersburg before Christmas, thinking she would do well trading if she had fresh merchandise. She left for Platland on 11 December, a misty Monday morning. It was fine when she got there and "Flossie, my dog, was overjoyed to see me". The next day's entry begins, "Had a jolly sleep last night in sheets and comfort." She spent the day organising things at Platland and prepared for the usual pre-dawn start on the 13th. She was up "early in the morning" but, as they left at 3 a.m. "middle of the night" might have been a better way of putting it.

They trekked to Buffels, a long day's haul up the mountain. She bought bread, milk and tinned salmon in the store and was given letters, including one from Dora, that had been waiting for her. Returning to the wagon she found Martin, the driver, had gone off with the *voorloper* to another store kept by a German named Lichtensteyn. She had intended trekking in the cool of the evening but both Africans became hopelessly drunk and allowed the oxen to stray. She sat up until after the moon went down, waiting for them, until she gave up and went to sleep in the wagon. Next morning they reappeared. Martin had met another wagon driver named Bushman who was "very fierce with drink" and there had been an almighty fight. The oxen were rounded up, inspanned and they set off again.

On Friday, the 15th, she arrived at 7 a.m. at Solomon Marais's farm, later the small town of Solomondale. She was taking it easy, intending to move on late that evening, outspan near Pietersburg and be in early next morning for business. However, Mrs Marais reminded her that the 16th was Dingane's Day and a public holiday, so that no business could be done before the Monday. Sarah, who had quite forgotten the holiday, was cross as now she might not get back to Ravenshill in time for the Christmas trade. She accepted Mrs Marais's invitation to spend the weekend with them.

After an early start she spent the whole of Monday in Kelly's store, and then put up at the Pietersburg Hotel, where the news was that "Birthdays", and all other Klein Letaba shares, were very low. The goldfields there were looking less promising than they had at the start.

"Baumann, resplendent in white waistcoat, new light suit, new teeth and eyeglass, came over to my table and informed me he was 'going once more into the bonds of matrimony', and further that he was appointed Manager of the 'Letaba Syndicate'. The machinery will start working in April." Sarah extracted a promise that if transport wagons were needed he would let her know.

247

On the way home the clerk at the Buffels store told her that "another Kaffir had been shot at Modjadje's. Did not seem to know why. Also read me part of a letter from Dicke in which he says the Kaffirs have stolen 150 head of cattle from him and that he means to punish them. That if they wanted war they should have it – that if the Government did not act quickly he was not going to wait to be shot treacherously. A digger – an Englishman – who was there said that the right thing to do was to force the Kaffirs into revolt so that they might be exterminated. He did not put it so elegantly".

She pushed on to the Koedoes River, disquieted at the way things were going. Next day, 22 December, she was back at Platland, after a bad journey and sticking in the drift. There was much to be done but the pumpkins, cucumbers, sweet potatoes, monkey nuts and garlic were all doing well. Daniel Erasmus told her he had heard nothing about an African being shot and that as Dicke only had 16 oxen he could not possibly have had 150 stolen. However, "things look uncomfortable".

The wagon was packed with the goods she had hoped to trade at Ravenshill over Christmas but the road was impassable after the rains and on Christmas Eve she abandoned the idea.

Christmas Day dawned fine and she took presents to Daniel Erasmus and his wife. A number of friends were gathered there and the talk was all of Johann Dicke who had, said Erasmus, "got all the neighbouring Boers on his side and they were egging him on to engage the Kaffirs so as to cause some outbreak that would ensure the Government punishing them, when these worthies would be able to seize cattle as formerly done… I told Erasmus that I should not allow injustice to be done to the Kaffirs in that way without bringing it to the notice of the British Government and that if so iniquitous a course were persevered in I should be prepared to go to Cape Town myself to see Sir Henry Loch about it". Sir Henry was the British Governor and High Commissioner. He paid a State visit to Pretoria in 1894.

As usual, Sarah took action. She wrote to the Secretary of the Society for the Protection of Aborigines. She received a reply on 19 March 1894, saying the Society "can do nothing to protect the Kaffirs if oppressed and are further of the opinion that any appeal to the Cape Government was useless", which left her wondering how the Society earned its name.

Two days later Sarah went up to Ravenshill and found Frank had nearly finished the house. There was a kitchen, a room which would be his mother's bedroom, a store and a room which would be sitting room, office and Sarah's bedroom all in one. On New Year's Eve she sat up late and when she went to bed could not sleep. She lay gazing into the dark, wondering what developments 1894 would bring and whether she was once more to be ruined as a trader by an outbreak of war, "so that I saw in the New Year somewhat completely".

18

The Soutpansberg disturbances

On New Year's Day 1894, Frank went down to Platland with the wagon to fetch his mother. The weather cleared and the farm work progressed well but the combined strain of the effort and worry, both about the tense political situation and her own health, was beginning to tell on Sarah. "Cannot write more. I had hardly any sleep last night and am going to sleep as I write," said the diary for 11 January. Two days later Kurtzhahn rode over to see her and gave yet another version of the affair at Dicke's farm. "He evidently thought Johann Dicke in the wrong." Later rumours reached them that the commission enquiring into the matter was likely to let it drop with merely a reprimand to both sides, as the Africans had spoiled their case with contradictory evidence.

Wood had to be cut for building pigsties. "The bush here is lovely. It seems a pity to touch a branch of it or tread down any of the beautiful undergrowth." She made her Africans cut in out-of-the-way places where it would not spoil the scene and they made it quite clear they thought her mad! On 21 January there was "a beautiful moonrise and I went for a walk. To my disgust I found that a largish and ornamentally placed tree had been cut down by a Kaffir to block up a cattle path that leads towards his mealie field". She restored the position by planting bella ombre trees which still flourish on Ravenshill 70 years later.

It was on 7 February that they first heard of fighting with Magoeba, a chief in the Woodbush, who was resisting orders to withdraw his people to the smaller location decreed for him. On 17 March, Tom Kelly, the Assistant Native Commissioner, was at the Medingen Mission to give notice to Modjadji's people on the nearby farms, including Ravenshill, that they must move back to the newly defined location, though it was patently too small to hold them all. On the 24th *The Star*, of Johannesburg, reported, "Modjadje's answer to the Superintendent of Natives' ultimatum is that the ground where her children are living outside of the location is hers, and was given by her to them, and that there is no need to talk further about the matter. It is reported that the Government has instructed the Native Commissioner to take action to remove the rebellious natives." Tom Kelly threatened action by the end of April.

Fritz Reuter said he thought nothing would come of the rumours of war with the tribes. Sarah did not agree and events proved her right. At the beginning of April Kelly put pressure on the Africans in his district for the payment of the hated hut tax and those in kraals on Ravenshill, Platland and Elandshoek (which was in Sarah Eland's name) appealed to Sarah for help in paying it, which she gave, saying they could repay her from their crops when they had harvested. If Africans failed to pay their taxes cattle were taken instead, but at a poor rate of exchange.

Sarah's labourers were terrified and told her stories of their people being tortured if they had neither money nor cattle. Sarah thought this unlikely but had no doubt they would be roughly handled.

There is a gap in the diary for the first half of April. "I have been busy during the day and too tired at night to make any entry," she wrote on the 15th. As she was invariably up at dawn or earlier and on her feet working all day it is no wonder. There is nothing further until the 29th, when she wrote, "Since my last entry things have not been going on pleasantly." She had been taken suddenly ill on the 16th, being "seized with the most violent rigor I ever witnessed... At its worst I thought, and so did Sarah, that I must surely die".

For these two women alone in such a lonely spot – Frank was away at Platland – it must have been frightening. When Sarah began to write again on the 29th she was still in bed with a severe infection of her right foot. As if this was not enough almost all her African labour disappeared as Modjadji was setting up her "schools". "Now this is a curious custom. The practice of circumcision obtains amongst the Kaffirs but does not take place in infancy. There appears to be combined with it a lengthened species of 'confirmation'. The Witchdoctors preside, and at intervals of some years all those who have not undergone the ceremony are called up by beat of drum and go they must for if not they are liable to be 'smelt out' by the Witchdoctor and put to death. The 'school' lasts for two or three months. The acolytes, however much they may have been accustomed to dress, have during the time to remain stark naked and sleep without blankets in the veld or forest." It was nearly winter and Sarah was anxious about the young men in her kraals who would go through this.

She said she had heard they were fed on nothing but large quantities of mealie pap (maize porridge) and were severely beaten, while reciting lessons and responses in a weird sing-song that was kept up night and day. No one could see the boys during this time, an intruder risking death. She did not know why they were whipped but "emissaries are continually being sent to me from the schools begging for ointment".

Modjadji sent a message to say she was sorry Sarah was being left short of labour but she could delay no longer in setting up the schools. The boys who had left Sarah in the lurch were not to blame.

Despite the alacrity with which Malata and his men had agreed to Sarah's terms of employment – paying 10/- a year for their huts and being paid wages – now that the rent was due they cried off because of their losses from the locusts. They argued and wheedled for several days while Sarah threatened to put them off her land if they would not stick to the agreed terms. In the end, however, she had to give in and allow them to do 20 days' work a year without payment instead of paying rent in cash. This was the system of free labour used by the Boers on their farms. She disliked it and thought it unfair to the Africans, reckoning they would work better for wages, but found it was not so. They still disappeared at inconvenient times to plough their own fields, bury their grandmothers or attend the elaborate and long-winded rituals the witch doctors decreed.

In the midst of these negotiations, and while she was still bed-ridden, a circular arrived from the veld cornet "giving notice to all the Burghers in the district immediately on receiving it to move all their belongings into one of the two townships of Houtbosdorp or Agatha, war with the Kaffirs being imminent".

Meanwhile on Ravenshill there was panic in the Dockerell family – bywoners who had a shack on the farm and helped with the work in payment for it. Sarah told Mr Dockerell that as his wife was expecting a baby he should take her and a friend, Mrs de Jager, who was staying with them, to a safer place but "as to obeying the order ourselves we did not think of it… They fled on foot, Mrs de Jager, who is very ugly, presenting a beautiful picture of panic with her petticoats tucked all round about, sun-bonnet strings flying and a big stick in her hand".

The next day a messenger from Modjadji arrived saying he knew Sarah was ill but he must see her. He would not be satisfied until he was let into her room where she was still in bed. "He talked in his funny lingo about the Boers being in camp and about my being his 'Captain' and that we need not be afraid. I assured him that we were not at all afraid and got Frank to lure him out with some snuff."

On 30 April Frank rode down to Platland and found several Boer families living there. He decided nothing could be done to evict them and so arranged to bring the animals and stores to Ravenshill, which was just as well as later the farm buildings were burnt out by marauding Africans. "Trade is paralysed and we do not know for how long," Sarah wrote in her diary. The swelling on her foot had burst and was discharging pus. It was now less painful but she still could not walk.

After more wild rumours of impending attack another notice from the veld cornet reached them on 14 May that everyone must go into laager at Houtbosdorp. "No one seems to mind the order particularly as far as I can see," said the diary, though the people encamped on Platland went. A bundle of newspaper cuttings had arrived from Johannesburg, which for the first time gave a clearer view of the situation, and the farm work went on as usual. "I am able to get up but I cannot walk as yet and am deplorably weak." She had been ill for a month.

On the 26th more mail and a bundle of copies of *The Star* arrived – full of "The Soutpansberg Disturbances". In Pretoria men were being commandeered – that is, called up for service without payment – to raise a force to march north. The *Uitlanders*, the new immigrants on the Rand goldfields who had no vote, were refusing to go and so were some burghers. Sarah appears to have been more amused than disturbed by it, though she was still not well. "My foot and ankle swell dreadfully on the least provocation ... the instep is very much inflamed still and there is sometimes a watery discharge from it. I am afraid it is a bad job, one that ought to have rest and treatment which I can't give it."

The month ended with a note to Dora that she enclosed cuttings from *The Star* to give the full picture and asking her to tell Stewart Semple that she had no time for a letter. He had to do with the diary, "which he sees", as a progress report. The many details of farm work and prices paid and obtained were evidently for Semple and her trustees to keep a watch on her investment.

The next section of the diary begins at the end of June.

News had reached them of the war against Malaboch. "Martin says that 30 White men and 60 Kaffirs were wounded but I hear that this quotation may be divided by ten. The inhabitants of Pietersburg mount guard every night and great alarm prevails there."

In mid July, Modjadji's "schools" broke up and for a week there was a prolonged beer drink ending with such a hullabaloo and firing of rifles that Sarah thought the war had begun in earnest, but it was merely the "purification" of the youngsters. Frank Eland told Malata that now the ceremonies were over he must bring all the men for the 20 days' work that had been promised. Things seemed quieter and the Dockerells came back, bringing the new baby.

On 14 July the diary records, "Feeling very ill and cough bad." She had cleared a large patch of brushwood, though hindered by a "long conference" with the Africans, about whose kraals were within her boundaries and whose were not. "They were inclined to be noisy but I dismissed them." She repeated to Malata that they must accept the agreed terms or leave the farm, to which he replied he could do nothing until he had consulted Modjadji. Sarah told him she did not wish to interfere in Modjadji's affairs, "but this farm belongs to me and not to Modjadji". If they would not obey her and neither pay the agreed rent nor do work in lieu of it then they would have to go.

"They talked a great deal, seeming sullen and flippant by turns. I told them if they refused both alternatives then I would destroy the huts. I gave them until Sunday to consider the matter and told Malata I held him responsible for letting all the Kaffirs on my estate know what was my word. I then turned and went back into the house."

When Sunday came the men arrived to see her and "after a great deal of talk agreed to my terms". It was a trying day as she still felt ill, her head ached and her eye was "troublesome".

Next day news reached them of the attack on Malaboch's kraal by Henning Pretorius, whom she remembered from the Siege of Pretoria, with a detachment of the *Staatsartillerie* (State artillery). "He has come here to settle matters and the Boers are disgusted as they say he favours the Kaffirs," said the diary. She regarded him as a just and capable man, the best of the Boer leaders.

On 21 July Dockerell brought her news that the veld cornet was inspecting farms to make up his roll of occupants. Elandshoek was recorded as having been unoccupied for 13 months and unless something was done quickly they would lose it. Mrs Eland was not expected to occupy it herself but had to provide an able-bodied substitute. Dockerell had told Tom Kelly not to act as he would occupy the place himself. Sarah thanked him for his presence of mind, and said he had better move there at once.

Troubles were not coming as single spies. Sarah Eland was ill, locusts again threatened, Daniel Erasmus' cattle strayed into their crops at Platland and Dockerell was commandeered for the war. However, there had been time to register him as the occupant of Elandshoek. For more than two weeks Sarah had no time to write up her diary. As at Groenfontein, 15 years before, she had started making bricks and digging foundations for a proper house. This time the house was completed, though not for several years and it is doubtful that she ever saw it finished. It still stood in the 1970s, though empty and the garden overgrown.

On 10 August Sarah sat up till past midnight writing and as she was going to bed "was seized with a sudden want of breath and weakness of heart. It passed off after a bit and I got up at 5.30 and got tea ready for Frank to be able to start early in the brick field". At noon she saw to the donkeys' bedding and, walking back up the slope to the shack "was seized and completely prostrated by another similar attack, so having nothing better to do I got out my sewing machine". After a hard spell of work the following day, during which she "found it hard to keep myself up", she remarked, "I cannot make out what causes these distressing feelings of breathlessness and faintness." Even if she did not recognise it, here was a clear warning that the punishing routine she had set herself was affecting her heart. The detailed record of her life at Ravenshill produces "a want of breath" in the reader. That she should have sustained a mild heart attack is not in the least surprising. She was now 55 and her lameness made standing tiring even when she was fit, which she was not. The tuberculosis which Nathaniel had diagnosed before he died was now re-asserting itself. However, she took no notice.

She was supervising a gang of Africans on the foundations of the new house on 4 August when "just before lunch two Mission Kaffirs, one resplendent in white trousers, frock coat, top hat and bare feet, came along and cheerfully informed me that all the buildings on Platland had been seen burning. Later I heard a report they were fired by a body of Mahupa's Kaffirs, the Woodbush Commando having attacked that chief yesterday". The local Africans suggested she should let Modjadji know what had happened. Two of them set off at a trot. Nothing had been saved at Platland except some wire Frank had buried and a few tools that were in the fields, but "what is perhaps the worst is that the locusts have eaten off all our crops".

A lesser woman would have given up and admitted defeat long before this, but the notion seems not to have entered Sarah's head and her thought was still for other people. Mrs Dockerell was extremely frightened so Sarah insisted that she should sleep in her already overcrowded shack. At nine that night the messengers returned from Modjadji, brandishing rifles and one of them wearing a feathered headdress. "They said Modjadje sent me word that if the damage had been done by her Kaffirs she would have punished them severely but it was done by Mahupa's. That I need have no fear, that she was a woman and I was a woman, that she counted me as her sister and her people as my children and that they would defend me as such." This simple message from the old, mysterious Rain Queen to the Englishwoman on her lonely farm is more deeply moving in the atmosphere of events now, than it was at the time it was sent.

Next day only three men turned up for work. "It is a great bore but my leg is very bad, paining and aching frequently in whatever position I am, and the breathlessness and weakness of heart occur frequently on the least exertion." Modjadji sent a message that she would do her best to protect Sarah but it was just possible that Mahupa's men might raid her so it might be wise for Sarah to seek safety at the Mission. Sarah told the induna who had brought the message that she was determined to remain where she was. He said Modjadji had armed pickets on the watch all round her borders, that she trusted Sarah and asked that, if there was anything she ought to know, Sarah would tell her. "I said I would. Looked to the arms and lay down dressed, keeping a light in the room."

None of the "boys" came to work the next day. She told one of the headmen that if she had no word before "next morning light" that the Africans would work their 20 days "I would undoubtedly burn their kraal down though I did not mean to harm the hair of even a cat, but to put everything out and then raze the kraal". The tension grew when grass fires along the mountains that night appeared to be an attack on their neighbours. Three of the older Africans came to the house with guns to stand guard. "Old Sprinkaan assured me he would, if necessary, remain and die here. The wind was so high and boisterous in the trees it was impossible to hear much if there had been anything to hear. Frank and I ate our supper but the other two could not. In the middle of it Sarah exclaimed, 'Here they come' but although we all jumped up it was only the wind."

It was nearly midnight before one of their Africans reported that the fires on the mountain were only accidental ones, and that the men would agree to her terms and do the work they had contracted to do. Next morning Modjadji sent Sarah a letter she had had from General Piet Joubert, who was at Dicke's farm, asking her to translate it for her. The letter told Modjadji that "she and her people will be in no way molested as she has been obedient and tells her to send one or more Indunas to hear what he has to say. The Kaffirs were greatly delighted. They seem to think that I have assisted towards this happy solution". On 20 August Modjadji sent another letter, this time from Henning Pretorius, to the effect that she must keep all her people within her boundaries and that Schiel and the white commandos had firm orders not to touch her people so long as this was obeyed. The induna with the letter told Sarah that Modjadji had said, "It is true I am a brown woman but henceforth you and I must be like sisters and never have any strife."

All day they heard heavy firing not far away. "Magoeba and five other Kaffir chiefs are fighting hard, I hear." The next day there was small arms fire quite close but the heavy guns seemed further off. Adolf Schiel sent word to Sarah that she must go into camp as they were in great danger at Ravenshill.

This was followed by a visit from a neighbour who had been at the camp. Henning Pretorius had said that the letters to Modjadji were only a blind to keep her quiet while they dealt with Mahupa and Magoeba and after that she would be "seen to". Sarah was appalled and said she could not believe the Government could be capable of such duplicity. The induna who had taken Modjadji's letter to Joubert had been kindly received and had been given a blanket which Joubert had pinned round his shoulders himself. Sarah distrusted Joubert and accepted that Ravenshill might now be in real danger. She told Mrs Dockerell that she should go into camp, though she herself "would not think of moving from here, danger or no danger".

Joubert had received many complaints about Modjadji from the local whites, including Fritz Reuter, whose mission Africans were afraid of the Lobedu. Henning Pretorius had said he refused to listen to such nonsense but Joubert had seemed inclined to believe them. Sarah kept her promise to Modjadji and sent Martin with a request that the Queen should send her most trusted indunas to receive a message. She sat up till one in the morning waiting for them, then lay on the bed in her clothes. At 5.30 a.m. she heard sounds and on getting up found the indunas at the door. She told them, through Martin, what she had heard, warning them they must not let anyone know she was advising Modjadji as it could harm them all.

On 24 August Modjadji sent two more of Joubert's letters, one of which accused her and two of her chiefs of harbouring refugees from the battles against Mahupa. The induna who brought the letters was plainly terrified. He said it might be true, though it would be against Modjadji's orders. Joubert also accused the Rain Queen of allowing crowds of her people to live outside the location, which was also true as there were far too many of them to live inside. There was more heavy fighting the next day and Dockerell appeared, looking exhausted. He said Magoeba was sure to be taken that day. (In fact he was killed and his head cut off.) "His account of the insubordination of the commando is wonderful. Sentries asleep at their posts and treating the matter as a joke, men refusing to obey orders jeering at their commanding officers and discussing whether to depose them and elect others." Sarah was shocked but Dockerell "seemed to think nothing of it". To herself Sarah thought, "if the Kaffirs had any pluck they could make mincemeat of the commandos". As it was the Africans had devastated all the farms from Agatha to Haenertsburg.

During the next few days some of the men reported for work but on the 30th Sarah wrote, "Lay down dressed last night as I felt a little anxious about the possible behaviour of the outside Kaffirs who are being driven into the locations. Got up at 3 a.m. and wrote letters until it began to get light." During the day Modjadji's messenger came to say that Joubert was threatening to burn down all the kraals of her people who were living on farms outside her location and asked Sarah to try to save the Ravenshill people. A few days later, looking down on Platland, she saw that the kraals there were being burnt. On 4 September there was more firing nearby and fires on the Woodbush Mountain. The next day she was feeling "very unwell" and the sound of cannon from the direction of Mametolas so frightened the Africans that "all work was at a standstill".

The net was now closing in on the Rain Queen and a large commando appeared at Ravenshill where they bivouacked, while others surrounded the location, though Modjadji had obeyed all orders and remained peaceful. Then the order came to disarm her people, which was done without a shot. Frank Eland went alone into the location and advised the people to deliver their arms to Sarah at Ravenshill as Joubert had orders to shoot everyone if there was any resistance. Several thousand head of cattle were taken as a fine on Modjadji and in taxes. In a final indignity the Rain Queen herself was forcibly taken from her kraal and exhibited at Joubert's camp, with no chance this time to send a substitute. "I met the poor old woman on her way back to her location and shook hands with her and expressed my sympathy. She is very old and was all of a tremble."

All that Modjadji had been able to obtain for her people through her efforts to meet the demands made on her was that three of her indunas were taken prisoner instead of the wholesale deportation of women and children inflicted on the tribes which had fought back. The Ravenshill kraals were burnt by the authorities but Sarah and Frank managed to save 60 head of their Africans' cattle and some of their mealies by claiming that they belonged to Sarah. After this it was decreed that no farm should have more than five kraals on it so Sarah arranged that she and Frank should "rent" portions of Elandshoek from Mrs Eland, and similarly at Platland and Ravenshill, so that they had 15 kraals. Such was Sarah's reputation among the Africans that there was great competition to get onto her land.

The diary ends here, in September 1894. Just before she closed it, Sarah went to Pietersburg and there saw a column of about 500 African women and children being marched south to Pretoria. This was the punishment for the "rebellious natives". These women and children were portioned out among Boers living around Pretoria where they were technically "apprentices". Many concerned white people could see no difference between this and slavery. The "fine" of forced labour was meant to last for only six months, but for many Africans it continued far longer than that and some never found their way back home at all.

"I saw the poor creatures on the march," wrote Sarah. "They were shamefully treated. One woman near her confinement tried to escape and was cruelly beaten. Another woman and her children were allowed to be ransomed for cattle by her husband who overtook the squadron on the march. He was told that if he gave the cattle he had brought and could find his wife he could have her. He went along the line calling her name, when she rushed out and threw herself into his arms."

It seems a cruel revenge but the Boers considered themselves aggrieved and most of them did not and could not see the Africans as human beings, with feelings like their own. To them the African was only a species of animal. It is a strange blind spot in a people who had such strong family feelings themselves and loved their own freedom so much that they had gone through incredible hardships to win it.

In the covering letter Sarah sent with this edition of the diary to Dora Scrimgeour she said, "The injustice to the Kaffirs makes me mad... Now, however, all one can do is to try to make as much good come out of the existing state of things as one can."

Peace returned to the Woodbush and Soutpansberg, and Sarah looked forward to showing it all to Dora, who was to come out on a visit early the following year.

19
Fresh schemes and a trip to England

By the beginning of 1895 Sarah's health was worrying even her. It was obvious that she could not continue working as she had been. In many ways the year and a half she had spent at Ravenshill had been the happiest time since Nathaniel's death, despite the alarums and excursions. She loved the place deeply and felt a real sense of achievement in her work there. She had provided a home and a means of livelihood for her cousin, Sarah Eland, and for Frank. He was now 21, and had adapted to the pioneering life and acquired the skills needed for it remarkably well. A quietly determined young man, he was a fine example of the best type of that sometimes maligned species, the White Settler. He was just and fair in his dealings with the Africans and they liked and respected him. It seemed to Sarah that he could now take over the management of the farms without her constant supervision.

Their African labourers had settled down and were working well. Sarah was not happy that her attempts to institute fair wages for them had failed. She now had abundant virtually free labour and found herself forced by competition to avail herself of it but she felt "sick at heart over the whole thing". There was nothing she could do about it and she did not waste time worrying over it. Instead she turned to another project which had simmered in her mind for so long: farm schools. Indeed, she had outlined the first vague idea to Nathaniel in the midnight talks at the cholera hospital nearly 30 years before. Over the years since she had gone as governess to the Jennings girls she had seen enough to convince her that at the bottom of the troubles and tensions of the Transvaal was the problem of rural education. The country, because of the franchise laws, was governed by farmers, or men with a rural background, who were largely ignorant of the world beyond the borders of their republic and many of them illiterate.

With the population so thinly spread schools could not be provided from taxation outside the towns, nor were most of the people living on farms able to afford school fees. The result was a rural people growing up ignorant and illiterate. Sarah saw the answer in farm schools, which would be self-supporting once established and could be run at little or no cost to the taxpayer. Staff and children could be fed from the farm produce and any surplus sold at market. They would give a good all-round education to boys and girls between six and 14, those from remote areas being boarders. In addition they would teach modern agricultural methods. The Boers were pastoralists and clung to primitive ways which did not make the best use of land and stock. If the country's agricultural potential was to be realised and the rural standard of living raised, better techniques had to be taught.

Dora Scrimgeour (who had written that she regarded her forthcoming visit to the Transvaal as a "moral tonic") was expected in Johannesburg in April and Sarah was to meet her. She would use the trip to consult her old friend, R.T.N. James, now president of the newly formed Transvaal Agricultural Union, and to talk to "little Sarah's" husband, George Hinds, who was an efficient, practical farmer. She wanted to be sure of her facts and work out the financial aspects of her scheme before she began to approach people in authority in an attempt to launch it. Education in the

Transvaal at this time was fraught with problems because of the language question – the Government insisting that Dutch be the medium of instruction against rising protests from the largely English-speaking inhabitants of the towns and some Boers who saw the advantage to their children of a sound knowledge of English. Much heat and little light was generated in public debate but Sarah, who had herself mastered Afrikaans, was quite prepared to walk into this minefield.

Frank drove Sarah to Pietersburg to catch the mail coach. She was delighted to find old friends among the passengers bound for Pretoria. She enjoyed the journey, which took 40 hours on the road, with only one stop – at Nylstroom – other than the brief halts to change horses. The fare was £9/10/0d. Sarah found it exhilarating to cover the 170 odd miles with such speed and comfort.

It was an emotional reunion when Dora arrived in Johannesburg – by train, the line from the Cape having been completed in 1892. The two friends had not met for seven years. They stayed at Hovell's Hotel while Sarah attended to business and helped Dora buy a light wagon and a team of donkeys with which they were to trek to Tobias-zynloop and Ravenshill. The main purpose of Dora's visit was to take transfer of her farm, but they did not go there directly. They were going first to Blaauwbank and Nooitgedacht. Dora, who evidently knew *A Lady Trader* almost by heart, was delighted to be meeting in person the various characters of the book. She kept a diary of the whole of her visit which shows how she revelled in the new experiences it brought. Her mother had died in 1892, and she was now an independent young woman of 32.

The two intrepid ladies set out on horseback, in riding habits and "wide-awake" hats. They were photographed beside their wagons – Dora mounted, Sarah standing by the donkeys – at the start of the trek. It was four in the afternoon as they left Johannesburg, threading their way through the traffic and negotiating the tramlines, which were a hazard to the donkeys' narrow hooves. That night they slept with the wagon, Dora inside it, Sarah on the ground as she said she preferred the open air – though it was the end of April and the nights were already nippy. They were up at 4.30 the next morning and made coffee by starlight as they waited for the dawn. They were in Krugersdorp that afternoon and put up at a hotel before riding the 20 miles to Blaauwbank the next day.

It was already dark as they rode up the sandy track to the house where Alice and Tom Hinds were now living. A lantern appeared on the stoep and Sarah called out, "Will you light us down the road, Mr Hinds?" and a cheerful, "Hullo there! Is that you, Mrs Heckford?" greeted them.

Dora was curious to see Alice, the first of the characters of Sarah's book she was to meet. Alice now had four sons and a new daughter, six weeks old. Next morning Sarah woke up feverish and ill. She insisted on getting up but had to return to bed. A concerned Alice "was very kind putting on hot flannels all day", while Tom took Dora off to watch him panning gold. The mining company, in which John and Jeremiah Jennings still had an interest, had bought part of the farm where the gold was worked but small quantities of alluvial metal were still found on the portion the family had retained.

The next day, a Saturday, Sarah was still very ill but on the Sunday she was well enough to be left for a few hours. Tom and Alice took Dora with them to St Thomas's Church, Thorndale, not far from Nooitgedacht, for the baby's christening. Dora was introduced to Mary Jennings, "Mrs Heckford's greatest friend" she told her diary, and to Sarah Hinds, "the 'little Sarah' of Mrs H.'s book who is now the mother of two children herself". Augusta, who was to be married a few days later, was the organist and the ceremony was performed by Bishop Bousfield, still Bishop of Pretoria. Dora was intrigued to see a bishop in full canonicals officiating at a christening in a tiny, primitive church.

That night Sarah was worse and in great pain. Dora sat up with her the whole night. On the Tuesday, however, she insisted on getting up in the face of Dora and Alice's protests, saying she had no intention of missing Augusta's wedding, which was to be on the following day, 1 May.

Sarah was with them when Tom, Alice and Dora drove again to Thorndale Church. There Dora was introduced to the beaming bridegroom, Harry Clement Hinds, brother of Tom and of "little Sarah's" husband, George. Dora thought it romantic that he had been Augusta's faithful adorer for 14 years, ever since she was 10 years old and he 14.

There was a "grand spread" with champagne at Nooitgedacht after the ceremony and the old homestead was crammed with relatives and friends. Bemused by introductions of "Cousin This" and "Aunt That", Dora began to wonder if everyone for miles around was related to everyone else. Bishop Bousfield opened the proceedings with a speech in which he likened himself to the grandfather and Mrs Heckford the grandmother of all assembled there.

She and Dora stayed with Mary for a month. Dora watched the cattle kraaled each evening and wondered how Sarah Hinds could know each one of the several hundred individually, as she obviously did. "She and her little girl, Gladys, go and sit on the wall of the kraal and watch the cattle in the evening." She added that the whole scene reminded her of "the days of the Patriarchs", sensing immediately the Old Testament quality of life in the Transvaal.

It was early June when they left Nooitgedacht for Pretoria, where they were to see to the legal business of Tobiaszyn-loop. They put up at the Fountains Hotel in Pretorius Street at 12/6d. a night – one of the more expensive hotels. It had been newly refurbished and boasted electric light, a French chef and "a Bath Room for Ladies upstairs and Shower Bath Room for Gentlemen downstairs".

Dora thought it beautifully kept and admired the wrought iron balcony all round it. "It seemed so funny to be suddenly in the midst of civilisation again after sleeping in the veld for two nights," she commented. Pretoria struck her as clean and attractive, with excellent shops and impressive public buildings. Everyone seemed to know Mrs Heckford.

They spent a week at the hotel, seeing the lawyer who handed over the title deeds and a chart of Tobias, and buying provisions for the trek. They left on 16 June. In two days they reached Hammanskraal and a hotel whose visitors' book described the place as "the end of civilisation", so they availed themselves of the luxury of baths, a good meal and comfortable beds while they might. They were now crossing the dry, sandy Springbok Flats – at one stop they were charged 1/–. for water. The 20 June saw them at Warmbaths (Bela Bela), then at the height of its "season". There was such a crowd they could not get a bath for themselves, though they stayed three days. Farmers were camped in wagons and tents, their cattle round them, spending a month or two at the spa. A guidebook of the time said it was "much patronised by sufferers from gout, rheumatism and cutaneous affections". The water wells up at 71°C (160°F) and it is still popular as a spa.

At Tweefontein, in the hills beyond Warmbaths, they stopped at the store. Dora was interested to see the numbers of Africans on the road, walking the 200 miles to find work on the mines or returning to their homes, carrying huge loads of blankets, cooking pots and other paraphernalia. They were starting off again when the storekeeper ran up to tell them that a commando with "several thousand prisoners" was coming down the road. He advised them to wait where they were as the column would be a long time in passing and the dust from the dirt road would be unpleasant.

They outspanned again and rode to meet the convoy. "It was a most extraordinary sight and a very harrowing one," wrote Dora in her diary. "They were arriving in the valley when we reached the bottom of the hill and in a few minutes this lonely spot was crowded with human beings, mostly women and children and a few old men – all carrying huge branches of trees on their heads besides their household goods. In a short time the whole place was covered with fires as they were camping there for the night. Many of the women had big babies on their backs besides all their other belongings. Those that were too big to carry had to walk and some poor little things looked dreadfully tired. The Boers are transplanting a whole tribe (or as many as they can catch of them) to a location near Pretoria." She said the Boers had been warring against this tribe for the past six months but had been able to bring matters to a close only when they had called in Swazi warriors to help them. That night the campfires were magnificent and lit up the sky around.

They reached Tobias-zyn-loop on 27 June. As soon as they were outspanned they were surrounded by the African women of the farm who knelt or squatted in a semi-circle round them. Dora gave each a little sugar, with extra for the numerous babies. "The drawing room being at an end the levee now commenced and we received the male population, headed by their Captain." The men were not as picturesque as the women, their tattered and dirty coats reminding Dora of "London cadgers with their faces blackened". Sarah took down the names of the men. There were about 200 Africans all told, including 33 men of working age. The law about five families to a farm did not seem to have been enforced. Dora gave each man a roll of tobacco, Sarah sitting in the background to indicate that Dora was *baas* (the boss) here.

They stayed at Tobias until 7 July, leaving at sunset and trekking by moonlight ten miles to a trading store. On the 9th they outspanned on the slopes of the Ysterberg and on the 11th they reached Pietersburg. Sarah took Dora to visit Joao Albasini's daughter, who was highly indignant about the removal of the tribe they had met at Tweefontein. When the column had passed through Pietersburg she had been to see the general in charge and had "given it to him hot and strong". She had argued so forcibly against the wholesale deportation of the Africans that he had given up about 30 of them to her care. A few days later a telegram had come from Pretoria ordering her to give them back. As Mrs Biccard's husband was a government official her action was seen as brave.

After a few days they trekked to Solomon Marais's farm, where they were met by Frank. They rode up to Ravenshill at sunset on 24 July, a cool breeze heavy with the scent of thyme greeting them as they crested the ridge. The moon was coming over the horizon as they dismounted at "the very romantic abode", to be treated by Sarah Eland to a hearty supper.

All through August and into September Dora watched and noted the work on the farms. On 12 September Sarah was plainly ill again but persisted in a day-long supervision of Dockerell at work on lengthening Dora's wagon. Next day Dora's diary said: "Mrs H. very ill, had to lie down all day and spitting blood." It was a week before she was better and able to sit outside making a blouse. She had a favourite style – seen in the photograph taken by Duffus Bros in Johannesburg in 1892. She had once taken the photograph into an outfitters and had asked the man behind the counter if he had a blouse like that in stock. He had taken one look, shuddered and said, "I sincerely hope not." Sarah often recounted this story to her friends, shaking with laughter each time. "The only way to be sure you get what you want is to make it yourself," she told Dora.

The 29 September was a Sunday, sunny and warm. "In afternoon went for a walk with Frank," wrote Dora. Imperceptibly the tone of her references to Frank changed. She had last seen him when he was a schoolboy and had been unprepared for the bronzed, good-looking young man he had become. He seemed older than his 22 years. The diary became less of a record of what Sarah did and said and more entries began with Frank's activities, whether ploughing or playing a prank on his mother – as when he put a stuffed snakeskin in her bed. "She had a particular horror of snakes, but Mrs Heckford mercifully let the cat out of the bag."

Time was going on and Dora's return passage to England was booked. The diary ends abruptly with an entry on 2 October, recording "a long and pretty walk with Frank", and she must have left soon after. Sarah went with her as far as Johannesburg and from there to spend Christmas at Nooitgedacht. Her arrival was celebrated with a picnic joined by all the cousins in the neighbourhood.

On Christmas Day a young tree in a clearing in a ravine above the house was decorated. In the evening wagons that had brought many of the Jennings and Hinds families were drawn up round the tree, illuminated by Chinese lanterns and a big campfire. There were fireworks and the children capered about in masks. The rocks of the mountainside reflected the glow and the mountain top was outlined against stars in a black velvet sky. Sarah thought she had never beheld so enchanting a scene.

She had long talks with George Hinds on the economics of farming in the Transvaal. He drew up several plans of farm management from which Sarah worked out that a farm school would need 100 acres and that the initial cost of establishment would be £10,000. The revenues from the Witwatersrand had filled the Republican government coffers, but a great deal was being dissipated in corruption and whether the Volksraad would vote money for a scheme such as Sarah had in mind was doubtful. The money would have to be raised as a charity. Sarah could not advance capital to start the project as she had in the case of the East London Hospital. By this time she had given away almost all her money, or had lost it in various ventures, and she had barely enough to live on. Though she was only 56 she was ailing and looked much older, but the former zeal still burned high, her sense of fun unimpaired. As she could not provide the money herself she would go to England and raise funds among the more wealthy and influential of her friends there.

She left during February 1896. In April Frank wrote to her at the Nicholsons with news of Ravenshill and Dora's investment at Tobias. He asked about "the progress of your farm schemes", beginning his letters "My Dear Coz" and sending messages to "Miss Scrimgeour". Her hosts and her sister Annie were shocked to see Sarah so ill but she refused to have a doctor, preferring to dose herself with homeopathic medicines to which she had been converted 20 years before and in which she had implicit faith. She relented only to the extent of seeing an eye specialist.

Exactly when Sarah returned to South Africa and whether she went alone or with Dora Scrimgeour is not known, but they were both back at Ravenshill by the middle of 1897. On 30 November Dora and Frank Eland were married at Nylstroom. Dora was nearly 12 years older than her husband but it was the happiest and most successful of marriages.

20
War once more

Work on the permanent brick farmhouse continued with fresh impetus now that it was to be Frank and Dora's home as well as his mother's. Whether Sarah Heckford felt that it was now Frank's place entirely, where she would be only a guest, or whether it was simply her health that prevented it, it seems that she never spent any considerable time at Ravenshill again after the end of 1897 and may indeed never have been there at all.

Early in 1898 she was in Pretoria sounding out various ways of proceeding with her farm schools project. She launched an association under the name of The Transvaal Women's Educational Union, enrolling members among the farming communities she knew. She felt that the mothers were those most acutely concerned over the provision of education for young children on the farms and that if they would band together in sufficient numbers they could bring some pressure to bear both on their menfolk – the voters – and on the government to do something about it. She enrolled an almost equal number of English and Boer women. This was deliberate policy as she saw the future of the country depended on the children growing up together, knowing each other's language and understanding each other's ways. The schools, she thought, must be bilingual, though this conflicted with Kruger's policy. How many women actually joined the Union is not known. A list of 25 names which includes Mary Jennings survives from 1900, but it is not clear whether this was the total membership or whether it was the Council of the Union, of which Sarah was the secretary.

At Nooitgedacht there were changes following Augusta's marriage. Mary Jennings divided the farm equally between her daughters and in 1898 work began on a house for Augusta and Harry on the eastern portion. It included Groenfontein and to distinguish it from her sister's property Augusta called it Fountains. Her only child, a girl, was born on 2 June of that year. Sarah was deeply moved when the baby was christened Muriel Heckford. Pleased as she had been to be godmother to "little Sarah's" daughter, this christening of Augusta's child with her beloved Nathaniel's name touched her more than she could find words to express.

The new house at Fountains was completed at the end of the year and Sarah returned to Nooitgedacht – as governess. This time her pupils were Willie and Gladys Hinds, then aged nine and five. George Hinds had enlarged the house and there was a comfortable schoolroom. Sarah's diary for this period has been preserved. It covers about two years and on it she based *Nooitgedacht: A True Tale of Peace and War*. About 3,000 words long, it was probably published in a magazine in 1901. It tells the story of the Jennings family from their arrival in the Transvaal, and life at Nooitgedacht from the time William and Mary took it over up to 1900. Sarah passionately espoused the cause of the long established English families in the Transvaal, like the Jenningses, who had become pawns between tricky British politicians and wily, hostile Boers. Loyal to the country of their fathers' birth, which most of them had never seen, they adopted the Transvaal as their home and became burghers. They played, or tried to play, a part in the affairs of their new country, never dreaming that their status as citizens could ever lead to their being commandeered to fight against Britain. The argument about British suzerainty over the Transvaal seems to have passed over their heads. They saw no conflict between their love of Britain and loyalty to their new country. Many of them had married into Boer families. They frequently had a touching faith in the virtues of British rule. All this had led to was that they were regarded with suspicion at best, outright enmity at worst, by most of the Boers while being disowned by Britain. The injustice of this stung Sarah into action.

Her story of Nooitgedacht contains her only surviving comment on the idiocy of the Jameson Raid. She thought it ill-judged, to say the least. While sympathising with the Reformers she was bitterly opposed to the means they adopted to gain their ends. She also understood the fears of Kruger and his supporters of being swamped if the *Uitlanders* in Johannesburg were given the vote, and of the liberalism of the newcomers. She saw, too, that the Boers could not understand the *Uitlander* demands for such fripperies as playing fields, schools, hospitals, piped water supplies and waterborne sewerage, amenities which they had never enjoyed themselves – except to some degree in Pretoria with its predominantly English population – and which they did not consider necessary. Her anger at the position in which the "loyal Africanders" had found themselves in 1881 and the treatment they had received over the years was directed not at the Boers but at the British Government.

From the time of the Jameson Raid it was obvious to Sarah, as to many others, that war was inevitable. It had nearly come in October 1895 when Kruger had made the blunder of closing the drifts on the Vaal River to overseas – in effect British – goods in an attempt to enforce his tariff policy, thus breaching the London Convention (which had superseded the Pretoria Convention of 1881). Britain had diverted troops en route to India to the Cape and had sent warships to Delagoa Bay. Gunboat diplomacy had paid off and Kruger had backed down on that occasion, but all who knew the Transvaal understood that this was not the end of the matter. With the annexation of Bechuanaland and Kosi Bay and the development of Matabeleland and Mashonaland as Rhodesia, the Boers, desperate for an outlet to the sea independent of the British, felt themselves hedged in and threatened.

When the crisis came, in September 1899, Sarah was still at Nooitgedacht. She was sitting in the schoolroom with Gladys and Willie when a man galloped up to the door on a lathered horse. Sarah's heart sank – she knew it meant news of war. Hurrying out of the room she heard the message the rider had brought: every man, horse, ox and African was to be at the veld cornet's by five o'clock. Though expected, it still came as a shock. George and Harry Hinds were just two of the Transvaal English who were caught in a cruel dilemma. The idea of fighting British soldiers, whom they regarded as their countrymen, appalled them; yet to disobey the order to join the commando could be dangerous – they had no illusions about the vengeance their Boer neighbours might exact. Both men told their wives that they would go but would never fire a shot at the British. Somehow they would throw away or hide their ammunition so that it would not be known how little they had used.

Sarah hurried to Augusta's house, knowing she would be on her own with the baby when Harry left. As she went, George said, "It will soon be over. In a fortnight I shall either be back and a free British subject, or I shall have been killed." Harry was more sombre when she saw him. "I know I shall never see you again," he said as he wrung her hand. "They can force me to go to the front because I am afraid of what might happen to my wife and child if I refuse, but I will never fire a shot against an Englishman – never." Many other men of English descent who found themselves in the same position took similar action. They were dubbed "traitors" by the British. The Boers appeared to understand them better.

Sarah's heart was ready to break for the two young men

and their wives and she thought also of Frank and Dora. Frank had left Ravenshill some weeks before, aiming to join the volunteers. When he reached Natal, just as the war had started, he heard that Dora, who had remained with his mother, was pregnant. Risking being caught by commandos he returned to Ravenshill to fetch her. He took her to England where their baby, Dora, was born, and then went back to join the Imperial Light Horse at Pietermaritzburg on 16 March 1900.

At Nooitgedacht Sarah kept the children hard at their lessons though she wondered privately whether it was not of more benefit to her than to them. They had no real news of the war for several weeks and then one evening as they were at supper, George walked in, grubby, exhausted, but unharmed. He had been released from the commando – perhaps the officers suspected that he lacked the will to fight – and allowed to return home on the understanding that he would till and sow the lands of Boers in the Hekpoort valley who were on commando, and generally look after the interests of their families. Within a few days Harry came home on the same terms.

The coming months brought a peculiar strain to the beleaguered families at Nooitgedacht. George Hinds had 36 Boer families to look after. He lent them oxen, seed and milch cows, gave them sheep, tilled their lands, supervised their African labourers and was even asked to flog their children when they were disobedient! On top of this when his fruit ripened, carts arrived which had to be loaded with fruit for the wives of the burghers on commando. Sarah protested. "These women had never been so well off in their lives." Most trying of all, everyone at Nooitgedacht had to listen unmoved to rejoicing over real or imaginary British reverses, not daring to reveal their real feelings for fear of a complaint being lodged with the veld cornet that they were friendly to the English.

As week succeeded week with no reliable news, Sarah found it difficult to keep up her courage. After a while another of the Hinds brothers, Fred, managed to have himself transferred to the Ambulance Corps. He was a great source of comfort as he arranged a code by which he could get news to them. If his letters said he had a headache, then the British had achieved a minor success; if he had a bad headache they had won a victory. If he had a toothache the Boers had triumphed. The number of casualties he mentioned was to be multiplied by four if he referred to the Boers and divided by two if to the British. He was with the Boer ambulance corps at the relief of Ladysmith. His letter to Nooitgedacht began, "I have a severe headache," and ended "My head is so bad I cannot write more," which was received with apparently unsympathetic jubilation.

Their Boer neighbours believed the war would be irretrievably lost if Ladysmith were relieved. After Cronje's surrender at Paardeberg, on the anniversary of Majuba, it became difficult to persuade them to remain on commando. As did other Boer generals in the field, Cronje had had his wife with him, looking after him and cooking his meals. It can fairly be stated that her presence contributed to his surrender and the capture of 4,000 men by the British.

When the work for which George and Harry had been released was done they feared they would be commandeered again, so determined to hide in the rocky recesses of the Magaliesberg above the farm. They had only just left when a Boer rode up towards the homestead. A resourceful African, who had seen his masters set out and knew they could not have gone far, kept the Boer in conversation until George and Harry had got clear away. When the Boer reached the house and showed Sarah Hinds his commandeering order she replied that her husband and brother-in-law were away "looking for cattle", which in the Transvaal was synonymous with "indefinitely".

The men continued hidden, returning to their homes only in darkness, until one bright morning at the end of May Sarah Hinds hurried into the schoolroom and said, "I can't help it – I must interrupt you. We can hear the guns!" They all ran out onto the stoep. They heard a low, ominous sound to the west of them, in the distance. Throughout the day it moved to the south-west and then to the south, growing louder and louder.

The women knew that the British were engaged along a line from Krugersdorp to Johannesburg and were not more than 25 miles from them. The firing died away at dusk but tension was too great to let them sleep and they listened till dawn for the cannonade to resume. When it did not they knew the British had taken Johannesburg.

Fugitive Boers called at the farm for refreshment for themselves and their horses, as anxious to escape their own commandos as to evade the British troops. It must be only a matter of days, Sarah thought, before Lord Roberts reached Pretoria. Wild stories circulated among the Boers of the valley of what the British would do to them. One woman sent her little boy to Sarah Hinds with a note, asking her to protect him as the British were coming down the valley murdering all the boys and taking the women and girls prisoners!

The next day, 1 June, Sarah, with Harry Hinds, tried to get through to Krugersdorp, ten miles away, to find out what had happened, but had to turn back when they came across a commando camped across the road. Cornelius Kruger, the veld cornet, was attempting to find reinforcements for Botha and to Sarah it seemed essential that the neighbourhood should be disarmed. News eventually filtered through that Lord Roberts had taken Pretoria on 5 June, and on the 11th Sarah set off on her own, intent on reporting to him the state of affairs in the Hekpoort valley. It is likely she saw Roberts himself. In any event Colonel Airey was sent with 300 of the New South Wales Bushrangers to occupy the valley as a result of her information. When she returned to Nooitgedacht she found that the Australian soldiers had made themselves highly popular with all the children around. Both Boer and English "Africander" alike were handing in their arms and taking an oath of neutrality.

As soon as the Australians withdrew the oath was ignored by the Boers. Two weeks later Sarah was with Augusta at Fountains when a party of Boers ordered Harry Hinds to join the commando then being assembled, under pain of confiscation of all he possessed. Harry flatly refused. Their spokesman demanded his horses. "I can't stop you taking them," said Harry. "You are armed but I gave up my guns. I will not break the oath I have taken. I am no longer a burgher."

"So much the worse for you," growled one of the party, who had taken the neutrality oath at the same time as Harry. "Mind you keep on your farm and reckon that everything you have is confiscated." With this they went off to the stables. After some debate they left Sarah's horse, as she was a British subject, but took another belonging to Harry. A third and more valuable horse had been sneaked out of the stable by an African farm worker while the Boers were at the house and was being held in hiding while this was going on. Sarah, who had seen what was happening, was terrified that the hidden animal would neigh and give itself away, but all was well. They managed to keep the horse out of sight for three months while the Boers, who knew it well, occupied the Magaliesberg above the farm and wondered where it had got to.

After dark George came across from Nooitgedacht to tell his brother he had received the same treatment. They were concerned that Lord Roberts should know the valley was in open insurrection, that hidden arms had been brought out and that the small bodies of British soldiers guarding Commandonek and Silkaatsnek were in danger. To Sarah it was obvious she must go. The family pleaded with her; she was ill and coughing badly – it was winter – but she refused to listen. She was up before dawn the next morning and this time she made no stop on the way to Pretoria. She rode the 60 miles in one day, warning the men at Commandonek as she passed. She had just celebrated her 60th birthday.

There was no going back. She stayed in Pretoria fretting

and fuming, knowing that the family were prisoners on Nooitgedacht. The British forces moved 25 miles west of Pretoria but it was some time before General Clements's men reached Hekpoort. When they were about 12 miles away George and Harry Hinds, warned by a friendly African that the Boers planned to arrest them the next day, managed to leave the farm at night and get through to the British lines. When the commando came to demand her husband, Sarah Hinds told them he had gone, and added, "Do you think I would wish to see him driven off in front of you, a prisoner, like my poor Uncle Jere Jennings yesterday? I would rather shoot myself." It was a risky speech but the Boers admired her for it.

The commando kept strict watch on the women after that and made frequent demands for food and stores. Not that the British Tommies, or "Khakis", as the locals called them, were any less of a nuisance when they arrived. One old woman hid her *kerkklere* (Sunday best) in a large tin when she heard they were coming. To her dismay the Tommies soon found it when they searched her house for arms, and she saw one of them arrayed in her precious finery for his mates' amusement. Sarah Hinds missed a bucket of freshly churned butter she had placed near the pantry window. She scolded the servant, who pointed out of the window. She glimpsed a British Tommy galloping off on his horse and that was the last she saw of the bucket or the butter.

General Clements marched to Hekpoort at the beginning of December 1900, and camped on the western side of Nooitgedacht. De la Rey and his commando were nearby, hidden in the mountains, and General Beyers was known to be coming from the north. Clements ruled that it was no longer safe for the women and, sadly, as they had 20 years before, they packed up and moved to the security of Pretoria.

Sarah, meanwhile, had been far from idle since her arrival nearly five months earlier. At the outbreak of war the schools in Pretoria had been closed. Sarah offered her services to the British authorities to help reorganise and reopen them, help which was accepted. She also turned with renewed enthusiasm to her work for the farm schools. If the Transvaal was to be once more under British rule there was a real chance of their being established and also a more urgent need for them. Sarah foresaw that once the war ended there would be hundreds, if not thousands, of destitute women and children who must be provided for. She had planned the schools on cottage lines with "House Mothers" in charge of small groups of children out of school hours – she was in favour of as many as possible being boarders. This would give work and accommodation to war widows. All through the final months of 1900 she worked on a report on the *Educational Needs of the Transvaal Colony from the Transvaal Women's Educational Union to the Education Department of the Colony*. She finally signed it "by order of the Union" as honorary secretary, on 12 March 1901, and sent it to the printers. With it was appended the agricultural plan which George Hinds had drawn up as a working basis in 1895.

She had also formed another plan, a project for adult education. A Boer friend had said to her, "All this would never have happened if my people had had a knowledge of history and had properly appreciated the relative position of Britain and the Transvaal and what all the fine words of the people in Europe were really worth." This had set her thinking. She saw that if the children were to have schooling it might cause a breach with their parents who had none, and that the best the teachers could do might be undone by ignorant or bigoted elders. She soon devised a practical method of dealing with the problem: popular lectures in world history and geography, illustrated by "magic lantern slides". Lecturers would travel the country districts, presenting lantern shows, recommending books for further reading and organising adult literacy groups for those who could not read. This scheme was outside the scope of what an education department could be expected to provide so she must go to England to raise the money for it there. She would also have to choose and buy the all-important lantern slides.

Mary Jennings and her children and grandchildren had scarcely reached Pretoria when the Battle of Nooitgedacht was launched before dawn on 13 December 1900. It raged over the farm but principally in the ravine below the pass where, five years before, they had held their Christmas party. This time the fireworks were deadly. The fighting was fierce and casualties on both sides heavy before Clements withdrew from Nooitgedacht to Yeomanry Hill, across the valley. It was a brilliant Boer victory but not as conclusive as it might have been. De la Rey had made the mistake of dismounting his men too far from the scene. Even then he and Beyers might have annihilated the British had their men maintained discipline and pressed home their initial success. Instead they descended on the camp near the Nooitgedacht homestead and started looting the abandoned tents and wagons. When they had grabbed as much as they could carry many of them mounted their horses and rode off home. Clements was thus given time to withdraw his guns and the remnants of his force. On the 19th he returned with reinforcements and drove the Boers back further to the west.

The wounded were taken to the military hospital in Pretoria, some of them Boers. Sarah visited the wards and talked to a number of the men. "Never," said one of the wounded Boer prisoners, "shall I forget the bravery of General Clements – it was more than human. I didn't think any man could be so brave." In the next bed a Tommy said to Sarah, "There was one of the 'Helios', he was on the edge of a precipice and he heliographed, 'Boers within 30 paces, ammunition spent, send relief', and rolled over the edge rather than be taken prisoner." Sarah looked at him in horror, seeing in her mind's eye the sheer mountainside with its rocky crown. It must have been a fall of several hundred feet at least. "Don't worry, Ma'am, he only broke three ribs. He's getting on fine," said the soldier. "I was with the ambulance and picked him up."

"Our men were heavily outnumbered," said Sarah. "That's all fair," said the ambulance man. "We've generally outnumbered them. They fought grandly. It's a pity to kill such men, but it's a pleasure to fight them. It was a beautiful battle. We knew we were outnumbered and we fought well, too, I can tell you. It was beautiful, the most beautiful battle in the whole campaign."

"This is like listening to a page from Froissart," thought Sarah, moved by the generosity of the man to his foes. "They treated the wounded well, too," he went on after a pause. "Gave them everything they wanted and looked after them as if they were friends. There was no ill-feeling between us. When we were leaving I shook hands with them and thanked them. One old fellow brought us some pumpkins and things and said we hadn't burnt his house so he must give us something."

"Now who could that have been?" Sarah wondered as she moved on down the ward. Meanwhile Nooitgedacht was a desert. The old homestead had been used as a hospital and so had not been too badly damaged but Augusta's new house was almost razed and had to be completely rebuilt after the war. Soldiers of both sides were buried there.

Sarah Heckford had no sooner finished her education report in March 1901 than she fell seriously ill. This time it was thought she was dying. She was staying with Mrs James, who had also moved to Pretoria. A night nurse was engaged while Ivy Scrooby, Alginy's daughter, came in to help during the day. Mary Jennings was a constant and anxious visitor and so was Frank Eland, who was now stationed at the Pretoria Depot of the Bushveld Carbineers. On 24 April Frank wrote to Dora, who had returned from England with the baby and was staying at Howick, in Natal, that Sarah was recovering. "She had a very bad attack of bronchitis and several times was given over by the doctor." A week or two later he wrote that Sarah was "better though still very weak" and intended leaving for England about 18 June.

She evidently did so as she wrote to Mary Jennings on 12 July on board the *Carisbrooke Castle*, giving her address as "near the Bay of Biscay". She now felt much stronger "and am less lean, I cannot say fatter". Sarah looked forward to hearing news of Mary and her family when she reached The Grange, where she would be staying for a while with the Nicholsons. "I don't suppose there will be anyone to meet me. I did not tell the exact ship I was coming by, for I do not like being met, it causes confusion," she continued with a flash of her habitual independence.

She arrived in England to find herself a minor celebrity. Letters she had written to the Press over the previous year had attracted a good deal of attention. The first, written from Pretoria on 26 July 1900 to *The Spectator*, had dealt over two columns with the British treatment of the "Africander Loyalists". Another shorter one to the same paper was published on 5 January 1901. In this Sarah told of a conversation between Boer prisoners on their way to Ceylon and the Englishman in charge of them. He had said, "You will return to the Transvaal to find all peaceful, and will live happily ever after under the Union Jack." "Never can we live under that flag," came an emphatic chorus in reply. "You treat the blacks, who are savages and murderers, as equals. In the Colony you will allow them to walk on the sidewalks. One might even have to sit next to a black woman in church." The comment Sarah added to this was: "When you get down to the rock-bed of the true and unsophisticated Boer's anti-British feeling it is always this. He wants, like the Southerner before the [American Civil] war, to be able to 'wallop his own nigger', and the dread, and indeed the knowledge, that he will not be able to do this if the British win make him ready to do and risk everything. It is the thought of the nigger on the sidewalk that maddens him, not the destruction of the Republic or the lowering of the Vierkleur."

On 20 April *The Spectator* published another long letter on the subject of education in South Africa. She said the Boers should not be blamed for the state of education in the Transvaal because matters were almost as bad in the Cape Colony, where few children went beyond Standard III or IV (Grade 5 or 6). She castigated the shortcomings of the Cape educational system, in particular the teaching of history, which did not begin until Standard V (Grade 7) and was totally inadequate then. The syllabus for 1900 covered English history only from 1066 to 1688 and the history of the Cape from the founding of the colony by the Dutch in 1652 to the outbreak of war in 1899. No other history, and no geography beyond that of South Africa, was included. She made a plea for teaching not "dates of kings and battles", but the history of men and ideas, of social development, of religion, from ancient Egypt and Rome to modern times, in all schools from an early stage. The history of the Christian religion should "take its due share, but not more, in universal history. In thus teaching history we also doom the religious bigotry of the Boers to slow but sure destruction". An editorial footnote read, "We print Mrs Heckford's eloquent and profoundly interesting letter with the greatest pleasure, and with strong hope that it will not pass unheeded by those on whom will fall the duty of dealing with the education problem in the new Colonies."

The letter was taken up by *The Natal Witness*, which expanded it into a lengthy article under the headline "Shaping the Future". This article mentioned another by Sarah which apparently was printed in several papers and magazines, in which she appealed for great care in choosing officials for the new colonies when peace came. Much had been made of "The crooked ways very common in Mr Kruger's regime", but Mrs Heckford pointed out that there had been British officials "who were very far from being straightforward themselves" and this must not happen in future.

As soon as she arrived at the Nicholsons, Sarah was overwhelmed with requests to speak on the subject of South Africa and the Transvaal. Before she could make plans Emily Hobhouse's first broadside against the concentration camps in which Boer women and children and a few old men were being held, was fired. Sarah, like many South Africans since, was infuriated when people visiting the country for a few weeks, looked at it with preconceptions formed in Europe and misinterpreted much of what they saw. On 5 August *The Times* published an article by Sarah headed: "We have received the following statement from Mrs Sarah Heckford, who has just returned to England after a residence of many years in the Transvaal. Mrs Heckford is not unknown in philanthropic circles in this country, and some readers may yet remember the description given by Charles Dickens of his visit to the children's hospital which Dr and Mrs Heckford had just brought into existence, and where they lived, in the neighbourhood of Shadwell. Mrs Heckford settled in the South African Republic more than 20 years ago, and has passed through both Transvaal wars. Having lived as a farmer among farmers, she has naturally acquired a peculiarly intimate knowledge of the Boer character and way of life."

Sarah's statement began, "Miss Hobhouse ... asserts that she is well qualified to give an opinion on the state of the concentration camps. Pray allow me the opportunity of asserting publicly that she is not." After this stinging commencement she went on to demolish the greater part of what Emily Hobhouse had said. With her own memories of the camp in the siege of Pretoria still vivid she said: "In a country distracted with war no camp can be otherwise than unhygienic." Miss Hobhouse's report was a vindication rather than otherwise of the British authorities. It was inevitable that children and feeble adults would suffer when war swept through a country, and "all hearts may well bleed when realising the cost of war. When, however, Miss Hobhouse harrows her own feelings and endeavours to harrow ours by describing what she imagines to be hardships to Boer women and children in the concentration camps she provokes a smile from those who know the habits of the Boers. They were used in their own homes to what people in England would regard as overcrowding to a shocking degree, and were indifferent to what many in Europe would regard as the elements of comfort". Sarah had seen too many Boer farmhouses to think otherwise. As for Emily's horror at women being housed in tents, Sarah was reminded "of many I have sat in when visiting well-to-do Boer families who were in the Bushveld with their cattle on what constitutes to large numbers of these people a sort of annual picnic". Sarah did not add that she herself spent many nights sleeping in a wagon or on the ground under the stars and considered that no hardship.

She went on to say that many Boers on commando were delighted to know that their women were safe and being fed and housed. It freed them from anxiety while they prosecuted the war and many whose wives were still on their farms had demanded that they be admitted to the camps. Sarah paid tribute to the bravery and hardihood of the Boer women, of whose lives during and after the Great Trek Miss Hobhouse seemed to know nothing. "Miss Hobhouse is, I conclude, unaware of how well the Boer women have served, and are still serving, the commandos as intelligence officers, spies and even as decoys. If she knew this she would hardly consider their being kept under some supervision a hardship, or wish them to be left at liberty. They cannot appeal to sympathy on the plea of harmless womanhood, for they have proved themselves to be dangerous enemies. We may admire their courage but they have forfeited the right to be considered non-belligerents."

It would be interesting to know whether Miss Hobhouse knew of women like Mrs Cronje, or of the Boer women who fought beside their men in the laagers when they were attacked by Africans in the early days. Sarah did know and had a great respect for these women. She suspected that

Emily saw them only as helpless drawing room ornaments, as so many middle class Englishwomen still were.

There was more in the same vein and Sarah took the opportunity of bringing up the subject of adult education in the Transvaal, for which she had come to raise funds, submitting that it was a question of political emergency rather than of education in the ordinary acceptance of the term. She had "no accurate knowledge except of the Transvaal, therefore I speak of it alone; but the South African problem is concentrated in the Transvaal". She was right in this analysis and it is still largely true now.

The battle was joined. Letters poured in supporting Sarah and others supporting Emily. "I see you annihilated Miss Hobhouse in a few sentences," read one. The clash of these two eccentric Englishwomen, both doughty champions against injustice, both waxing emotional in the causes they took up, each absolutely sure she was right, provided fine entertainment for newspaper readers and those who attended their meetings. There was impressive support for both sides.

21

The end of the story

In the midst of her contest with Emily Hobhouse Sarah was stunned by news of Frank Eland's death. He had been killed in action at Duiwelskloof, only a few miles from Ravenshill. His body was taken there to his mother and he was buried on the hillside, just below the house. In due time his mother, his wife and his daughter's husband were buried near him. To stand by the graves, with the wind rustling the grass and trees and to look out over the plain where Frank first learnt to handle a plough, to the ranges of mountains beyond, brings the visitor close to understanding what drew Sarah and Frank and other pioneers before them to this beautiful part of Africa.

Shaken with grief, Sarah wrote to Dora, who replied in a calm, brave letter on black-bordered paper. Private grief, however, was not going to deter Sarah from the work she felt called to do. She stayed with friends in Wales while she planned the lantern lectures to be used by the Transvaal Women's Educational Union in their adult education project. She kept up her letters to the Press. On 19 August 1901, *The Times* printed an immensely long letter from her on Boer treatment of Africans in the Transvaal, in which she took Sir William Harcourt to task for remarks during a House of Commons debate in which he claimed that the Pass Laws "were only a mild measure of police". She described their operation as she had seen it, the exactment of hut tax and the treatment of Africans in Soutpansberg while she was there – in particular what had been done to Modjadji and her people. She recounted a story of Kruger on commando in the early days which had been told her by an eyewitness. The letter ended, "Mr Labouchere, in the same debate, says that 'the real truth was that there were only two things a black man wanted, and they were a bottle of brandy to get drunk and a gun to shoot his neighbour'. This statement was received with laughter. It is much to be regretted that members should not have more regard for their own dignity than to laugh at such a manifest falsehood, the flippancy of which should be as offensive to our legislators as it certainly would be to numbers of respectable, although very ignorant, Kaffirs. I am no negrophilist, but I do not think we, who are even now trusting so much to the self-restraint of our Kaffir subjects, should allow such a remark to pass unchallenged."

One of *The Times* correspondents who backed Sarah up was Sir Bartle Frere, who had been in Pretoria and may have known her personally.

Christmas of 1901 was spent with childhood friends at Portsmouth and was a happy interlude after several months of reading and research for her lectures on history and geography. She had spent much time looking at lantern slides and selecting the ones that best illustrated her themes. It had been a strain on her failing sight and she was glad to rest her eyes for a few days. The house was full of children and "there was any amount of merry racket on Christmas Day, and all sorts of games. A drum and trumpet were performed on with wonderful perseverance during the rest of my visit". The house brought back memories of her happy time with Nathaniel, for paintings she had done as a girl and which had decorated the wards of the East London Hospital hung on the walls. There was also a picture of the hospital dog, Poodles, who had been given to these friends when Sarah left England. The original drawing of the New

Year's Eve party at the hospital, which showed Poodles, Sarah and Nathaniel, and which had been published in *The Illustrated London News*, was there also.

She went back to Totteridge to the Nicholsons – Sir Charles was now 93 but still went up to his office in the City occasionally (he died on 8 October 1903). On January 15 she wrote to Mary Jennings, "I am always thinking of you although I have been rather remiss about writing. I hope you will all know that it is because I really cannot get time. I seem to do nothing but write unless when I am seeing people. I am writing the lectures now and selecting the slides. It is pretty hard work." This letter shows clearly how homesick Sarah was for South Africa, that she felt herself now more South African than English. She had been remembering the Christmases she had spent at Nooitgedacht and thinking of her Transvaal friends. "It is very nice over here and people are most kind but I wish I could see you all, and have a talk and really know how you all are."

Among messages to the children, to Harry Hinds and to the rest of the family she reverted to the subject of the lectures. "They must be written." For the first time she seemed to admit that she may not herself be able to carry through the adult education scheme but was determined to set things up so that others may continue the work should she have to abandon it. She was still travelling the country on speaking engagements. "I think I am doing some good in enlightening people's minds and I seem to produce an impression on my hearers for many come up to me and say they understand things as they never understood them before."

From the moment the small figure limped onto the platform Sarah held her audience. She was an emotional speaker but she marshalled her facts and knew how to drive them home with anecdotes from her own experience. She could "think on her feet" and deal cogently with questions and firmly with heckling. Soon after she had written to Mary Jennings she went to Cambridge where, on a snowy day, she addressed a meeting of the Ladies' Discussion Society on "Opportunities for Women in South Africa". These, she said, ranged from buying a farm for those with about £3,000 in capital, or a market garden near a town if £600 to £800 was available, to employment as a dressmaker or a children's nurse.

She also spoke to the British Women's Emigration Association on this subject and to their South African Expansion Department on the topic of education, being the principal speaker at meetings in London. On 18 February *The Times* published a reply by Sarah to a correspondent at the Cape, protesting at his suggestion of "a large measure of amnesty" and a policy of compromise and "peace at any price". An editorial introduction to the letter said Sarah was in England as president of the "Transvaal Women's Education Association" and that she spoke for "the real loyalists of South Africa". It indicates that Sarah was by this time well known. She spoke "for the men of plain, heroic breed ... for the loyal Africanders who have stood devotedly by the English flag throughout the war. These are the people whom Mr Gladstone gave away in 1881 – one of the most shameful episodes in the history of the Empire".

Sarah protested vigorously against suggestions that when Boer prisoners of war returned home they should be absolved from an oath of loyalty and given money and grants of land to rehabilitate themselves. This would be an insult to the loyal Boers and Africanders, many of whom had been driven from their farms and who had lost everything at the hands of those Boers who had fought. A reward for past loyalty should surely be the first call on public funds. "I think it desirable," she wrote, "to draw attention to the feelings of truly loyal Africanders and to point out what they consider loyalty to mean." She recounted her experiences in the 1881 war and during the second Anglo-Boer War, then drawing to a close, instancing William Jennings and the Hinds brothers as examples of the loyalists she had in mind.

It was a long letter, at the end of which she reverted to the correspondent from the Cape. "The appeal to be tender of the honour of our brave enemies is admirable. How well these wily Boers know the weak point of an English audience and how well they know how to play to the gallery. They have misled us so often and have laughed at our folly. Let us beware of being misled now. The Boer leaders and those who have followed them must guard their own honour as best they can. If we are to pardon rebels and spend money on our enemies what does our honour require us to do for the numbers of truly loyal Africanders who have stood devotedly by the British flag? If we were to allow the Boers any terms but unconditional surrender how shall we English be able to look these people in the face at the termination of the War?"

This letter, dated from Totteridge on 13 February, was reprinted in pamphlet form by a London printer and given wide circulation.

In March Sarah wrote to many publications, including *The Times*, the *Pall Mall Gazette*, the *St James's Gazette* and *The Spectator*, appealing for funds to launch the adult education scheme. A thousand pounds, she urged, was all that was needed to provide lanterns and slides, to print the lectures and pay a team of operators. Some of the papers simply printed the letter, others expanded it into articles on education in South Africa and recounted Sarah's part in the scheme and her past philanthropic works.

On 30 May 1902, Sarah wrote to Mary, "I think peace is very near now and I shall be coming out soon." She asked Mary to find her "board and lodging. I can't afford a hotel". The Treaty of Vereeniging, which ended the war, was in fact signed the next day, 31 May, but it was some time before Sarah was able to leave.

The catalogue of her activities in 1901 and 1902 gives no hint of it but her health was rapidly worsening. She was now blind in one eye and had partially lost the sight of the other. The Nicholsons, her sister Annie and her friend Dr Frances Hoggan all begged her to give up any idea of returning to the Transvaal, but whether or not she could work when she got there she was determined to go. In September she paid a farewell visit to relatives of Nathaniel near Nottingham – she had remained on close and affectionate terms with his family ever since his death and also with their adopted daughter Marian Longobardi and her family in Naples. As soon as Sarah arrived she had to take to her bed and when she recovered a little she asked for a solicitor to have a fresh will drawn up. It was signed on 19 September, the straggling signature sad testimony to her weakness and increasing blindness. The will forgives her opulent cousin in Australia, Thomas Strettle, a debt he had owed her for 40 years. It appoints Annie Goff as executrix in England and Dora Eland in South Africa. Any personal effects in England she leaves to Annie and all her personal effects in South Africa to Mary Jennings. The residue of her estate, including any property she might have, whether in England or South Africa, is to go to Dora.

There is no further mention of Marian Longobardi in her memoir. She may well have assumed that since Marian had married into a good family in Naples, that she would have been well provided for. A portrait of Marian painted in 1929 has recently come to light and shows a distinguished old lady. Sarah kept photographs of her in her album, which was among the effects inherited by Mary and was still at Nooitgedacht in 1978, but the last mention of her in any surviving papers is a payment in her favour of £77 from Sarah's account with Coutts in 1882. However, they did in fact keep in touch until Sarah's death. Marian Longobardi lived on into the 1930s and had four children, Ernesto Cesare, Gabrielina, Cesare, and Eva. Her descendants are still living in Italy.

Sarah recovered and returned to Totteridge, but at the beginning of November 1902 Lady Nicholson wrote to Mary that Sarah was again forced to stay in bed and had had to abandon a plan to address a meeting. Lady Nicholson said this was just as well as it was snowing. Sarah had been kept amused by the antics of a kitten which had been brought up to her room but she fretted at being inactive and unable to read much. Lady Nicholson drew a pencil portrait of her. Perhaps one way of keeping her quiet was to make her pose! Sarah gave the picture to Mary and it hung in Augusta's house on Nooitgedacht.

By the end of the year the precious lectures were complete. She stayed for Christmas at Totteridge – Sir Charles's present to her was a copy of his book *Aegyptiaca*, the first catalogue of Egyptian antiquities and containing portions of *The Book of the Dead*. Immediately afterwards, with her magic lantern and boxes of slides, Sarah sailed for South Africa. Mary had found lodgings for her with a Mr and Mrs Springle in Norval's Cottages at the corner of Schoeman and Du Toit streets, Pretoria. When she arrived Sarah was too weak to embark on lectures and the lantern and slides were put into a furniture store, the Springles' cottage being too small to accommodate much luggage.

By April she was confined to bed, coughing and spitting blood. Dr Kay called frequently and after a few days brought in a Sister Faith to nurse her. Late on the evening of Friday, 17 April 1903, Sarah Heckford died, two months before her 63rd birthday.

The next day *The Pretoria News* announced her death "from an affection of the bronchial tubes" with regret "that will be shared by hundreds of old Transvalers". The obituary, which bears all the hallmarks of having been written by the editor, Vere Stent, said, "She was a worker among women whom we can ill afford, as a community, to lose. She took an advanced and more serious view of women's position in the economy of the State than is customary and her death is a serious loss indeed to the capital." It commends her books as "displaying a deal of literary merit and capability".

The funeral was on the Sunday afternoon, the cortège leaving the Springles' cottage at 3 o'clock. A long procession followed the coffin to the Old Cemetery in Church Street West, where they buried Sarah in the Wesleyan Methodist plot. The simple granite headstone records that she was the widow of Nathaniel Heckford and, her proudest achievement, that she was "co-foundress with him of the East London Children's Hospital". It adds that "later she adopted the Transvaal as her country, and devoted herself to its best interests". Whoever chose her epitaph chose well: "To thine own self be true."

The Times published a telegram announcing the death of Mrs Heckford the following morning and the next day, 21 April, carried the lengthy obituary which was quoted in the first chapter of this book. This was picked up and used by *The Star*, Johannesburg, and there were others.

What did Sarah actually achieve?

She was very much a woman of her times. She was an imperialist in that she believed with honesty and sincerity that the greatest good for all men everywhere was to come under British rule, that British justice and sense of fair play were her country's greatest gifts to the world. But she was far from believing "my country, right or wrong". When she thought it wrong, she said so, loud and clear. Likewise when she thought her country's enemies right or badly treated she spoke up and was quick to commend bravery and honesty wherever she found them. This independence of judgement made her unpopular in some quarters. It also accounts for her reputation as "pro-Boer", when in fact she did not like them, once even writing – in 1894 – "I loathe oppression and this 'War' [the Soutpansberg campaign] has made me hate the very sight of a Boer." Yet in the midst of the greater war that followed she could praise the courage and hardihood of Boer women, while they were fighting the British.

A Lady Trader in the Transvaal is fairly well known in South Africa, though not in England. When Mary Jennings went to collect the magic lantern and slides from store, she found they had been stolen. The lectures, however, were printed in London in 1905 by George Philip and Son, together with lists of the slides to be used and "Hints to Operators", so presumably the scheme went ahead. Farm schools were established – there was one near Pretoria.

The combination of an improvement in child health, which would have delighted Sarah and which lessened the need for children's hospitals in the East End of London, together with the workings of the National Health Service, have meant that the name of Sarah and Nathaniel's hospital has disappeared, though the work continues.

It is tempting to speculate what her story would have been had Nathaniel lived. He was the greatest single influence on her. Why, when *The Times* could call her "one of the most extraordinary women to whom the British nation has given birth" and say that her country cannot afford to let her memory "pass into oblivion", was she forgotten when others of no greater worth at least survived in reference books? She would want to be remembered as Nathaniel's wife and "cofoundress with him of the East London Hospital". It is sad the name has been lost in that form but the London Hospital is still there. It has a museum which holds the portraits of Sarah and Nathaniel.

She was obviously a powerful personality and a brave woman and this is what so strongly impressed her contemporaries. Her real memorial is her life and, perhaps her greatest achievement, that she lived every hour of every day. She fought ill-health and lameness from the age of nine, and had a virtual sentence of death pronounced on her by Nathaniel before he died, yet for another 30 years she remained true to herself and her philosophy of life, working for the betterment of others and refusing to give in either to illness or to the buffetings of fortune which so often snatched from her what she had dearly achieved. Her energies and considerable talents were dissipated in many different directions, though always with one end in view: to give to those who had less than she had. She espoused "la vie simple" and "self-sufficiency" many years before it became fashionable.

If Kipling could have conceived of his famous poem as applying to a woman one could think that it was Sarah Heckford who inspired it. If anyone ever filled "the unforgiving minute with sixty seconds worth of distance run" it was her. And she was notable for keeping her head when others were losing theirs. But perhaps after all we should remember her for her escape from young-lady-dom. It is thanks to Sarah and women like her that women today can have an independent existence, instead of being mere appendages of father or husband. We can be thankful that she leapt those "barriers armed with painfully sharp spikes" to a "wider life" and encouraged others to do the same.

Index

Afrikaanse Patriot, Die 193
All the Year Round magazine 66
Anderson, Elizabeth Garrett 10, 15, 59, 75, 76, 77, 78, 81
Anderson, Skelton 61, 75, 76, 77, 80, 81, 82
Anstruther, Lt.-Col 204
Argus 157

Baines, Thomas 142
Barclay, Experience, *see* Clibborn Family
Barnes, Dr 58, 59
Begam, Shah Jahan 94, 95
Bellairs, Col. 201, 204, 205, 212
Beyers, Gen. 283, 285
Bezuidenhout, Piet 194, 196
Birthday Mine 234, 235, 236, 237, 238, 247
Blaauwbank 142, 152, 153, 227, 228, 267, 268
Blackwell, Dr Elizabeth 29, 30
Bousfield, Bishop 151, 268, 269
British Medical Journal, The 61
British Women's Emigration Association 296
Brodrick, Albert 153
Bronkhorstspruit, Battle of 204
Burgher Right 232

Caesar, A.A. ("Julius") 58, 60, 68, 77, 81
Cambridge, Duke of 51
Carnarvon, Lord 192
Cetshwayo 103, 104, 105
Chelmsford, Viscount 105
Clark, Duncan and Malcolm 235
Clements, General 283, 285
Clibborn, Abigail 17, 18, 19, 20
Clibborn family 16, 17, 25
Clibborn, Mary, 17
Colley, Sir George 201, 204, 211, 212
Colquhoun 121, 122
Cooper, Advocate Henry 151, 198
Coutts, bankers 8, 20, 55, 60, 70, 91, 169, 298
Cronje, Commandant Piet 194, 198, 201, 280

Daily Telegraph, The 51
Deecker, Charles 207
De la Rey, General 283, 285
De Wet, Judge 198
Dicke brothers 244, 245, 246, 248, 251, 259
Dickens, Charles 64, 65, 66, 67, 68, 69, 70, 289

303

Dingane 103
Dingane's Day 201, 247
Dunn, John 104
Du Toit, S.J. 192
Du Val, Charles 9, 207, 219

East London Hospital for Children 8, 16, 59, 61, 65–83, 87, 95, 111, 139, 165, 220, 223, 273, 294, 300, 301
East London Hospital, The Story of 56, 80, 220
Eland, Dora (née Scrimgeour) 9, 222, 224, 225, 226, 228, 229, 231, 232, 233, 243, 245, 246, 247, 255, 257, 262, 263, 266, 267, 268, 269, 270, 271, 272, 273, 274, 275, 279, 286, 293, 298
Eland, Frank 9, 231, 233, 234, 239, 243, 244, 245, 249, 251, 253, 254, 256, 257, 258, 259, 262, 265, 267, 272, 273, 274, 275, 279, 286, 293
Eland, Sarah (née Fetherstonehaugh) 220, 225, 231, 233, 234, 252, 257, 265, 272
Elizabeth, Princess 65
English, Dinah, *see* Clibborn family
Englishwoman's Journal, The 25
Erasmus, Daniel (of Platland) 238, 246, 248, 257
Excelsior 9, 23, 56, 136, 219, 229

Ford, Edward 140
Frere, Sir Bartle 104, 105, 192, 294

Garrett, Elizabeth, *see* Anderson
Genootskap van Regte Afrikaners 193
Geskiedenis van ons Land, Die 193
Gildea, Lt.-Col. 203, 205, 207

Gladstone, William Ewart 32, 296
Gladstone, Mrs 32
Goff, Annie 17, 18, 19, 21, 24, 25, 33, 50, 51, 52, 53, 54, 55, 220, 222, 274, 297, 298
Goff Family 8, 16, 17, 25, 36, 83
Goff, Gerald 96
Goff, Robert 18, 19, 20, 21, 27
Goff, William 16, 17, 18, 25
Great Ormond Street Hospital 57
Grobler, Cornelis 235

Harcourt, Sir William 293
Hartley, Fred 228
Hartley, Henry 142, 228
Heckford Family 8, 70
Heckford, Marian, *see* Longobardi
Heckford, Dr Nathaniel 8, 16, 24, 35, 36, 37, 40,41, 43, 44, 47, 48, 49, 50, 51, 52, 53, 54, 55, 56, 57, 58, 59, 60, 61, 62, 63, 64, 65, 66, 67, 69, 70, 71, 72, 73, 74, 75, 76, 77, 78, 79, 80, 81, 82, 83, 85, 86, 91, 92, 94, 136, 162, 174, 221, 223, 258, 265, 266, 276, 289, 294, 295, 298, 300, 301
Heckford, Nathaniel (Master Mariner) 36, 58
Heys, George 223
Hicks-Beach, Sir Michael 192, 193
Hinds, Alice (Jennings) 145, 146, 148, 151, 154, 157, 159, 161, 209, 224, 268, 269
Hinds, Clifford Augusta (née Jennings) 142, 143, 144, 146, 148, 151, 152, 155, 164, 165, 224, 229, 268, 269, 276, 278, 282, 286, 299
Hinds, Fred 279
Hinds, George 224, 266, 269, 273, 276, 278, 279, 280, 282, 283, 284

304

Hinds, Gladys 276
Hinds, Harry Clement 269, 276, 278, 279, 280, 281, 282, 283, 295
Hinds, Sarah Hannah Maud (née Jennings) 142–149, 154, 155, 224, 268, 269, 276, 280, 281, 283
Hinds, Thomas 209, 224, 268, 269
Hinds, Willie 276
Hobhouse, Emily 289, 290, 291, 293
Hoggan, Dr Frances 91, 297
Hudson, George 205
Hugo, Victor 25

Illustrated London News, The 9, 71, 159, 295

James, R.T.N. 210, 220, 222, 266
Jennens, James 140
Jennens, Mary 140, 141
Jennens (Jennings), James 140, 141, 142, 145, 148, 151, 157, 161, 162
Jennings, Ada 145, 146, 148, 151, 153, 154, 157, 159, 161
Jennings, Alice, *see* Hinds
Jennings, Clifford Augusta, *see* Hinds
Jennings, James William ("William") 9, 136, 137, 139, 140, 142, 143, 145, 147, 149, 152, 153, 154, 157, 158, 159, 160, 161, 164, 165, 166, 168, 169, 170, 176, 209, 213, 214, 216, 276, 296
Jennings, Jeremiah ("Jere") 152, 268, 283
Jennings, John 152, 268
Jennings, Mary (Reiken) 9, 140, 142, 143, 145, 148, 149, 152, 153, 154, 155, 157, 158, 159, 161, 162, 164, 166, 171, 176, 209, 213, 219, 224, 230, 268, 269, 276, 285, 286, 287, 295, 297, 298, 299, 300
Jennings, Sarah Hannah Maud, *see* Hinds
Jennings (Jennens), Sarah (Saunders) 142, 145, 148, 151, 157
Jennings, Walter 150
Johnson, Mrs 70, 80, 90
Jones, The Rev. E.R. 58
Joubert, Commandant-General Piet 193, 198, 200, 212, 213, 239, 241, 259, 260, 261, 262

Keate Award, The 192
Keightley, Illa 220
Kennedy, The Rev. J. 82
Kensington Children's Hospital 57
Klein Letaba Goldfields 234, 237, 247
Kotze, Chief Justice John 151
Kruger, Paul 160, 176, 183, 193, 197, 198, 212, 238, 275, 277, 288, 294

Lady Trader in the Transvaal, A 97, 209, 219, 300
Lanyon, Sir Owen 192, 194, 201, 202, 204, 205
Leonard, Charles 227
Life of Christ, and its bearing on the Doctrines of Communism, The 86, 139
Lithauer, Isaac 227, 228, 232
Loch, Sir Henry 248
Longobardi, Enrico Guiseppe Cipriano 94
Longobardi, Marian (Heckford or Matthews) 70, 86, 92, 93, 94, 165, 298
Loreto Convent 205

305

Louder, The Rev. C.F. 32
Louis Moore Mine 236
Louis Philippe, King 18

Magoeba 252, 260, 261
Majuba, Battle of 211, 212, 280
Makapan 182, 183, 184, 185, 187
Manchester Children's Hospital 57
Mapela 187, 211
Martineau, Harriet 15
Martineau, The Rev. James 54
Matthews, Francis Claughton 165
Matthews, Marian, *see* Longobardi
Medingen Mission 9, 243, 244, 252
Modjadji, the Rain Queen 240, 241, 244, 245, 246, 252, 253, 254, 256, 258, 259, 260, 261, 262, 294
Moffat, Robert 119
Mpande 103
Munnik, G.G. 234
Murray, Dr 61, 62, 64
Mzilikazi 119, 128, 129
Macmillan's Magazine 65

Natal Witness, The 288
News of the Camp, The 9, 209, 211, 212
Nicholson, Sir Charles 220
Nicholson, Lady Sarah 9, 221, 222, 298, 299
Nightingale, Florence 23, 30
Nil Desperandum Mining Company 152
Nixon, Mr 33
Nooitgedacht (Surprise) 7, 9, 97, 142, 145, 146, 150, 151, 153, 154, 155, 160, 161, 162, 165, 166, 170, 175, 216, 224, 229, 267, 268, 269, 273, 276, 277, 278, 279, 280, 281, 282, 283, 285, 286, 295, 298, 299
Nooitgedacht, Battle of 143, 285
Nourse, Henry 203

Paardekraal 197, 198
Philip, George, publishers 23, 229, 301
Pigott, prospector 236
Pollock, Alfred 19
Potgieter, Hermanus 145
Pretoria News, The 299
Pretorius, Andries 103, 164, 198
Pretorius, Henning 213, 256, 260
Pretorius, M.W. 197

Rain Queen, *see* Modjadji
Retief, Piet 103
Reuter, Dr Fritz 243, 244, 252, 260
Reuter, Mrs 243
Richardson, The Rev. 136, 137, 150
Roberts, Lord 281, 282

Sanders, Muriel Heckford (Hinds) 9, 276
Schiel, Capt. Adolf 240, 260
Schoeman, Hendrik 201, 213, 214, 216
Schoon, Robert 119
Scott, Canon 32
Scrimgeour, Dora, *see* Eland
Scrooby, Harriet 154
Scrooby, Mary (née Jennings) 152, 161
Scrooby, Walter 150, 154, 157, 159
Seidewitz, Baron von 78, 80
Sekhukhune 104
Semple, Stewart 225, 228, 255
Settlers, the 1820 140, 141, 142
Shaka 103, 128
Shaw, George Bernard 80

Shepstone, Sir Theophilus 95, 104, 192
Siege of Pretoria, the 7, 9, 205, 207, 208, 209, 211, 215, 216, 257, 289
Smith, "Solo" 235
Spectator, The 287, 288, 297
Star, The 252, 255, 300
Story of the East London Hospital, The, see *East London Hospital, The Story of*)
Surprise, *see* Nooitgedacht

Teck, Duchess of 92
Times, The 9, 15, 33, 76, 289, 293, 294, 296, 297, 300, 301
Transvaal Argus 207
Transvaal Farming Trading and Mining Association 165
Transvaal Women's Educational Union 275, 284, 293
Treaty of Vereeniging, *see* Vereeniging, Treaty of
Trichardt, Louis 119

Victoria, Queen 75
Vereeniging, Treaty of 297
Vierkleur 198, 201, 287
Volkstem 157
Vryheidsoorlog 201

Warner, Ashton 74, 81, 91, 97, 165
Warner, George ("Jimmy") 96, 97, 100, 103, 106, 108, 109, 110, 111, 112, 113, 115, 117, 119, 120, 121, 149, 150, 152, 157, 161, 162, 163, 164, 165, 166, 167, 170, 175, 195, 196, 199, 200, 216, 217, 218
Westminster, the Duke of 91
Woodman, Dr W. Bathurst 35, 37, 44, 49, 50, 52, 53, 54

Zeederberg brothers 223
Zenana Medical Mission 94

Xhosa 104, 140, 141